French Cheeses

FOREWORD BY
JOËL ROBUCHON

WRITTEN BY
KAZUKO MASUI AND TOMOKO YAMADA

PHOTOGRAPHY YOHEI MARUYAMA
WINE CONSULTANT ROBERT VIFIAN

CONSULTANT
RANDOLPH HODGSON

LONDON, NEW YORK,
MUNICH, MELBOURNE, AND DELHI

Published by Dorling Kindersley

Senior Editor   Claire Nottage
Senior Designer   Anne Fisher
Managing Editor   Deirdre Headon
Managing Art Editor   Marianne Markham
Production Controller   Heather Hughes

Produced for Dorling Kindersley by Blue Island Publishing

Art Director   Stephen Bere
Designer   Ian Midson
Editorial Director   Rosalyn Thiro
Associate Editor   Michael Ellis

First published in Great Britain in 1996
by Dorling Kindersley Limited
80 Strand, London WC2R 0RL
Penguin Group (UK)

Reprinted with revisions 2000
This edition published 2005

Copyright © 1996, 2000, 2005
Dorling Kindersley Limited, London
Copyright © 1993 Bungeishunju Ltd.
for the original Japanese edition
English text copyright © 1996, 2000, 2005
Chihiro Masui Black
and Gerd Christian Seeber

A CIP catalogue record for this book
is available from the British Library

ISBN 978 1 4053 1211 0

Printed and bound by L. Rex Primting in China
Repro by Colourcan in Singapore

See our complete
catalogue at
www.dk.com

CONTENTS

Foreword
10

How to Use this Book
12

INTRODUCTION

The Origins of Cheese
16

Types of French
Cheese
18

Cheese, Wine,
and Bread
22

French Cheese Today
26

The Appellation
d'Origine Contrôlee
(AOC)
28

Buying, Storing, and
Tasting Cheese
30

A DIRECTORY
OF FRENCH
CHEESES

Map of France
34

A
36

B
44

C
86

D–G
162

L–N
184

O–P
198

R
210

S
220

T
228

V
262

Glossary
276

Cheese Shops
in France
278

AOC Cheese
Producers
280

Index
282

Acknowledgements
286

Foreword

At last – and what a pleasure for me to say so! Because among all the cheese books published to date – including that admirable work by Pierre Androuët – none as far as I know is based on so many valuable photographs for the identification and choice of a cheese ripened to perfection.

This book is for people who care for the good things in life, for amateurs with a love of cheese and serious gourmets alike. It takes you on a journey through the many regions of France, teaching you all you ought to know about cheese, and helping you in your choice. Expert knowledge is the key to an appreciation of pure and authentic flavours. Here is a reliable handbook for those who wish to share those flavours with their friends, and a clear and easy-to-follow initiation into the secrets of cheesemaking. Connoisseurs may read it with interest and pleasure. Amateurs will give it pride of place among their books and profit whenever they consult it.

Writing this preface fills me with a sense of duty, so that others may share what I know. Yes, I love cheese! It's a marvellous product, inscribed in that great trinity of the table, which it forms with bread and wine.

Cheese is part of what we have been eating from the beginning of time. A national French food for as long as people recall, it reflects nature as much as their own history. A concentrate of that life-giving liquid, namely milk, it allows us to conserve its many qualities. The extent of our range of cheese, remarked on already by the Roman naturalist Pliny the Elder, mirrors the diversity of our land as well as the art of dairymen and women and of social and economic developments over the ages. The example of monastic cheesemakers or that of cheese such as *tommes* or *reblochons* given in lieu of tax demonstrate the point.

To conclude then, what could be more satisfactory than to know for oneself which cheese to choose in preference to another? It's an informed choice, which shows understanding and results in joy.

Joël Robuchon

How to Use this Book

This book is the ideal quick-reference guide to selecting and identifying French cheeses at home, in your local cheese shop, or travelling in France. More than 350 cheeses are organized alphabetically. Similar cheeses of the same family or type are grouped. Details are given on where the cheeses are made, methods of production, appearance, smell, and taste. Special feature boxes that appear throughout the book give useful background information. At the end of the book, useful terms are explained in a concise glossary, which is followed by selected lists of cheese shops in France and the AOC cheese producers. The book concludes with a comprehensive index.

A whole Emmental

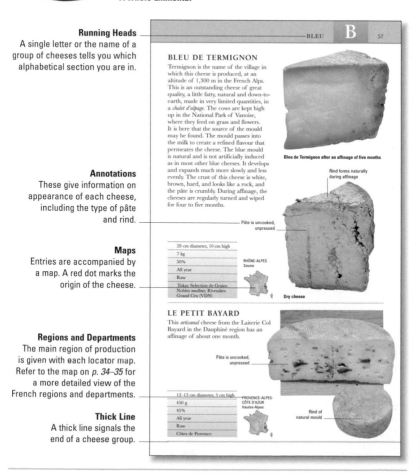

Running Heads
A single letter or the name of a group of cheeses tells you which alphabetical section you are in.

Annotations
These give information on appearance of each cheese, including the type of pâte and rind.

Maps
Entries are accompanied by a map. A red dot marks the origin of the cheese.

Regions and Departments
The main region of production is given with each locator map. Refer to the map on *p. 34–35* for a more detailed view of the French regions and departments.

Thick Line
A thick line signals the end of a cheese group.

BLEU **B** 57

BLEU DE TERMIGNON

Termignon is the name of the village in which this cheese is produced, at an altitude of 1,300 m in the French Alps. This is an outstanding cheese of great quality, a little fatty, natural and down-to-earth, made in very limited quantities, in a *chalet d'alpage*. The cows are kept high up in the National Park of Vanoise, where they feed on grass and flowers. It is here that the source of the mould may be found. The mould passes into the milk to create a refined flavour that permeates the cheese. The blue mould is natural and is not artificially induced as in most other blue cheeses. It develops and expands much more slowly and less evenly. The crust of this cheese is white, brown, hard, and looks like a rock, and the pâte is crumbly. During affinage, the cheeses are regularly turned and wiped for four to five months.

Bleu de Termignon after an affinage of five months

Rind forms naturally during affinage

Pâte is uncooked, unpressed

28 cm diameter, 10 cm high	
7 kg	
50%	RHÔNE-ALPES Savoie
All year	
Raw	
Tokay Selection de Grains Nobles *moelleux*, Rivesaltes Grand Cru (VDN)	

Dry cheese

LE PETIT BAYARD

This *artisanal* cheese from the Laiterie Col Bayard in the Dauphiné region has an affinage of about one month.

Pâte is uncooked, unpressed

12–13 cm diameter, 5 cm high	
450 g	PROVENCE-ALPES-CÔTE D'AZUR Hautes-Alpes
45%	
All year	
Raw	
Côtes de Provence	

Rind of natural mould

LANGRES (AOC)

As the name indicates, this *artisanal* cheese originates from the high plains of Langres, in Champagne. It is shaped like a cylinder and has a 5-mm deep well on top called a *fontaine*, a kind of basin into which Champagne or *marc* may be poured. This is a pleasant way to eat this cheese and is characteristic of wine-producing regions.

The surface of the cheese is sticky, wet, and shiny, and has a pronounced smell. The pâte is firm and supple, and melts in the mouth, releasing a complex mixture of aromas. The salt too is strong, yet Langres is a milder cheese than Epoisses de Bourgogne (p. 166). The cheeses shown are completely ripe.

Langres is produced in a large and a small version. Affinage usually takes five to six weeks within the areas specified by the AOC. The cheeses are placed in a cellar at a humidity of 95%, where they are regularly rubbed with brine, either using a damp cloth or by hand. The minimum permitted affinage is 21 days for large cheeses and 15 days for small ones. A red dye extracted from the seeds of the American annatto tree is applied to colour the rind. This is called *rocou* in French and is also added to other cheeses and butter.

White to light-beige pâte, becomes softer towards centre; uncooked, unpressed

Smooth, fine-textured, washed rind, brick-red to light brown

16–20 cm diameter, 5–7 cm high (large); 7.5–9 cm diameter, 4–6 cm high (small)

800 g min. (large); 150 g min. (small)

42 g min. per 100 g cheese

50% min., 21 g min. per 100 g cheese

All year

Pasteurized

Marc de Champagne

CHAMPAGNE-ARDENNE Haute-Marne; LORRAINE Vosges; BOURGOGNE Côte d'Or

AOC Regulations: Langres

1 The sliced curd must be neither washed nor kneaded. (Concentrated or reconstituted milk is not allowed.)
2 It is permitted to add annatto to the brine, applied when rubbing the cheese, in order to impart a red colouring to the rind.

AOC GRANTED 1975

Cheese Names
Cheese groups and individual cheeses are listed alphabetically. Where a cheese is given two or more names, the first is the local name used in the region of origin, followed by any other names by which the cheese is known. "AOC" means Appellation d'Origine Contrôlée (*see below*).

Main Entries
These give information on place of production, appearance, flavour, and smell. For some AOC or more important cheeses, details are also given on production methods.

Essential Facts
These give dimensions, shape, weight, fat content, dry matter, and best season to buy and eat a cheese (*see below for key to symbols*).

AOC Regulations
These boxes list some of the most important guidelines in the making of a cheese as outlined by the AOC (*p. 28*).

Common Terms

Affinage is a French word that means both the ripening and curing of a cheese.

AOC stands for Appellation d'Origine Contrôlée (*p. 28*), which is a government body that controls the quality and production of important cheeses.

Fermier, **artisanal**, **coopérative**, and **industriel** refer to the method of production (*p. 28*).

Pâte is a French word that refers to all that is within the rind or crust of a cheese.

VDN stands for Vin Doux Naturel (naturally sweet wine), which is a type of fortified wine.

See also the Glossary (*p. 276*).

Key to Essential Facts Symbols

The boxes give at-a-glance information about each cheese.

⊖	Shape
⚖	Typical weight
⁂	Dry matter – the residue after all the water in the cheese has been eliminated
𝔻	Fat content – the amount of fat contained in the dry matter. "Not defined" indicates that the fat content is not stipulated
✓	Season indicates when the cheese is usually eaten
♨	Cow's milk is used – raw, pasteurized, skimmed, etc
◎	Sheep's milk is used
⚘	Goat's milk is used
Ⅱ	Goes well with the named beer or cider
⬙	Goes well with the named Champagne
⬗	Goes well with coffee
▼	Goes well with the named red wine
♀	Goes well with the named white or *rosé* wine
⬛	Goes well with the named spirits (e.g. *marc*)

INTRODUCTION

The Origins of Cheese

"Rest with me on green foliage: we have ripe fruit, soft chestnuts, and plenty of fresh cheese." VIRGIL, 42 BC

CHEESE IS ONE of the most ancient forms of manufactured food. The first real evidence of cheese is in ancient Sumerian writings from around 3000 BC, which refer to around 20 soft cheeses. Remains of cheesemaking equipment discovered in Europe and Egypt also appear to date back to around 3000 BC. However, we can only guess at when the craft of cheesemaking actually started. The most likely theory is that in around 10,000 BC, when sheep and goats were domesticated, early herdspeople began to take advantage of the fact that sour milk naturally separates into curds and whey. If drained off, shaped, and dried, the curds provided them with a

Cow's-milk Cheeses
Since their domestication thousands of years ago, cattle have been bred selectively for the quantity and quality of milk they produce for cheesemaking.

simple and nourishing food. Cow's-milk cheeses came two or three thousand years after the sheep and goat's-milk cheeses as cattle were not domesticated until considerably later.

Cheese in Ancient Greece
References to cheese and cheesemaking are dotted through ancient literature, including the *Old Testament*. Homer's *Odyssey* tells how Ulysses and his men hide in the Cyclops' cavern, while the one-eyed giant milks his ewes and goats, then curdles half the milk, drains the curds, and sets them to one side in wicker baskets.

Roman Cheeses
The Romans enjoyed eating cheese both raw and cooked in little cakes called *glycinas* made from sweet white wine and olive oil. In a treatise on farming written in AD 60–65, Roman agricultural writer Columella tells how

cheeses were made from fresh milk, which was curdled by the addition of coagulum – rennet extracted from the fourth stomach of a lamb or kid.

The curds were pressed to expel the whey, and then sprinkled with salt and left to harden in a shady place. Columella explains that, apart from enhancing the flavour, the salt helped to dry and preserve the cheese, and so the process of salting and hardening was repeated. The ripe cheeses were washed, dried, and packed for shipping, perhaps to an army depot, since cheese was included in a legionnaire's daily ration. Caesar himself is said to have eaten a blue cheese at Saint-Affrique, just to the west of Roquefort, where one of the world's most celebrated blue cheeses is still produced today.

The Fromager
The makers and sellers of cheese are known in France as *fromagers*. Many of these crafts-people still make and ripen cheeses in family businesses following traditional techniques passed down the generations.

Cheese and Language
The vast network of Roman roads set up communications that influenced language. The Latin word for cheese, *caseus*, became Italian *cacio*, German *Käse*, and English cheese, as well as Spanish *queso*, and *queijo* in Portuguese. The Italian *formaggio* and French *fromage* also derive from Latin, although the root of these words is in the Greek *formos* – the Cyclops' wicker basket.

After the Romans
Soon after the collapse of the Roman Empire, Barbarian invaders overran much of Europe. Subsequent invasions by the Normans, Mongols, and Saracens, followed by successive outbreaks of the bubonic plague, devastated the continent. The ancient cheesemaking recipes and techniques, developed over thousands of years, were gradually forgotten, surviving only in the mountains and in remote monasteries. It was there that some of the oldest traditional cheesemaking methods were preserved for us to appreciate today.

Ancient Affinage
Many of the techniques for ripening and airing cheese date back thousands of years. This process, known as affinage, intensifies the flavour.

Types of French Cheese

"Age is something that doesn't matter, unless you are a cheese." LUIS BUNUEL.

THE ARRAY of French cheese is so great that it can be daunting to enter a cheese shop, or *fromagerie*, and understand the difference between varieties. However, there are basic distinctions in the milk used, e.g. cow, goat, or sheep's milk (*p. 21*), and the methods of production. These factors affect the characteristics of the mature pâte and rind.

This book includes a fact box for each cheese, which shows the type of milk used, along with information about typical size, weight, percentage of dry matter, fat content, and availability. Captions to the pictures indicate the type of pâte and rind. Details about the length and method of affinage (curing and maturing) are also described for many.

On the following pages is a brief summary of the main cheese groups, which are defined by their production method and type of pâte and rind.

Fresh, Rindless Cheeses
These cheeses are shaped and kneaded during production, but they have not had any affinage (curing time). Examples include the family called *fromage frais* ("fresh cheese"; *p. 176–180*) and Boursin (*p. 257*).

Soft Cheeses
Many French cheeses have a soft pâte and can be grouped according to what kind of rind they have. Camembert (*p. 92*) and Brie (*p. 80*) are probably the best-known examples of soft cheeses with a white mould. Others include Chaource (*p. 102*), Neufchâtel (*p. 196*), and many *triple-crème* and *double-crème* cheeses (*p. 256–261*).

Some soft cheeses have a washed rind. Munster (*p. 192*) and several of the cheeses from Corsica are good examples. There is also a grouping of soft cheeses that have a natural mould. Many goat's-milk cheeses, such as Chèvre de la Loire and Chèvre de Coin (*p. 104–111*), fall into this group. Some of them are covered with salted ashes or charcoal powder during affinage, which adds to the flavour, e.g. Sante-Maure de Touraine (*p. 108*).

Blue Cheeses
The Bleu family (*p. 51–57*), Persillé (*p. 204*), and the famous Roquefort (*p. 216*) are excellent examples of soft cheeses with veins of blue mould.

Goat's-milk Cheeses during Affinage
The length of affinage varies from a few days to many months depending on the type of cheese. Goat's-milk cheeses often have two to four weeks.

Cow's milk is used in a great variety of French ▶ cheeses, ranging from soft Brie to hard Beaufort

Sheep and Cheesemaking
The villagers of the Pyrénées have a long tradition of using ewe's milk to produce uncooked, pressed, semi-hard cheeses with a natural mould.

Pressed Cheeses

During affinage, some cheeses are placed in a press in order to eliminate some percentage of water. Exactly how much pressing will determine if the mature cheese is classified as semi-hard or hard. (Unpressed cheeses are classified as soft.)

Semi-hard Cheeses

The group of semi-hard cheeses includes many with a natural mould, such as Saint-Nectaire (*p. 224*), the Brebis des Pyrénées family (*p. 66–79*), Cantal and its relatives (*p. 94*), and many types of Tomme de Savoie (*p. 231–238*).

Other semi-hard cheeses have a washed, rubbed, and waxed rind. Beaumont (*p. 47*) and Port-du-Salut (*p. 209*) are good examples. Both are *industriel* cheeses.

Milking
In one year, a cow can produce nearly 10 times more milk than a goat, and 30 times more milk than a ewe.

Hard Cheeses

Comté (*p. 142*) and Beaufort (*p. 48*) are examples of cheeses with a hard pâte that has been pressed during affinage. They are both very popular.

The pâte of the majority of French cheeses is not cooked during the process of affinage. Cheeses such as Comté and Beaufort, which involve the heating of milk during production, are referred to as "cooked".

Cheeses Started with Whey

Fromage de lactosérum (*p. 181*) and the Corsican Brocciu (*p. 146*) are the best examples of these mild, spreadable cheeses.

Other Cheeses

This book includes products based on cheese, such as *fromage fort* (*p. 173– 175*). Some products are cheeses that have been marinated in wine or covered with herbs. Processed cheeses (*p. 23*) are another group.

TYPES OF MILK USED IN FRENCH CHEESE

French cheeses are made from the milk of either cows, goats, or sheep, or a combination of milk from these animals. The type of milk used to make a cheese determines its taste. The most highly concentrated milk of all is ewe's milk, which gives strong, robust, full-flavoured cheeses, with a lingering aftertaste.

The annual quantity of milk produced by one cow over 305 days of milking is 6,065 kg; a goat produces 644 kg over 240 days; and a ewe produces 200 kg over 180 days.

Cheese may be made from either raw or pasteurized milk. Raw milk is not heat-treated prior to cheesemaking and is usually used shortly after milking or within 12 hours; if chilled immediately to 4°C, it may be stored for up to 24 hours. Raw milk contains natural bacteria and is considered to produce cheese with complex taste and flavour. All *fermier* cheeses belong to this category. Raw milk is compulsory for some AOC cheeses (*p. 28*).

Pasteurized milk is treated at low or high temperatures. At low temperatures this usually involves heating the milk to between 72°C and 85°C for 15 seconds and immediately chilling it to 4°C. This reduces the level of bacteria, allowing the milk to be stored for a long time, and is widely used in factory-produced cheeses. (It is not to be confused with the definition of a cooked cheese: see opposite.) Mass-produced cheeses made from pasteurized milk are simple in taste.

Weight and Composition of Different Types of Milk

	Cow's Milk	Goat's Milk	Sheep's Milk
Fats	35–45 g	30–42 g	65–75 g
Proteins	30–35 g	28–37 g	55–65 g
Lactose	45–55 g	40–50 g	43–50 g
Minerals	7–9 g	7–9 g	9–10 g
Water	888–915 g	892–925 g	838–866 g
Approx. net weight	1,032 g	1,030 g	1,038 g

(Figures from *Les Productions Laitières*, Vol. 1,1996, Tableaux des Calories, 1992)

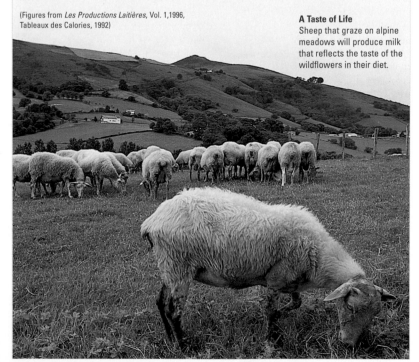

A Taste of Life
Sheep that graze on alpine meadows will produce milk that reflects the taste of the wildflowers in their diet.

Cheese, Wine, and Bread

*"Cheese is probably the best of all foods, as wine
is the best of all beverages."* PATIENCE GRAY, 1957

IN FRANCE, cheese and wine have been considered natural allies for as long as people can remember. This view remains valid today, but we must not forget bread, which cements the union. Indeed, there can be few greater pleasures in life than a good, ripe *fermier* cheese, matched with a glass of quality wine and a chunk of freshly baked bread. The great advantage of this union is that cheese, wine, and bread are all foods that can be enjoyed in their "raw" state, with little or no preparation, making them an ideal choice for quick snacks or picnics. It is no coincidence, therefore, that generations of French farmworkers have relied on local cheeses, wines, and bread to fortify them while they work in the fields.

Wine with Cheese
Suggested wines to match with different cheeses are included throughout this book.

The "Holy Trinity" of the Table
Because of their close association, cheese, wine, and bread have occasionally been called the Holy Trinity of the table, an expression that may have been coined by the French humanist François Rabelais, whose writings attest to a great liking for

food. Born at Chinon in around 1494, he would, of course, have tasted at least some of the outstanding goat's-milk cheeses Touraine is still famous for today. Rabelais was a Roman Catholic monk for much of his life and was familiar with the concept of the Holy Trinity – inseparable God the Father, Jesus Christ the Son, and the Holy Spirit – yet even he admitted that some cheeses are better served with fruit, than bread: "There is no match you could compare to Master Cheese and Mistress Pear".

The Action of Yeasts and Bacteria
Although bread, cheese, and wine are produced from very different base ingredients – bread is made from grain, wine from grapes, and cheese from milk – they all depend on yeasts and bacteria for their development. Without the changes brought about by fermentation, bread doughs would not rise, wines would be devoid of alcohol, and cheeses would simply not taste like cheese. In addition, it is the action of the fermentation that makes all of these products keep.

Just as the flavour, body, and bouquet of a wine depend on the grape variety, production techniques, and the technique and length of ageing, so the taste, texture, flavour, and aroma of cheeses depend on the milk from which they are produced – cow, goat, ewe, or mixed milks – and the methods used to make and ripen them (*p. 18–21*).

Crusty French Bread
This long crusty baguette is traditionally eaten fresh from the bakery. With a hunk of cheese and a good wine it makes a simple, hearty meal.

Accompanying Breads

The combination of foods is a matter of harmony and contrasts, be it in looks, textures, temperatures, flavours, or smells, all of which are subject to personal likes and dislikes. A simple rule of thumb might be that the more delicate the cheese, the whiter and less salted ought to be the bread to go with it, while spiced breads, which are often made with sour milk and thus already contain a dairy flavour, are most enjoyable with a powerful blue cheese.

Which Wine to Choose

Although much advice is given on which wines should be selected to accompany a particular food or dish, there are no hard and fast rules. The best selections are almost always based on individual tastes because different people naturally prefer different combinations. The only way to know and develop your own preferences is to sample as many wines with as wide a variety of foods as you can.

An Alternative to Meat
Cheese is a valuable source of protein and an appetizing alternative to meat as a main meal served with potatoes, fresh green salad, and a good wine.

PROCESSED CHEESE

Processed cheese was invented in around 1908 by the Swiss, who were looking for a way to use up surplus cheese. In 1911, it was made with Emmental and commercialized by the Swiss firm Gerber. At the same time, processed cheese was being developed in the United States.

The first European factory for the mass production of processed cheese was opened in 1917 in the Jura, France by the Graf brothers, and in 1921, the trademark for La Vache Qui Rit cheese was registered by Léon Bel. In 1953, a French decree laid down strict guidelines as to what exactly a processed cheese should contain in terms of minimum fat and dry matter, and established a law, which was revised at the end of 1988.

Processed cheese has little to do with real cheese. One or several ripened cheeses are heated and mixed, then pasteurized at high temperature (130–140°C) after other dairy

Bonjura
This is a type of canned processed cheese spread specially produced twice a year for the French Army. It keeps for a long time and is available in plain or ham flavour.

products, such as liquid or powdered milk, cream, butter, casein, whey, and seasoning, have been added. The flavour of the original cheeses alters during processing. The main, or only advantage of processed cheese is that it has a long shelf life.

Some processed cheeses are made with several ripened cheeses of the same type, others with cheeses of different types. The most often used are Emmental and Cantal, but Saint-Paulin (*p. 226*) or Roquefort (*p. 216*) may be used to vary the taste. They are sometimes seasoned with pepper, herbs, ham, onions, mushrooms, or even seafood.

The Produce of Normandie
Normandie is known for its fine butters and world-famous cheeses such as Camembert and Pont l'Evêque. Such cheeses can often be successfully paired with the local Calvados (apple brandy).

Many of the wines recommended in this book by Robert and Isabelle Vifian come from the same region as the cheese with which they are matched. Their choice is often based on the combinations of wine and cheese favoured by local people. Wine is not the only drink that goes well with cheese, however. In areas such as Normandie where little or no wine is produced, the cheeses are often better matched with a good local beer or cider, or sometimes even coffee. With cheeses that have been cured in *eau-de-vie* it is worth trying a good *marc*. It is also important to remember that the wine suggestions in this book are merely pointers. Your own taste and pleasure count most of all.

Compared with a dish composed of a number of ingredients, cheese is a unique product that may be matched relatively easily with a wine. Matches are usually made in terms of texture and taste rather than smell, and a particular wine is often selected to accompany a particular cheese on the basis of similarities, contrasts, or complementary characteristics.

A smooth, fatty cheese may go very well with a similarly smooth, slightly oily wine, while a cheese with high acidity often contrasts very well with a sweet, alcoholic wine. Very salty cheeses may be complemented by a wine with good acidity. It is worth bearing in mind that, as a general rule, the longer a cheese is left to ripen the more it will dominate and "attack" the flavour of a wine.

Many people erroneously believe that cheese should be eaten exclusively with red wine. One of the principal reasons for this may be that cheeses are usually served at the end of a meal, when it is difficult to return to a dry white wine after a red, especially if the red is full-bodied. It is, however, true to say that white wines go better with many cheeses than reds and it is well worth sampling a few combinations for the experience.

NUTRITIONAL VALUES OF CHEESE

Cheese is recommended for children and old people because of its high nutritional value. Compared with milk, it contains the same nutrients although in greater concentration, with fats, proteins, minerals (calcium, phosphorus), and vitamins (A, B), but less water. The proteins change into amino acids which the digestive system can absorb. Calcium joins with the amino acids and can similarly be absorbed. Cheese also contains a lot of beta carotene (vitamin A); the only elements lacking are vitamin C and fibre. Eaten with fruit and vegetables, cheese offers an almost complete diet.

Nutritional Values per 100 g

	Proteins	Fat Content	Calcium	Energy
Fromage frais (fresh cheese)	6.5–9.6 g	0–9.4 g	75–170 mg	44–160 kca
Soft cheese (e.g. Camembert)	20–21 g	20–23 g	150–380 mg	260–350 kcal
Uncooked, pressed cheese (e.g. Tomme)	24–27 g	24–29 g	657–865 mg	326–384 kcal
Cooked, pressed cheese (e.g. Comté)	27–29 g	28–30 g	900–1,100 mg	390–400 kcal
Blue mould cheese (e.g. Roquefort)	20 g	27–32 g	722–870 mg	414 kcal

Regional Specialities
Northeast France is the home of Langres cheese, which is traditionally paired with the local *marc* de Champagne.

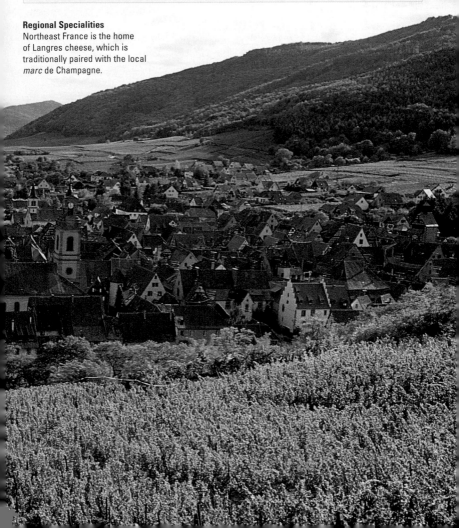

French Cheese Today

"How can anyone be expected to govern a country with 325 cheeses?" GENERAL CHARLES DE GAULLE

SINCE CHARLES DE GAULLE made his famous statement over 40 years ago, the number of cheeses produced in France has, according to recent estimates, increased to around 500 – a count that could be higher still if we include local, homemade cheeses that are unlikely to be found outside their region of production. We might deduce from these figures alone that French cheesemaking is prospering, an impression that is confirmed by official statistics as well as the wide range of cheeses on offer in many shops, restaurants, and supermarkets.

A Wide Variety
The increased demand for a wider variety of cheeses has led to the mass-production of cheeses such as Camembert, which is now available worldwide.

Changing Attitudes
A growing preference for vegetarian foods and a modern tendency for people to browse during the day rather than sit down to cooked meals, both favour cheese. Little could be easier, tastier, or more nourishing than a light meal of a few good pieces of cheese, with bread, salad, and fresh fruit on the side. No doubt we shall continue to see cheeses being offered at the end of a formal lunch or dinner. However, more and more people accept that unless we plan our menus in order to leave room for cheese, only the heartiest of appetites can do them justice.

The Effect of the Supermarket
One of the greatest changes to the sale and production of French cheeses has been the increase in numbers of supermarkets. Even in traditionally rural areas of France, supermarkets are gradually replacing the village shops that used to sell a wide variety of household goods, food, and drink. Despite constant criticism by people who have forgotten the frustrations of not finding what they want in the village shop, supermarkets have brought down prices and offer a wider variety of fresher produce. Cheeses, however, pose a problem for supermarkets as most of them require expert care if they are to be allowed to reach maturity when their textures and flavours are at their peak. While the village grocer might have had the knowledge and patience to mature some Camembert or Brie, he also took the risk of being left with some rather smelly, old cheeses that no one would buy. Supermarkets, which rely on a quick turnover and are best at selling large quantities of uniform goods, cannot afford to take this risk and prefer to stock mainly *industriel* (factory), rather than *artisanal* (artisan) or *fermier* (farmhouse) cheeses.

Specialist Cheese Shops
It is at the specialist cheesemonger – be it in a small market town or a great city – where the best cheeses can be bought. Just like people with a passion for good wines, lovers of cheese have become both better informed and more demanding in their choice. What they are looking for is character and flavour, the attributes given to a cheese by the care and attention of

the artisan cheesemaker who uses traditional methods rather than by the technician applying science in a factory.

The traditional cheesemaker is backed up by the careful husbandry of the farmer producing the finest milk. However, it is not only the traditional cheeses that are proving so popular. New cheeses, too, are being developed and made by hand, in limited numbers, on small farms in many areas of France.

Into the Future

Over the last 50 years or so, French cheese-making has been subject to a number of European regulations that are too often based on the methodology of the factory and do not take account of the advantages of the farm. They tend to be drawn up by scientists and, as a result, are unsympathetic to the needs of France's many *artisanal* and *fermier*

cheesemakers, several of whom have been producing traditional cheeses for generations. Unless people discover for themselves the superiority of a good, handmade, *fermier* cheese over one that has been mass-produced in a factory they will never understand why it is so important – and worthwhile – to protect and promote small-scale cheesemaking.

Ultimately, the future of France's many traditional cheeses depends on people being aware of what is actually available, knowing what to select or buy in a shop or a restaurant, and being prepared to ask for it if it is not already on display. This book will provide you with all the information you need to locate them.

Cheese Markets
Some of the best regional *fermier* and *artisanal* cheeses can be found in cheese markets, where local cheesemakers often have their own stalls.

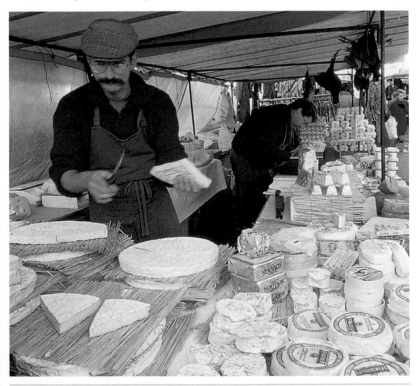

The Appellation d'Origine Contrôlée (AOC)

"Roquefort should be eaten on one's knees."
GRIMOD DE LA REYNIÈRE, 1838

CURRENTLY 42 French cheeses have the status of Appellation d'Origine Contrôlée, or AOC, which applies to French wines, *eaux-de-vie*, and dairy and farmhouse products. The AOC label guarantees that a product of quality has been made within a specified region of France following established methods of production. For AOC cheesemakers, the strict laws mean that inferior cheeses cannot be passed off under their name. For consumers, the AOC label provides a useful marker, not only of quality but also a distinction between cheeses that may be confusingly

Obligatory mark for all AOC cheeses

similar, such as Brie de Meaux (*p. 80*) and Brie de Melun (*p. 82*).

Many AOC cheeses have a long history. For example, the ripening of Roquefort (*p. 216*) was granted by Charles VI in 1411 solely to the people of Roquefort. This cheese was also mentioned in a decree dating from 1666, from which the AOC jurisdiction was later developed.

The Law for the Protection of the Place of Origin was first established on 6 May, 1919. Nowadays, a branch of the French Ministry of Agriculture – the Institut National des Appellations d'Origine, or INAO – is responsible for enforcing the AOC rules.

AOC CATEGORIES AND CONDITIONS OF PRODUCTION

The four main categories of production permitted by the AOC are *fermier*, *artisanal*, *coopérative*, and *industriel*.

The category of *fermier* is not a guarantee of quality – it merely implies that a cheese is made according to traditional methods.

Category	Conditions of Production	Quantities Produced	Where the Cheeses are Sold
Fermier (Made in a farmhouse, *chalet d'alpage*, *buron* or other mountain hut)	An individual producer uses the milk of animals (cows, goats, sheep) raised on his or her farm to make cheese following traditional methods. Milk from neighbouring farms is not allowed. Only raw milk may be used.	Small	Regional markets and a few *fromageries* in large towns. Some are exported to other countries.
Artisanal	An individual producer uses the milk of animals raised on his or her farm, or buys in milk to make cheese. (The producer is the owner of the dairy but all the milk may be bought elsewhere.)	Small to medium	Regional markets, and *fromageries* in towns and suburbs.
Coopératives (also *fruitières*)	The cheese is made in a single dairy with milk provided by members of the cooperative.	Medium to large	All of France.
Industriel	The milk is bought from a number of producers, sometimes from distant regions. Production is industrial.	Large	All of France; sometimes exported to other countries.

THE AOC CHEESES

In the table below, the AOC cheeses are listed alphabetically along with the year in which they were awarded the AOC and the basic type of milk used in production. The right-hand column gives the places in this book where you will find more details about individual AOC cheeses. For the most popular AOC cheeses, the details include a summary of the most important points of current regulations. The official journal of the AOC gives a precise description of each qualifying cheese, such as the type of milk used, regions, methods of production, and the length of affinage. The AOC laws are taken seriously by producers – any violation is liable to prosecution, and penalties consist of imprisonment of three months to one year, and a fine.

AOC cheeses are easily recognizable with their trademark Appellation d'Origine Contrôlée stamp. At the back of the book is a full list of the AOC producers with their contact details, along with the details of the INAO.

Cheese	Year of AOC	Milk Type	Page
Abondance	1990	🐄	40
Banon	2003	🐄🐐	46
Beaufort	1976	🐄	48
Bleu d'Auvergne	1975	🐄	51
Bleu des Causses	1979	🐄	52
Bleu du Haut-Jura	1977	🐄	53
Bleu de Sassenage	1998	🐄	56
Brie de Meaux	1980	🐄	80
Brie de Melun	1980	🐄	82
Brocciu	1983	🐐🐑	146
Camembert de Normandie	1983	🐄	92
Cantal	1980	🐄	94
Chabichou du Poitou	1990	🐐	105
Chasource	1977	🐄	102
Chevrotin	2002	🐐🐄	109
Comté	1976	🐄	142
Crottin de Chavignol	1976	🐐	104
Epoisses de Bourgogne	1991	🐄	166
Fourme d'Ambert /	1976	🐄	167
Fourme de Montbrison	2002	🐄	167
Laguiole	1976	🐄	98
Langres	1991	🐄	186
Livarot	1975	🐄	187
Maroilles	1976	🐄	188
Mont d'Or (Vacherin du Haut-Doubs)	1981	🐄	273
Morbier	2000	🐄	194
Munster	1978	🐄	192
Neufchâtel	1977	🐄	196
Ossau-Iraty-Brebis Pyrénées	1980	🐑	66
Pelardon	2000	🐐	203
Picodon	1983	🐐	206
Pont-l'Evêque	1976	🐄	208
Pouligny-Saint-Pierre	1976	🐐	104
Reblochon	1976	🐄	213
Rocamadour	1996	🐐	88
Roquefort	1979	🐑	216
Sainte-Maure de Touraine	1990	🐐	109
Saint-Nectaire	1979	🐄	224
Salers	1979	🐄	96
Selles-sur-Cher	1986	🐐	110
Tome des Bauges	2002	🐄	233
Valençay	1998	🐐	111

Mountain Goats
Goats in the lower Rhône area provide the milk used for Picodon AOC.

Buying, Storing, and Tasting Cheese

Buying Cheese

Choose a reputable, well-managed shop, with helpful assistants. (A selected list of cheese shops in France can be found on *p. 278*.)

The shop should be clean, and the cheeses should be cut in front of you. More important than variety is the quality and condition of the cheeses on sale. Learn to choose cheese first by eye and then by taste. With time, your eyes and tongue will begin to work together.

Do not buy more than you can eat. Larger pieces of pressed or cooked pressed cheeses (e.g. Emmental) usually keep well, as do well-ripened goat's-milk cheeses. Avoid pre-packed cheeses since they are often inferior to those cut in a shop.

Keeping and Storing Cheese

Cheeses contain living organisms that must not be cut off from air, yet it is important not to let a cheese dry out. As a rule, big pieces of cheese keep well. The ideal place for storing cheese is a cool, dark, well-ventilated room. Although dark, refrigerators are often too airless. Cover the cut sides of a cheese only and let it breathe through its rind or crust. Wrap soft cheeses loosely. Use greaseproof or waxed paper rather than cling film.

Do not store cheese with strong-smelling foods; as it breathes, it will absorb other aromas and may spoil.

Small quantities of cheese may be stored in a refrigerator for short periods as long as they are wrapped in waxed or greaseproof paper as described above.

Tasting Cheese

Let cold cheese warm up for about half an hour before eating to allow the flavour and aroma to develop. Cover it with a damp cheesecloth if the air is very dry. Cut the cheese into pieces, with an equal portion of rind as well as the heart and outer bits of the pâte. Remove hard crusts depending on the taste.

Preferably offer bread and wine with the cheese. There is nothing to beat well-matured cheese, crusty fresh bread, and a good wine.

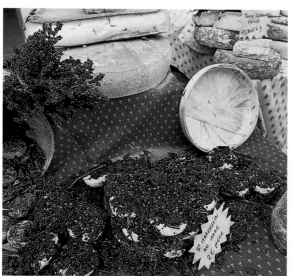

Cheese Display
This food stall in Provence is selling Saint-Marcellin, which has been ripened in *marc* and is liberally covered with pressed grape stalks to intensify the flavour.

Philippe Oliver cheese shop, Normandie ▶

HOW TO CUT CHEESE

The most important thing to bear in mind when cutting a cheese is to give everybody a chance to enjoy each part of the cheese, from the rind to the heart. The way a cheese is cut depends largely on its shape and size. The illustrations show typical cuts for some of the cheeses in this book.

Valençay (*p. 111*)

Emmental (*p. 164*)

Camembert (*p. 92*)

Brie (*p. 80*)

Charolles (*p. 119*)

Pont l'Évêque (*p. 208*)

Picodon (*p. 206*)

Epoisses (*p. 166*)

Tomme (*p. 231*)

A Directory of
French
Cheeses

Map of France

THROUGHOUT THIS BOOK are minimaps of France with
red spots that give a rough indication of where each
cheese is produced, accompanied by the regional names.
The large map on these pages shows more detail of the
administrative regions (*régions*) of France, each of which
is made up of several standard-sized departments
(*départements*). In total there are 22 regions and 96
departments, all of which are listed below with
their official administrative
numbers. Many of the
departments are named
after rivers.

Alsace
Bas-Rhin (67),
Haut-Rhin (68)

Aquitaine
Dordogne (24),
Gironde (33), Landes (40),
Lot-et-Garonne (47),
Pyrénées-Atlantiques (64)

Auvergne
Allier (03), Cantal (15),
Haute-Loire (43),
Puy-de-Dôme (63)

Bourgogne
Côte d'Or (21), Nièvre (58),
Saône-et-Loire (71),
Yonne (89)

Bretagne
Côtes-d'Armor (22),
Finistère (29),
Ille-et-Vilaine (35),
Morbihan (56)

Centre
Cher (18), Eure-et-Loire
(28), Indre (36),
Indre-et-Loire (37),
Loir-et-Cher (41),
Loiret (45)

Champagne-Ardenne
Ardennes (08), Aube (10),
Marne (51),
Haute-Marne (52)

Corse
Corse-du-Sud (2A),
Haute-Corse (2B)

Franche-Comté
Doubs (25), Jura (39),
Haute-Saône (70),
Territoire de Belfort (90)

Ile-de-France
Paris (Ville de) (75),
Seine-et-Marne (77),
Yvelines (78),
Essonne (91),
Hauts-de-Seine (92),
Seine-Saint-Denis (93),
Val-de-Marne (94),
Val-d'Oise (95)

**Languedoc-
Roussillon**
Aude (11), Gard (30),
Hérault (34), Lozère (48),
Pyrénées-Orientales (66)

Limousin
Corrèze (19), Creuse (23),
Haute-Vienne (87)

Loire (Pays de la)
Loire-Atlantique (44),
Maine-et-Loire (49),
Mayenne (53),
Sarthe (72), Vendée (85)

Lorraine
Meurthe-et-Moselle (54),
Meuse (55), Moselle (57),
Vosges (88)

Midi-Pyrénées
Ariège (09), Aveyron (12),
Haute-Garonne (31),
Gers (32), Lot (46),
Hautes-Pyrénées (65),
Tarn (81),
Tarn-et-Garonne (82)

Nord-Pas-de-Calais
Nord (59),
Pas-de-Calais (62)

Normandie (Haute-)
Eure (27),
Seine-Maritime (76)

Normandie (Basse-)
Calvados (14),
Manche (50), Orne (61)

Picardie
Aisne (02), Oise (60),
Somme (80)

Poitou-Charentes
Charente (16),
Charente-Maritime (17),
Deux-Sèvres (79),
Vienne (86)

**Provence-Alpes-
Côte-d'Azur**
Alpes-de-Haute-
Provence (04),
Hautes-Alpes (05),
Alpes-Maritimes (06),
Bouches-du-Rhône (13),
Var (83), Vaucluse (84)

Rhône-Alpes
Ain (01), Ardèche (07),
Drôme (26), Isère (38),
Loire (42), Rhône (69),
Savoie (73),
Haute-Savoie (74)

Nord-Pas-de-Calais
62
59
80
76
Picardie
02
rmandie
(Haute-)
60
08
95
55
57
93
51
Lorraine
67
78 92 75 94
Champagne-
54
Alsace
91
77
Ardenne
Ile-de-France
10
88
28
52
68
45
89
90
41
21
70
Centre
Bourgogne
25
18
58
Franche-
Comte
36
71
39
03
74
23
01
87
69
Limousin
63
42
19
Auvergne
Rhône-Alpes
73
15
43
38
46
07
26
05
48
12
04
82
30
84
06
Midi-Pyrénées
81
Provence-Alpes-Côte-d'Azur
31
34
13
83
Languedoc-
Roussillon
09
11
66

2B
Corse
2A

0 kilometers 100
0 miles 100

FRENCH CHEESES

A

ABBAYE DE CÎTEAUX

Although the Abbey of Saint-Nicolas-lés-Cîteaux dates back some 900 years, production of this *fermier* cheese began as recently as 1925. It is as soft to the eye as it is to the palate, and rather milder than the majority of washed-crust cheeses. Sixty tons are made every year from the milk of 70 Montbéliard cows. Most of the cheeses are eaten locally.

Semi-hard pâte;
uncooked, unpressed

⊖ 18 cm diameter, 3.5 cm high	
⚖ 700 g	
🏷 45% min	
✓ All year	
🜂 Raw	
🍷 Beaujolais or Bourgogne, young and fruity, chilled	

BOURGOGNE
Côte d'Or

Smooth, washed,
greyish-yellow rind

ABBAYE DE LA JOIE NOTRE-DAME

This *fermier* cheese has been produced by the nuns of the Abbaye de la Joie Notre-Dame since 1953. The recipe was passed on to the convent when it became independent from the Abbaye de la Coudre (*p. 252*). This fine and elegant cheese is one of the numerous descendants of Port-du-Salut (*p. 209*), the very first French monastery cheese, which it resembles both in appearance and taste. During affinage it is washed with brine for four to six weeks.

Semi-hard pâte;
uncooked, pressed

Washed rind

⊖ 20 cm diameter, 4 cm high	
⚖ 1.4 kg	
🏷 50%	
✓ All year	
🜂 Raw	
🍷 Bordeaux, young and fruity	

BRETAGNE
Morbihan

◀ **Cattle grazing on a hillside in the Pays Basque region**

ABBAYE DU MONT DES CATS

Monks at an abbey near Godewaersvelde started production of this *artisanal* cheese in 1890 using the Port-du-Salut recipe (*p. 209*). The cheese shown has been cured using modern methods and is not yet ripe. The small holes are characteristic. It is often served as a breakfast cheese with coffee. Affinage takes at least one month, during which the cheese is washed with a red dye.

Hard pate; uncooked, pressed

Rind washed in brine dyed with *rocou*, a reddish extract of annatto seeds

⊖	25cm diameter, 4 cm high
⚖	2 kg
🜄	45–50% min
✓	All year
🜲	Raw
🍷	Graves

NORD-PAS-DE-CALAIS Nord

ABBAYE DE LA PIERRE-QUI-VIRE

Both this cheese and the Boule des Moines (below) are *fermier* cheeses made by monks at the Abbaye de la Pierre-qui-Vire. Both cheeses are organic. During the affinage of two weeks the cheese is washed with brine. It should be eaten when young.

Washed rind

Soft pâte, smooth and supple; uncooked, unpressed

⊖	10 cm diameter 2.5 cm high
⚖	200 g
✓	All year, best in summer and autumn
🜲	Raw
🍷	Beaune

BOULE DES MOINES

This soft, fresh version of the above cheese was launched to boost sales. The flavoured pâte has a strong smell of garlic.

Boules des Moines

Soft pâte, mixed with garlic, chives, and pepper

BOURGOGNE Yonne

⊖	5–7 cm diameter
⚖	100–150g
✓	All year, especially summer and autumn
🜲	Raw
🍷	Irancy, young and fruity

ABONDANCE (AOC)

This medium-sized mountain cheese from Haute Savoie in the Rhône-Alpes is produced using milk from cows of the Abondance, Montbéliard, and Tarine breeds. The animals must not be fed any silage or other fermented fodder. The *fromage d'alpage (p. 78)* shown here was made in September at an alpine *chalet*. It has a strong smell and a distinct and complex flavour, with a balance of acidity and sweetness and a long aftertaste. The crust, including the grey layer beneath, should be removed before eating. *Artisanale, coopérative,* and *industriel* versions of Abondance are produced, but around 40% of the 348 tonnes made each year are *fermier* cheeses, and production is increasing. *Fermier* cheeses have an oval, blue *casein* label on the side, while all other versions have a square label. Affinage takes at least 90 days, during which time a maximum of three samples are taken from the core of the cheese with a cheese iron.

Creamy to pale yellow pâte, supple without elasticity, with small, even holes; half-cooked at 45–50°C, pressed

Dark yellow to brown rind, with cloth traces and a blue casein label on the side

Abondance *d'alpage fermier*, affinage of ten months (*above and below*)

⊖	38–43 cm diam., 7–8 cm high
⚖	7–12 kg
♣	58 g min. per 100 g cheese
🗗	48% or 27.84 g min. per 100 g
✓	Autumn onwards for cheeses made at a *chalet d'alpage*
⟁	Raw, whole
🍷	Vin de Savoie, Côte de Nuits Villages, Morey St. Denis, Fixin

RHÔNE-ALPES
Haute-Savoie

AOC Regulations: Abondance

1 The milk may be heated once to a maximum of 40°C, but only at the renneting. Systems or machinery that would allow the rapid heating to above 40°C before renneting may not be kept on the premises.
2 Salt is applied to the surface of the cheese either directly or with brine.
3 A *casein* label must bear the following information: France; Abondance; the ID number of the place of production; *fermier* for the farm category.

AOC GRANTED 1990

Abondance *d'hiver fermier*, affinage of seven months

HOW ABONDANCE IS MADE

It takes 100 litres of milk from cattle grazing in the mountain pastures to make a single Abondance of 9.5 kg.

Renneting and Coagulation
After the wooden mould is made (**1**), the rennet is added and the milk heated to 32–35°C. Coagulation (**2**) takes 35 minutes.

Cutting the Curd (*le décaillage*)
The curd (*caillé*) is carefully cut into small pieces and stirred vigorously to separate out the whey. As it separates, the curd turns grainy (**3**). The whey, which is usually thrown away, contains proteins and sugars.

Scalding
The curd is heated to 30°C and on to 50°C, over 45 minutes. The whey continues to separate, while the curd turns into grains the size of wheat, with a milky colour, rubbery consistency, and sugary taste. Scalding dries the curd and cooks it. If the curd is heated too quickly or too much, the pâte may break or swell during affinage.

Drawing Off (*le soutirage*)
The curd is gathered ("drawn off") in a linen gauze (**4**).

First Pressing
The curd is pressed (**5**) into a wooden hoop mould lined with gauze. A rope can be tightened to adjust the width of the cheese, which expands above and below the hoop (**6**). Seven or eight filled hoops are stacked (**7** and **8**) and pressed for 20 minutes. The curd grains begin to stick to each other.

Labelling and Second Pressing
The moulds are turned immediately and *casein* labels slipped in on the side. After the fourth turning, in the evening, when the wet gauze is changed for a dry one, the moulds are pressed at maximum force. The curd

grains fuse, and the cheese takes its final shape. The cheese is taken out of the mould and left for a day in a room at 13–16°C to let the pâte cool without drying the crust.

Salting
The cheese is soaked in brine for 12 hours to speed up the formation of the crust, improve its appearance, and reduce the risk of mould. It is allowed to dry naturally for 24 hours at 12–14°C.

Affinage
The affinage takes place over a minimum of 90 days in a well-ventilated cellar at 12°C and 95% humidity. On alternate days the surface of the cheese is rubbed with coarse salt and wiped with a cloth soaked in morge. (This is made by mixing brine with the sticky, light-brown substance found on the crusts of old cheeses.) The abrasive action of the salt limits the growth of mould and helps build up the strong crust (**9**) that conserves these large cheeses for a long time.

AISY CENDRÉ

This *artisanal* cheese from Bourgogne is made by burying a young cheese in ashes for a month. A number of cheeses can be used as a base for Aisy Cendré but the one shown here is a young Epoisses de Bourgogne (*p. 166*), a strong, washed cheese. It is not yet matured and would be perfect for people who prefer an unripe centre. The heart is white, with a texture of plaster, and is surrounded by a more creamy pâte. The salty taste indicates that it is still young.

Soft to slightly hard pâte; uncooked, unpressed

⊖	1 cm diameter, 3 cm high
⚖	200–250 g
🗋	50% min
✓	All year
⚗	Raw, whole
🍷	Hautes Côte de Nuits Villages

BOURGOGNE
Côte d'Or

Rind covered with ashes

Fermier cheeses are produced on small farms in rural areas such as this, whereas *industriel* cheeses are made in large-scale creameries

ARÔMES AU GÈNE DE MARC

This is an *artisanal* cheese available at the end of autumn. It is produced in the wine-growing region of Lyons, using a traditional method of curing. Ripe cheeses such as Rigotte (*p. 214*), Saint-Marcellin (*p. 222*), Pélardon (*p. 203*), and Picodon (*p. 206*) are placed in a barrel or large jar of *marc* for a minimum of one month. The *marc*, which consists of the damp skins, pips, and stalks left after the grapes have been pressed, permeates the cheese.

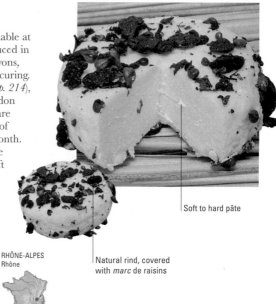

Soft to hard pâte

Natural rind, covered with *marc* de raisins

⊖ 6–7 cm diameter, 2–3 cm high	
⚖ 80–120 g	
✓ End of autumn, winter	RHÔNE-ALPES Rhône
🍶 Not defined	
🗓 Not defined	
◻ *Marc* de Côtes du Rhône	
♀ Muscat de Beaumes de Venise	

ARÔMES AU VIN BLANC

This cheese is made by filling the bottom of a large jar with white wine and placing a goat's-milk cheese, for example Saint-Marcellin (*p. 222*), on a wire rack just above the wine's surface. The jar is then sealed tightly and left for two to three weeks. As the wine evaporates, the cheese absorbs its aroma, while the pâte grows soft and moist. This is a refined and sought-after cheese, worthy of Lyons, the city of gourmets. It should not be eaten on its own.

Soft, moist pâte

No rind

⊖ 6–7 cm diameter, 2–3 cm high	
⚖ 80–120 g	
✓ End of autumn, winter	RHÔNE-ALPES Rhône
🗓 Not defined	
🍶 Not defined	
♀ Bourgogne, St. Romain	

FRENCH CHEESES

B

BANON (AOC)

The small mountain cheese shown is called Banon à la Feuille. It was made by a couple from the village of Puimichel near the town of Banon in Provence. After an affinage of two weeks, the cheese is dipped in *eau-de-vie* and wrapped in a chestnut leaf. Other versions include Banon Poivre and Banon Sarriette. The AOC was awarded in 2003.

Fine, soft white pâte, not too elastic; uncooked, unpressed

Dried chestnut leaf softened and sterilized by boiling in water and vinegar

Rind of natural mould

⊖	6–7 cm diameter, 2.5–3 cm high
⚖	90–120 g
🛢	45% min
✓	All year (cow's); spring to autumn (goat's)
🡒	Raw
🡒	Raw
🍷	Vin de Cassis
🍶	*Marc* of the region

PROVENCE

POIVRE D'ÂNE / PÈVRE D'AÏ

The cheese used as a base for Poivre d'Âne is the same as for Banon à la Feuille and may be made solely with either goat's or cow's milk, or a mixture of the two. Affinage, in dried savory, takes one month and *fermier*, *artisanal*, and *industriel* versions are produced. Pèvre d'Aï is the old Provençal name given to *Satureia hortensis* or summer savory, a southern European herb similar to thyme and mint, with a peppery bite that is used to flavour this cheese.

Soft pâte; uncooked, unpressed

Rind covered in dried savory

⊖	6–7 cm diameter, 3 cm high
⚖	100–120 g
🛢	45%
✓	All year (cow's); spring to autumn (goat's)
🡒	Raw
🡒	Raw
🍷	Coteaux d'Aix *rosé*

PROVENCE-ALPES-CÔTE-D'AZUR
Alpes-de-Haute-Provence

BARGKASS

Le Thillot, where this *fermier* cheese is produced, is a little village in the Vosges mountains of northeast France, famous for its cheeses, the best-known being Munster (*p. 192*). In the local dialect, *barg* means mountain, *kass* cheese. Bargkass has a soft but firm pâte, which is slightly elastic, with a few small holes. It has a light, soft smell and a rounded, relaxed taste with a slightly acid aftertaste. The cheese is best eaten with black sourdough bread. Affinage takes between six and eight weeks, during which time the cheese is brushed and turned once a week.

Light brown or brown rind, marked by the cloth during pressing

Slightly elastic pâte; uncooked, pressed

⊖	30 cm diameter, 6 cm high
⚖	7–8 kg
🏷	Not defined
✓	May to October
🐄	Raw
🍷	Pinot Noir

LORRAINE
Vosges

BEAUMONT

This *industriel* cheese was first made in 1881 at Beaumont, near Geneva in Switzerland, using the same method as for Tamié (*p. 230*). It is one of the first mass-produced cheeses to use raw milk. Affinage takes four to six weeks, during which time the cheese is washed.

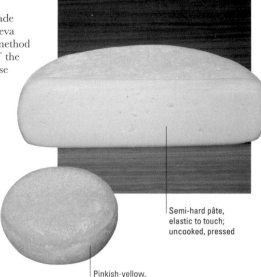

Semi-hard pâte, elastic to touch; uncooked, pressed

Pinkish-yellow, washed rind

⊖	20 cm diameter, 4–5 cm high
⚖	1.5 kg
🏷	48% min
✓	All year
🐄	Raw
🍷	Vin de Savoie, Hautes Côtes de Beaune

RHÔNE-ALPES
Haute-Savoie

BEAUFORT (AOC)

Beaufort is a large, round mountain cheese produced in the province of Savoie in the French Alps. Large cheeses with cooked and pressed pâtes are commonly called *gruyères* in France (not to be confused with Swiss Gruyère).

The average weight of a Beaufort is 45 kg, or all the milk produced by a herd of 45 cows in a day. Around 12 litres of milk make 1 kg of Beaufort. The cheese should have a moist, sticky crust and a concave surface due to the *cercle de Beaufort* used to shape it (*p. 41*).

Beaufort, affinage of five to six months

Hard, yellowish rind forms during affinage

Slightly concave circumference

⊖	35–75 cm diameter, 11–16 cm high
⚖	20–70 kg
⁂	62 g min. per 100 g cheese
🗁	48%
✓	All year; autumn if made in a *chalet d'alpage*
⌘	Raw, whole
♀	Seyssel, Chablis

RHÔNE-ALPES
Savoie,
Haute-Savoie

Types of Beaufort

Three versions of Beaufort are produced: Beaufort, Beaufort *d'été* (summer Beaufort) and Beaufort *d'alpage*, which is made in *chalets* in the mountains. The pâte of a winter cheese is white, that of a summer cheese, pale yellow. It is said that the chlorophyll from the grass and carotene from the alpine flowers give the summer cheeses both colour and flavour.

Production and Affinage

Fermier, chalet d'alpage, coopérative, and *industriel* versions of Beaufort are made. Affinage takes at least four months from the date of production, within areas specified by the AOC at below 15°C with at least 92% humidity, during which time the cheese is constantly wiped and rubbed with brine.

In November, five- or six-month-old Beauforts (shown above) appear at the Parisian markets and are the first of the *fromages d'alpage*. They have a soft, clear scent of milk, butter, flowers, and honey. The supple pâte has a flowery aroma, as well as a hidden acidity and salt. The taste lingers on the palate. Beaufort of this age goes well with white wine.

Some Beauforts are allowed an affinage of one year in a dark, cool cellar at 8–9°C and 98% humidity. Twice a week, the cheese is washed with brine and turned. A year-old cheese has a moist crust, under which there is a thin, grey layer that gradually melts into the pâte. The flavour is complex, with a stronger aroma than the younger cheeses and a more subtle taste of salt.

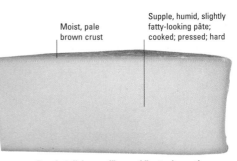

Moist, pale brown crust

Supple, humid, slightly fatty-looking pâte; cooked; pressed; hard

Beaufort *d'alpage*, affinage of five to six months

Beaufort *d'alpage*, affinage of approximately one year

Creamy to pale yellow pâte

Fine horizontal cracks and small holes are common in older cheeses

Beaufort *d'alpage*, affinage of one-and-a-half years

Cows grazing in the foothills of the French Alps

Beaufort Cows

The mahogany-coloured Beaufort cows are indispensable in the making of Beaufort cheese. This ancient mountain breed, originally from the Indo-Asian continent, crossed Central Europe before reaching France. The cows were named Tarines in 1863 and were entered in the *Herd Book* in 1888. During the winter they are kept in sheds to protect them from the snow, and according to AOC regulations, they are not allowed to be fed any silage or other fermented fodder. In spring, they are taken to high alpine meadows, and in autumn they descend to the lower meadows.

The milk of the Tarines is of excellent quality, with a fat content of 36.3% and protein content of 31.8%. In the 10 years of its working life, each cow produces an average of 4,338 kg of milk. Some of this milk is used to make several other great mountain cheeses such as Tomme de Savoie (*p. 231*) and Emmental (*p. 165*).

Cutting a Beaufort
The double-handled knife, known as a *guillotine*, is lightly moistened. It is then pushed towards the centre of the cheese in a firm, rolling, see-sawing manner.

Cheese Iron
This is used for taking samples from the inside of a cheese. The pâte of young Beaufort is elastic and yields easily to the knife.

Cheese Cellar
A cellar in Chambéry where up to 1,000 cheeses may be stored in November. The temperature is 8–9°C, with a humidity of 98%.

AOC Regulations: Beaufort

1 The milk must be taken into the dairy immediately after milking. Only where refrigeration tanks are in use on the farm may it be transported once a day. If the milk is refrigerated, the rennet must be added within 24 hours of milking, or 36 hours in winter.

2 No system or machinery that would allow the milk to be heated above 40°C before renneting is allowed on the premises.

3 The name of the cheese must be shown in blue *casein* letters that must always remain legible.

4 The terms *été* and *alpage* may be used only as follows: *été* for dairy products from June to October, including those made at a *chalet d'alpage*; *alpage* for summer products made twice a day at an alpine *chalet* with the milk from a single herd (no other milk may be mixed with it).

5 The salt must be applied to the surface of the cheese either directly or with brine.

6 If the cheese is sold cut and prepacked, the pieces must show a portion of the crust that is characteristic of Beaufort AOC.

AOC GRANTED 1976

Bleu

BLEU D'AUVERGNE (AOC)

There are two different sizes of Bleu d'Auvergne. The larger size has a diameter of 20 cm, with a height of 8–10 cm and weight of 2–3 kg. The smaller size is 10 cm in diameter, varies in height, and weighs anything from 350 g to 1 kg. Although these cheeses are traditionally round, a rectangular version is produced for export and prepack sale. This is 29 cm long, 8.5 cm wide, 11 cm high, and weighs 2.5 kg. The cheeses shown here were made with raw milk. The pâte is sticky, moist, and crumbly, with an even spread of veins, and its taste is tart. The spice of the mould blends perfectly with the well-integrated salt. This cheese is delicious in salad dressings, with chicory, nuts, or raw mushrooms. It also makes an excellent seasoning for piping-hot, fresh pasta.

Both *coopérative* and *industriel* versions of Bleu d'Auvergne are made within the areas specified by the AOC. Affinage takes a minimum of four weeks from the date of production for cheeses weighing over 1 kg, and two weeks for those weighing below 1 kg. The AOC was granted in 1975.

Natural rind

Pâte evenly veined with blue mould; uncooked, unpressed

⊖	20 cm diameter, 8–10 cm high (large); 10 cm diameter, variable height (small)
⚖	2–3 kg (large); 350 g–1 kg (small)
♣	52 g min. per 100 g
⅁	50%
✓	All year
⟁	Raw or pasteurized
♀	Sauternes, Maury (VDN)

AUVERGNE Cantal, Haute-Loire, Puy-de-Dôme; MIDI-PYRÉNÉES Aveyron, Lot; LIMOUSIN Corrèze; LANGUEDOC-ROUSSILLON Lozère

BLEU DES CAUSSES (AOC)

This commercially produced *coopérative* or *industriel* cheese is a mild cow's-milk version of Roquefort (*p. 216*). The solid flavour is a result of the affinage, which lasts at least 70 days, and usually three to six months, and takes place in natural caves called *fleurines* in the limestone plateaus of the Causses. The pâte of the summer cheeses is moist and ivory-yellow; winter cheeses are white and have a strong taste. They are best when matched with a naturally sweet white wine of good acidity, especially at the end of a meal. The AOC was granted in 1979.

Yellowish or white pâte with veins of blue mould; uncooked, unpressed

Natural rind

⊖	20 cm diameter, 8–10 cm high
⚖	2.3–3 kg
♣	53 g min. per 100 g cheese
⬡	45%
✓	All year
⟳	Raw, whole
♀	Barsac *moelleux*, Banyuls (VDN)

MIDI-PYRÉNÉES
Aveyron, Lot;
LANGUEDOC-
ROUSSILLON Gard,
Hérault, Lozère

BLEU DE COSTAROS

This traditional *fermier* cheese from the village of Costaros in the Auvergne is known locally as *fromage à vers*, meaning cheese eaten by worms – a reference to the cheese mite (*le ciron*) that lives in it. The slightly hard, elastic pâte is irregularly punctured by small holes and is sticky, with a faint smell and flavour of mould. Affinage takes two months. A local cheesemaker says that she eats the crust: "Oh, yes, all of it, even the worms."

Veins of natural concentrated mould

Uncooked, unpressed pâte

Hard natural rind forms during affinage

⊖	10 cm diameter, 7–8 cm high
⚖	550–600 g
⬡	Not defined
✓	All year
⟳	Raw
♀	Loupiac, Rivesaltes (VDN)

AUVERGNE
Haute-Loire

BLEU DU HAUT-JURA (AOC)

This mild blue cheese is also known as Bleu de Gex or Bleu de Septmoncel, but its official name is Bleu du Haut Jura. The rind is covered with a layer of white, powder-like mould that should be gently wiped off before eating. The pâte's aroma evokes the milk of rich pastures. Locally, it is often eaten with boiled potatoes.

The cows that are milked to make this cheese graze in the mountains of the Jura. It is said that the mould of the mountain grass and flowers passes into their milk, where it flourishes. Today, spores of the blue mould *Penicillium glaucum* are introduced into the milk. During affinage, air is inserted with a syringe into the pâte to allow the mould to grow internally.

During the affinage of around one month within AOC specified areas, the cheeses are dried and ripened naturally in the cellars of a *coopérative* at a humidity of 80%. The AOC was granted in 1977.

Gex is stamped on surface

Holes where air is inserted with syringe

Soft, ivory pâte, evenly marbled with pale green mould; uncooked, unpressed

Rind forms naturally; thin yellowish with a dry powdery mould, may show red spots

⊖	36 cm diameter, height not specified
⚖	7.5 kg
⋰	52 g min. per 100 g
⬚	50%
✓	All year; best in summer
⌕	Raw
♀	Sainte Croix du Mont (VDN)
❢	Port

RHÔNE-ALPES Ain;
FRANCHE-COMTÉ
Jura

BLEU FONDU À LA POÊLE

To make this tasty recipe, simply cut the cheese into slices and melt them slowly in a frying pan. These slices of cheese make an excellent topping for chicken breasts, or are equally delicious spread on slices of country bread and accompanied by a glass of Vin jaune d'Arbois.

BLEU DE LANGEAC

Locally, this *fermier* cheese from the town of Langeac in the Auvergne goes by the simple name of *fromage de la région*, meaning cheese of the region. It has a completely dry crust and a slight aroma. The pâte is firm and has a definite taste of mould. This is a salty and solid cheese, made from good, strong milk. Affinage takes two months.

Yellowish pâte, veined with natural mould; uncooked, unpressed

⊖	10–12 cm diameter, 4 cm high
⚖	450–500 g
🗗	Not defined
✓	All year
⟁	Raw
♀	Cérons *moelleux*, Sauternes *meilleur marché*, Banyuls (VDN)

Rough, dry rind forms naturally during affinage

AUVERGNE
Haute-Loire

BLEU DE LAQUEUILLE

Antoine Roussel from the village of Laqueuille first made this cheese in 1850 with mould grown on rye bread (his statue can be seen in the village). The pâte has a slight smell of the cellar and tastes of blue mould. Bleu de Laqueuille belongs to the same family as Fourme d'Ambert (*p. 167*). Today, production is limited to an *industriel* version. Affinage takes three months.

Soft pâte with blue mould; uncooked, unpressed

◇	49 cm diameter, 9.5 cm high
⚖	2.5 kg
🗗	45%
✓	Summer, autumn
⟁	Pasteurized
♀	Monbazillac *moelleux*, Rivesaltes (VDN)

Rind forms naturally during affinage

AUVERGNE
Puy-de-Dôme

BLEU DE LOUDES

The pâte of this *fermier* cheese from the town of Loudes in the Auvergne is firm and elastic, sticky, and slightly sour, with no particular smell. The presence of the mould is not immediately obvious. The cheese shown has been cut and exposed to the air for 24 hours. Affinage takes six weeks.

Firm pâte with traces of natural blue mould and a few holes; uncooked, unpressed

Hard, dry rind forms naturally during affinage

⊖	11 cm diameter, 6 cm high
⚖	600–650 g
🗗	Not defined
✓	All year
♻	Raw
♈	Sainte Croix du Mont *moelleux*, Rivesaltes (VDN)

AUVERGNE
Haute-Loire

BLEU DU QUERCY

A mild, commercially produced *bleu industriel* from the Quercy region suitable for the uninitiated who have yet to acquire a taste for blue cheeses. Affinage takes three months.

Pâte regularly veined, with natural green mould; uncooked, unpressed

Rind appears naturally during affinage

⊖	18 cm diameter, 9–10 cm high
⚖	2.5 kg
🗗	45%
✓	All year
♻	Pasteurized
♈	Cérons *moelleux*, Maury (VDN)

MIDI-PYRÉNÉES
Lot

BLEU DE SASSENAGE (AOC)

This traditional mountain blue, with a delicate flavour, was granted the AOC in 1998. Sassenage – a town on the plain near Grenoble – is included in the name because the 14th-century Counts of Sassenage had ordered their subjects to pay their taxes in cheeses, which increased production. However, the cheese is produced exclusively in the mountains, not in Sassenage. Efforts are being made to increase *fermier* production using the milk of three breeds of cattle: Montbéliard, Abondance, and Villard. Affinage takes two to three months.

Uncooked, unpressed pâte

Natural rind

⊖	30 cm diameter, 8–9 cm high
⚖	5–6 kg
🜄	45%
✓	Summer, autumn
⌀	Raw, pasteurized
♀	Barsac *moelleux*, Banyuls (VDN)

RHÔNE-ALPES
Isère

BRESSE BLEU

This commercially produced *industriel* cheese was first made after World War II in the province of Bresse in southern France. The soft pâte is peppered with small patches of blue mould. Three different sizes are produced. The large size is around 10 cm in diameter, 6.5 cm high, and weighs 500 g. The medium size is 8 cm in diameter, 4.5 cm high, and weighs 225 g. The small size is just 6 cm in diameter, 4.5 cm high, and weighs 125 g. Affinage takes two to four weeks.

Soft, supple pâte; uncooked, unpressed

Rind of white mould

⊖	6–10 cm diameter, 4.5–6.4 cm high
⚖	125–500 g
🜄	55%
✓	All year
⌀	Pasteurized
♀	Monbazillac *moelleux*, Rivesaltes, Rasteau (VDN)

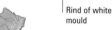

RHÔNE-ALPES
Ain

BLEU DE TERMIGNON

Termignon is the name of the village
in which this cheese is produced, at an
altitude of 1,300 m in the French Alps.
This is an outstanding cheese of great
quality, a little fatty, natural and down-to-
earth, made in very limited quantities, in
a *chalet d'alpage*. The cows are kept high
up in the National Park of Vanoise,
where they feed on grass and flowers.
It is here that the source of the mould
may be found. The mould passes into
the milk to create a refined flavour that
permeates the cheese. The blue mould
is natural and is not artificially induced
as in most other blue cheeses. It develops
and expands much more slowly and less
evenly. The crust of this cheese is white,
brown, hard, and looks like a rock, and
the pâte is crumbly. During affinage, the
cheeses are regularly turned and wiped
for four to five months.

Bleu de Termignon after an affinage of five months

Rind forms naturally
during affinage

Pâte is uncooked,
unpressed

Dry cheese

⊘ 28 cm diameter, 10 cm high	
⚖ 7 kg	
⊐ 50%	
✓ All year	
⊘ Raw	
♀ Tokay Selection de Grains Nobles *moelleux*, Rivesaltes Grand Cru (VDN)	

RHÔNE-ALPES
Savoie

LE PETIT BAYARD

This *artisanal* cheese from the Laiterie
Col Bayard in the Dauphiné region
has an affinage of about one month.

Pâte is uncooked,
unpressed

Rind of
natural mould

⊖ 12–13 cm diameter, 5 cm high	
⚖ 450 g	
⊐ 45%	
✓ All year	
⊘ Raw	
♀ Côtes de Provence	

PROVENCE-ALPES-
CÔTE D'AZUR
Hautes-Alpes

BOULE DE LILLE / MIMOLETTE FRANÇAISE

The name Boule de Lille allegedly derives from the *cave d'affinage*, or ripening cellar, in the city of Lille where affinage originally took place. The name Mimolette derives from *mi-mou* or half-soft. Some say this cheese originated in Holland, while others maintain that it has always existed in France. The true story behind its origins is probably that during the 17th century, the French minister Colbert forbade the import of foreign goods, including cheese, and the French began making Mimolette themselves. The method of production is the same as for the Dutch cheese Edam.

This is a northern *coopérative* or *industriel* cheese, about the size of a baby's head, flattened at top and bottom, with no distinct aroma. The pâte is semi-soft at the beginning, then slowly hardens and dries as the cheese ripens and finally cracks. Results of ripening vary, depending on the level of humidity in the cellar. The minimum affinage takes about six weeks; three months for a young Mimolette; six months for a *demi-étuvée* or *demi-vieille* (half-old); twelve months for a *vieille en étuvée* (old); and two years for a *très vieille* (very old) cheese. The colour of the pâte changes from carrot to orange brown, and with it the taste. The dry cheese can be grated and used for cooking.

Affinage of 18 months

Semi-hard to hard pâte; half-cooked, pressed

Hard, dry, yellowish-orange to light brown rind

Pâte varies in colour from yellowish-orange to red, with a few small holes

Affinage of 24 months

⊘	20 cm diameter, 15 cm high
⚖	2–4 kg
⁂	54 g per 100 g cheese
⊔	40%
✓	All year
⟁	Pasteurized
♀	Banyuls (VDN)

NORD-PAS-DE-CALAIS
Pas-de-Calais

Bresse Bleu and Bleu de Sassenage are among several ▶
blue cheeses made in the mountainous Rhône-Alpes region

Brebis de Pays

BREBIS DE PAYS DE GRASSE

This *fermier* cheese is made in the area around the town of Grasse. The ewes whose milk is used to make the cheese feed on the grass and lavender of the arid mountain plateaux, exposed to the pure air of the Alps and the Mediterranean breezes. The taste is light, and slightly acid for a sheep's-milk cheese made with quality milk. Brebis de Pays de Grasse is a perfect accompaniment to a baguette hot out of the oven. Affinage takes about six weeks.

Semi-hard pâte; uncooked, unpressed

Dry, natural rind

⊖	12 x 20 cm, 5–6 cm high
⚖	1.5–2 kg
❖	54 g per 100 g cheese
🄳	40%
✓	All year
⚵	Raw
♀	Cassis

PROVENCE-
ALPES-CÔTE-
D'AZUR
Alpes-Maritimes

BERGER PLAT

This *fermier* cheese is produced on a farm called Le Berger des Dombes in the province of Lyon. It was first made as a result of the introduction of Lacaune sheep into the region, the same breed as the ewes of Roquefort (*p. 216*). The rind is white or beige with a pale blue mould. Berger Plat is a cheese of gentle scent and taste. During affinage, the cheeses are left to rest on a bed of straw for 15–21 days.

Soft pâte; uncooked, unpressed

Rind of natural mould

⊖	8 cm diameter, 2.5 cm high
⚖	110 g
🄳	45%
✓	All year
⚵	Raw, whole
♟	Coteaux du-Lyonnais, Beaujolais

RHÔNE-ALPES
Ain

BREBIS DE BERSEND

This *fermier* cheese from the village of Bersend is one of the few sheep's milk cheeses produced in the province of Savoie. Until the 19th century, many ewes were reared in this mountainous area, close to the Swiss and Italian borders. Their numbers fell but at last appear to be on the increase again. Affinage takes a minimum of two months in a natural cellar.

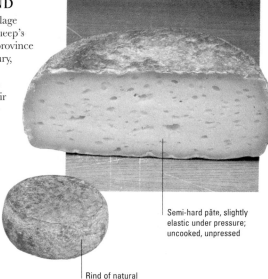

Semi-hard pâte, slightly elastic under pressure; uncooked, unpressed

Rind of natural white, brown, or grey mould

⊖	12 cm diameter, 5 cm high
⚖	580 g
🗋	45%
✓	Best in summer
⚱	Raw
⚱	Roussette de Savoie

RHÔNE-ALPES
Savoie

BREBIS DU LOCHOIS

This *fermier* cheese is a recently introduced sheep's-milk cheese in an area dominated by goat's-milk cheeses. There are only two producers in the whole of the Touraine. The cheese shown here was made in the village of Perrusson near the town of Loches. Affinage takes at least two weeks.

Soft pâte; uncooked, unpressed

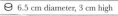

Rind of natural mould

⊖	6.5 cm diameter, 3 cm high
⚖	120–130 g
🗋	45%
✓	Best from end of winter to summer
⚱	Raw
⚱	Menetou Salon

CENTRE
Indre-et-Loire

LE CAUSSEDOU

This mild, gentle *fermier* cheese is produced by La Ferme Poux-del-Mas in the Quercy region. In French a *causse* is a limestone plateaux, for which the Quercy is famous, and *doux* means soft, describing the nature of the Caussedou. A natural blue mould appears on the rind after a few days. Affinage takes a minimum of 15 days at 13°C.

Soft pâte; uncooked, unpressed

Rind of natural mould

◇	7 cm square, 2–3 cm high
⚖	170–180 g
⊓	45% min
✓	All year
♧	Raw
⚑	Cahors

MIDI-PYRÉNÉES
Lot

FROMAGE DE BREBIS

This is a rich *fermier* cheese produced by GAEC Saint-Pierre in the village of Meyrueis. It is thick, with a robust flavour. In a cheese weighing 95 g, 25 g are fat, which accounts for a lot of calories! Affinage takes five to ten days.

Soft pâte; uncooked, unpressed

Rind of natural mould

◇	Square base, 2 cm high
⚖	95 g
⊓	50% min.
✓	All year
♧	Raw
⚑	Minervois

LANGUEDOC-
ROUSSILLON
Lozère

FROMAGE FERMIER PUR BREBIS

This *fermier* cheese is produced by the GAEC La Bourgeade near Saint-Hilaire Foissac on the western edge of the Massif Central. The cheese shown here looks soft at the centre and harder at the edges because it was bought at the beginning of its affinage from the farm where it was made. The flavour is slightly sour, with a well-balanced saltiness and a subtle sweetness that leaves a pleasant aftertaste. Affinage takes one to four weeks.

Soft pâte; uncooked, unpressed

Rind of natural mould

⊖	6–7 cm diameter, 2 cm high
⚖	85–100 g
🗋	45%
✓	March to December
⚐	Raw
❦	St. Pourçain

LIMOUSIN
Corrèze

FROMAGEON FERMIER AU LAIT CRU DE BREBIS

Although it is made from the same ewe's milk as Roquefort (*p. 216*), the Fromageon is a very different cheese, with a mild flavour. It is produced according to traditional *fermier* methods on a farm owned by J. Massebiau at La Cavalerie in Rouergue. Affinage takes a minimum of 10 days.

Soft pâte; uncooked, unpressed

Rind of natural mould

⊖	6–7 cm diameter, 2 cm high
⚖	85 g
🗋	Not defined
✓	End of winter to summer
⚐	Raw
❦	Côtes du Roussillon

MIDI-PYRÉNÉES
Aveyron

LE LACANDOU

In the northern part of the Aveyron, where the mountains stretch as far as the eye can see, M. Lacan makes the Lacandou following traditional *artisanal* methods. The farmer who produces the milk does not feed any silage to his ewes, allowing them to graze on the mountainside. Affinage takes three weeks.

Soft pâte; uncooked, unpressed

Rind of natural mould

⊖	10 cm diameter, 1.5 cm high
⚖	200 g
🗋	45% min
✓	All year
♘	Raw
♈	Côtes du Roussillon, Crozes Hermitage

MIDI-PYRÉNÉES
Aveyron

MOULAREN

Two women make this *fermier* cheese in the village of Montlaux, at an altitude of 600 m, where it snows occasionally. The ewes stay outdoors for eight months of the year and lamb in both October and March, enabling them to produce milk all year round. As with many washed-rind cheeses, the surface of Moularen cheese is pale orange. The pâte is creamy and thick and pleasant in the mouth. Affinage takes three weeks.

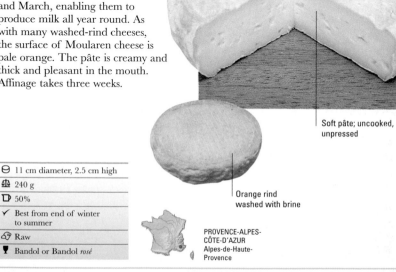

Soft pâte; uncooked, unpressed

Orange rind washed with brine

⊖	11 cm diameter, 2.5 cm high
⚖	240 g
🗋	50%
✓	Best from end of winter to summer
♘	Raw
♈	Bandol or Bandol *rosé*

PROVENCE-ALPES-
CÔTE-D'AZUR
Alpes-de-Haute-
Provence

PÉRAIL

This *fermier* or *artisanal* cheese is made according to traditional methods on the limestone plateaux of the Causse du Larzac in the province of Rouergue. It has a smell of ewe's milk and a smooth texture like very thick cream. The flavour is soft and velvety. Affinage takes at least one week.

Soft pâte; uncooked, unpressed

Rind of natural mould

⊖	8–10 cm diameter, 1.5–2 cm high
⚖	80–120 g
�□	45–50%
✔	Winter to summer
⚘	Raw
🍷	St. Chinian

MIDI-PYRÉNÉES
Aveyron

TRICORNE DE MARANS

The Tricorne was extinct for many years, but in 1984 production was started up again at the coastal town of Marans. The flavour is rich and slightly sweet and sour. The quality of the milk results in a high fat content. Cow's and goat's milk may be used if the ewe's milk is in short supply. For a goat's-milk cheese, 1.5 litres of milk are needed, but for a sheep's-milk cheese of the same size, just 0.7 litres are sufficient. This *fermier* cheese is usually eaten fresh, although it may be ripened for two or three weeks to three months.

Fresh or soft pâte; uncooked, unpressed

Rind: none when fresh; depends on the ripening

⊿	8 cm sides, 3 cm high
⚖	250 g
�□	48%
✔	All year; best at end of winter for ewe's-milk cheese
⚘	Raw
⚘	Raw
⚘	Raw
🍷	Haut Poitou

POITOU-CHARENTES
Charente-Maritime

Brebis des Pyrénées

The cheeses shown here are from the rugged Béarn and Basque regions
in the western Pyrénées, where there is a long tradition of making sheep's-
milk cheeses. Most are *fermier* cheeses made from whole raw milk, with
an undefined proportion of fat. A long affinage makes them hard.

They are usually simply called "mountain cheeses" or "sheep's cheeses".
Due to the limited amounts of ewe's milk available and the short period
of production, most of them are sold and eaten locally. The AOC
Ossau-Iraty-Brebis Pyrénées was granted in 1980.

Cut this cheese a while before eating to allow it to breathe. Brebis des
Pyrénées goes well with white wines such as Jurançon *sec* and Bordeaux *sec*.

OSSAU-IRATY-BREBIS PYRÉNÉES (AOC)

These cheeses are made with the
milk of mainly Manech ewes, and
fermier, *artisanal*, *cooperative*, and
industriel versions are produced.
There are three main sizes: small
(Petit-Ossau-Iraty-Brebis Pyrénées);
intermediate (non-*fermier*); large
(*fermier*). Affinage takes at least
90 days; 60 days for the small
version. The temperature of
the cellar must be below 12°C.

⊖	18–28 cm diameter, 7–15 cm high (sizes vary according to production)
⚖	2–7 kg (depending on size)
♣	58 g min. for 100 g cheese
⬭	50% min.
✓	All year, depending on affinage; autumn for mountain cheeses
⟐	Whole
♀	Irouléguy, Graves *sec*

AQUITAINE
Pyrénées-
Atlantiques

Stamp of Quality
The producer imprints
his initials into the rind
of the cheese using
special metal stamps.

AOC Regulations: Ossau-Iraty-Brebis Pyrénées

1 No ewe's milk may be made into
cheese until 20 days after lambing.
2 Renneting must take place
within 48 hours.
3 Coagulation must be obtained by
renneting. Any other enzyme,

especially of fungal or microbial
origin, is forbidden.
4 The term *montagne* may be used
only for cheeses made from the milk
of ewes grazing on summer pastures
between 10 May and 15 September.

5 Any cheese not conforming to the
regulations must be sold as *fromage
de brebis*, or sheep's-milk cheese.

AOC GRANTED 1980

ABBAYE DE BELLOCQ

This *fermier* cheese is made from the milk of red-nosed Manech ewes. The milk is bought in from neighbouring farms and taken to the Abbaye de Notre-Dame de Bellocq in the Pays Basque, where it is made into cheese. The cheese shown has a fine, dense pâte that is rich in fat. The strong, lingering flavour, like caramelized brown sugar, is the result of a long affinage of six months, a similar effect to a stew that has been simmering for a long time. It is hard to believe that the only additive is salt. Bread and wine go well with this cheese, which is one of the few Pyrenean sheep's-milk cheeses to be found in Paris.

Grey layer beneath rind | Semi-hard pâte; uncooked, lightly pressed

⊖	25 cm diameter, 11 cm high
⚖	5 kg
🝙	60% minimum
✓	All year
🐄	Raw, whole
🍷	Pacherenc du Vic-Bilh, Bordeaux *sec*

Grey, light brown, mahogany, or beige natural rind

AQUITAINE
Pyrénées-Atlantiques

ARDI-GASNA (1)

In the Basque language, *ardi* means ewe and *gasna* is cheese. This type of Ardi-Gasna is made by a shepherd near Saint-Jean-Pied-de-Port. In May he moves up to the mountains, where he milks his ewes and makes the cheese. A local shop owner then ripens each cheese with great care. The rind is yellow, orange, beige, and slightly moist. The pâte under the rind is greyish, the taste refined. This is a *fermier* cheese with an affinage of at least three months.

Semi-hard pâte; uncooked, pressed

Natural rind

⊖	19 cm diameter, 7 cm high
⚖	3 kg
🝙	50%
✓	All year, depending on affinage
🐄	Raw, whole
🍷	Margaux, Madiran

AQUITAINE
Pyrénées-Atlantiques

ARDI-GASNA (2)

This *fermier* cheese is made at the farm of Aire-Ona high in the Pyrénées, where 250 ewes and 60 cows are reared. In the Basque language, *aire* means air and *ona* pure or good. In spring, the animals are taken up to graze on the lush alpine pastures. The spring cheese, made from ewe's milk, is highly recommended. During winter the animals come down from the mountains and are fed on corn and hay. Affinage may last up to two years, but the young cheese, ripened for two to three months only, has a pleasant aroma.

Natural rind

Semi-hard pâte; uncooked, lightly pressed

⊖	27 cm diameter, 8–9 cm high
⚖	4 kg
🗓	Not defined
✓	Best in spring
🐏	Raw, whole
🍷	Irouléguy, Côtes de Bordeaux (young)

AQUITAINE
Pyrénées-
Atlantiques

FROMAGE DE VACHE BRÛLÉ

These two *fermier* cheeses are also made in the Pays Basque from cow's milk. The Fromage de Vache Brûlé is scented by charring the rind over oak charcoal. The pâte is fine and sour.

Pâte is semi-hard; uncooked, slightly pressed

Charred rind

CAILLÉ DE LAIT DE VACHE

This is made by mixing fresh cheese with sugar or honey. It is eaten with coffee, or with sugar and Armagnac for dessert.

⊖	13–15 cm diameter, 5–6 cm high
⚖	1–1.3 kg
🗓	Not defined
✓	Best in spring
🐄	Raw, whole
🍷	Bergerac, light and fruity
☕	Coffee (*caillé de lait de vache*)

AQUITAINE
Pyrénées-
Atlantiques

AUBISQUE PYRÉNÉES

The letter "F" stamped on this young *fermier* cheese is the initial of one of three shepherds, who, according to local people, are the only producers of this cheese in the Vallée d'Ossau. It is made from a mixture of ewe's and cow's milk, the proportions of which vary according to season and availability. The flavour is mild and smooth. Generally, the higher the percentage of cow's milk, the softer the flavour. The mixture requires a shorter affinage of two months than that required by a pure ewe's-milk cheese.

Semi-hard pâte; uncooked, pressed

Natural rind

⊖	26–30 cm diameter, 10 cm high
⚖	5 kg
⬥	Not defined
✓	Spring to autumn
⟁	Raw
⟲	Raw
♥	Madiran (young), Côte de Blaye

AQUITAINE
Pyrénées-Atlantiques

BREBIS PAYS BASQUE, LE CAYOLAR

A young *fromager* goes to market in a van that doubles as a mobile cheese shop. His *fermier* cheese has a brown rind, a viscous grey and shiny pâte, and holes due to the pressure applied in the manufacturing process and during the affinage of seven months. The proportion of fat is probably very high. The name could not be more straightforward: Brebis, Pays Basque, le Cayolar, in other words a ewe's-milk cheese made in a *cayolar*, or mountain hut of the Basque Country. This one was bought in Saint-Jean-Pied-de-Port.

Semi-hard pâte; uncooked, pressed

Hard, natural rind

⊖	19 cm diameter, 7.5 cm high
⚖	2.5 kg
⬥	Not defined
✓	Best at the end of summer
⟲	Raw, whole
♥	Pacherenc du Vic-Bilh

AQUITAINE
Pyrénées-Atlantiques

BREBIS

This *fermier* cheese, which was bought in the little mountain village of Izeste in the Vallée d'Ossau, is made in a *cayolar*, or mountain hut. It is surprisingly strong given the smooth, mild flavour of the milk. The letters "C" and "D" stamped in the rind are the initials of the shepherd and owner – M. Daniel Casau. Affinage takes three months.

| Natural rind | Semi-hard pâte; uncooked, slightly pressed |

⊖	26 cm diameter, 8 cm high
⚖	4.05 kg
⮻	Not defined
✓	Best at the end of summer
⬧	Raw, whole
♥	Irouléguy, Graves *sec*

AQUITAINE
Pyrénées-
Aquitaine

MIXTE

A stream, the Gave d'Ossau, passes through the village of Izeste from its source on the Pic du Midi d'Ossau, which reaches a height of 2,887 m. In the village there is a little house, at the entrance of which a small sign reads: "cow, goat, ewe". The locals come here with their churns to buy milk. Just inside the door two or three cheeses are displayed, which the owner of the house cuts on a wooden board. The flavour of these cheeses is compact, with an aroma that fills the mouth. The strength of this cheese is surprising considering that the milk is so mild and smooth. Affinage takes three months.

| Natural rind | Semi-hard pâte; uncooked, slightly pressed |

⊖	27–31 cm diameter, 8 cm high
⚖	5.1 kg
⮻	Not defined
✓	Best at the end of summer
⬧	Raw, whole, 50%
⬧	Raw, whole, 50%
♥	Irouléguy, Graves *sec*

AQUITAINE
Pyrénées-
Aquitaine

BREBIS PYRÉNÉES

At the market in the town of Saint-Jean-de Luz, a *fromager* and his daughter sell large, hard *fermier* cheeses that no one is allowed to touch. They have been produced on a farm near Arudy, a town in the Vallée d'Ossau. Affinage takes six to ten months.

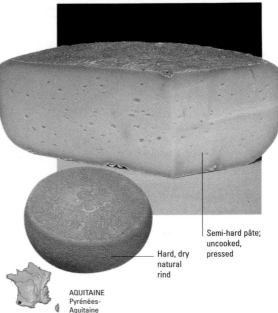

Semi-hard pâte; uncooked, pressed

Hard, dry natural rind

⊖	26–28 cm diameter, 9–10 cm high
⚖	5–6 kg
🗋	Not defined
✓	All year, depending on affinage
🝙	Raw, whole
🍷	Pacherenc du Vic-Bilh

AQUITAINE
Pyrénées-Aquitaine

FROMAGE DE BREBIS

The region where this *fermier* mountain cheese is produced is often snowbound in the winter, with limited means of transport. Cheese is an important food since it can be made with the plentiful summer milk and stored for months. Fromage de Brebis is made for six to seven months of each year, and has an affinage of eight months. It is a large and heavy cheese, with a reddish-brown rind. The yellow pâte is compact, and the rind, which preserves it, quite solid. This is a tasty cheese that should be chewed for a while to allow all the flavours to develop. Most of the production is consumed in the region.

Semi-hard pâte; uncooked, pressed

Natural rind

⊖	25 cm diameter, 9 cm high
⚖	5 kg
🗋	Not defined
✓	Best in autumn
🝙	Raw
🍷	Pacherenc du Vic-Bilh, Côtes de Blaye

AQUITAINE
Pyrénées-Aquitaine

FROMAGE DE BREBIS ET VACHE FERMIER

This *fermier* cheese is made from a mixture of cow's and ewe's milk. The "S" on the rind is the initial of the cheesemaker, M. Sauche, who makes only 200 cheeses in a year and sells them wholesale to M. J-C. Chourre when they are still *blanc*, or fresh. There are always some 1,500 cheeses ripening in M. Chourre's cellar, which has been in his family for generations. The quality of the cheeses depends on the milk – the ewes that give the best milk are two to three years old. Affinage takes around three months.

Hard pâte with small holes; uncooked, slightly pressed

Natural, reddish-yellow rind

⊖	24–26 cm diam., 8 cm high
▦	3.5 kg
🗗	Not defined
✓	All year, best in summer
⬧	Raw
⬧	Raw
♀	Irouléguy

AQUITAINE
Pyrénées-Atlantiques

FROMAGE DE BREBIS VALLÉE DE L'OSSAU (AOC)

A superb *fromagerie*, or cheese shop, can be found at the port of Saint-Jean-de-Luz. Here you can buy sheep's-milk cheeses from the two main cheese-producing regions of the Pyrénées: the Béarn and the Pays Basque. The owner is a *maître affineur*, a master cheese ripener. His cheeses are refined and elegant, a perfect union of mountains and soil, ewe, shepherd, and *affineur*, with all the balanced flavours this imparts to the palate. Affinage lasts five months. The AOC was granted in 1980.

Semi-hard pâte; uncooked, slightly pressed

Natural, hard rind

⊖	26 cm diameter, 9 cm high
▦	5 kg
🗗	50%
✓	Spring to autumn
⬧	Raw, whole
♀	Irouléguy, Entre Deux Mers *sec*

AQUITAINE
Pyrénées-Atlantiques

FROMAGE FERMIER AU LAIT DE BREBIS

This sweet, salty *fermier* cheese, is produced at the Penan farm in the province of Béarn. The owner of the farm milks the ewes, makes the cheese, and sells it at the town market. Of her cheeses she says, "People now prefer young cheeses, not too salty. I make them to be eaten immediately. It is better to sell them quickly, especially the heavy ones. But a minimum of salt is necessary. It is really best to leave them a while, but then they become smaller and more expensive." At the start of affinage the cheeses are wiped, then brushed over four months.

Semi-hard pâte; uncooked, pressed

Natural rind

⊖	9–26 cm diam., 5–11 cm high
⚖	0.5–6 kg
🗋	Not defined
✓	Summer to winter
ᗡ	Raw, whole
♀	Jurançon *sec*

AQUITAINE
Pyrénées-
Atlantiques

FROMAGE FERMIER AU LAIT DE VACHE

This cow's-milk cheese, like the ewe's-milk cheese shown above, is another *fermier* cheese produced by the Penen farm in the province of Béarn. It comes in three different sizes: large, medium, and small. During affinage it is wiped and brushed, sometimes with salt, then left for at least two months.

Semi-hard pâte; uncooked, pressed

Velvety, natural rind

⊖	11–20 cm diameter, 5–6 cm high
⚖	1–2 kg
🗋	Not defined
✓	All year; best in spring
ᗡ	Raw
♀	Madiran

AQUITAINE
Pyrénées-
Atlantiques

FROMAGE D'OSSAU, LARUNS

This *fermier* cheese is made in the Hameau de Bagès, in the department of Laruns, one of the cheesemaking centres of the Ossau Valley. It has a robust flavour and is traditionally eaten at the end of a meal consisting of a nourishing local soup called *garbure* (made from leeks, cabbage, celery, white beans, bacon, goose confit, and goose fat simmered together for three to four hours) followed by roast lamb. Affinage takes five months.

Semi-hard pâte; uncooked, pressed

Hard, natural rind

⊖	25 cm diameter, 12 cm high (not level)
⚖	6 kg
🗋	Not defined
✓	Best at the end of summer
🐏	Raw, whole
♀	Jurançon *sec*

AQUITAINE
Pyrénées-
Atlantique

FROMAGE DE VACHE

This is a *fermier* cheese made in Hameau de Bagès, in the department of Laruns in the Ossau Valley. Surrounded by mountains and just 29 km from the Spanish border, the town perches high in the Pyrénées at an altitude of 531 m, where the air is pure and cold. The cheese has a rich, complex flavour. Affinage takes at least two months.

Pâte is semi-hard; uncooked, pressed

Natural rind

⊖	24 cm diameter, 6 cm high
⚖	3 kg
🗋	Not defined
✓	Spring
🐄	Raw
♟	Madiran

AQUITAINE
Pyrénées-
Atlantique

FROMAGE DE PAYS, MIXTE

A sign in the shop in the area of the Col d'Aubisque where this cheese was bought says simply Fromage de Pays, or regional cheese. Most of the farms in the area raise cows and ewes. When there is not enough ewe's milk for making cheese, cow's milk is added. The pâte is sweeter, closer to butter, yellower, and less dry when the two milks are mixed. The usual affinage of this *fermier* cheese is eight months.

Semi-hard pâte, yellowish; uncooked, pressed

Natural rind

⊖	25 cm diameter, 9 cm high
⚖	4.6 kg
�ï	Not defined
✓	All year, depending on affinage
⋌	Raw
ᘓ	Raw
⚲	Jurançon *sec*

AQUITAINE
Pyrénées-
Atlantique

Farms in Aquitaine produce many variations of Brebis des Pyrénées, which are uncooked, pressed, semi-hard cheeses with a natural mould

LARUNS

Every year, a cheese fair is held in Laruns, where shepherds from all over the region come to show and sell their products, and price levels are fixed for the next year. Because ewe's milk is more concentrated than cow's milk, only 5.5 litres are needed to make 1 kg of cheese, compared with 10 litres of cow's milk. The rind of the *fermier* cheese shown here is dry, while the pâte is grey, very crumbly, with the colour of a ripe ewe's-milk cheese. The affinage of six months has given the cheese a balanced blend of acidity, salt, and fat. The strong animal smell of sheep adds flavour to the cheese. A total lack of softness is another characteristic.

Semi-hard pâte; uncooked, pressed

Hard, dry, natural rind

⊖	28 cm diameter, 9 cm high
⚖	5 kg
◨	Not defined
✓	All year, Laruns; October, Montagne *d'été*
⊕	Raw
⚲	Jurançon *sec*

AQUITAINE
Pyrénées-Atlantique

MATOCQ (AOC)

This *artisanal* cheese is named after its maker, M. C. Matocq, who produces it from sheep's milk in the town of Asson in the Béarn. It is a solid, well-structured cheese with a salty flavour. Affinage takes six months to one year.

Matocq is one of the few cheeses to have a label and an AOC. It falls into the AOC category of Ossau-Iraty-Brebis Pyrénées, which was granted in 1980.

Pâte is semi-hard; uncooked, pressed

Natural rind

⊖	26 cm diameter, 9 cm high
⚖	4.2 kg
◨	50%
✓	All year; best from end of spring to autumn
⊕	Raw, whole
⚲	Jurançon *sec*

AQUITAINE
Pyrénées-Atlantique

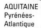

MATOCQ

The cheese shown is a cow's-milk Matocq. It is as rich as the sheep's-milk version. Annual production of sheep's-milk cheeses amounts to 200 tonnes, mixed-milk cheeses (half ewe's milk, half cow's milk) to 110 tonnes, and cow's-milk cheeses to 200 tonnes. Their affinage takes some six to eight months in cellars at 8–10°C, although some are left to mature for a year. M. Matocq's cheeses are exported to Germany, Belgium, and the United States in increasing numbers each year.

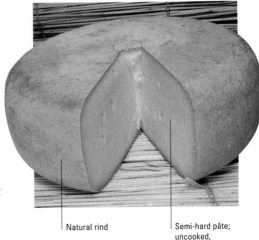

Natural rind

Semi-hard pâte; uncooked, pressed

⊖ 24 cm diameter, 9 cm high	
⚖ 4.2 kg	
🗁 50%	
✓ All year	
🗁 Whole	
♀ Jurançon *sec*	

AQUITAINE
Pyrénées-Atlantique

OSSAU FERMIER

This *fermier* cheese has an affinage of four-and-a-half months. Cheeses from the Pyrénées are never ripened in a hurry. The one shown here is a little young but perfect, with small holes spread evenly throughout the pâte. In the mouth, this cheese seems dry and salted. It has a good scent of well-integrated fat. As it is chewed, the sour-sweet flavour and aroma are released. This is a strong cheese with nothing soft or flamboyant about it.

Semi-hard pâte; uncooked, slightly pressed

⊖ 26 cm diameter, 9 cm high	
⚖ 4 kg	
🗁 Not defined	
✓ All year, depending on affinage	
🗁 Raw, whole	
♥ Madiran (type Château Montus), Pauillac	

AQUITAINE
Pyrénées-Atlantique

Natural rind

MAKING CHEESE IN THE MOUNTAINS

Summer arrives late in the French Alps, but each year, as soon as the last of the winter snow has disappeared, the *alpage*, or summer migration of herds, begins. In mid to late June, herds of cattle, often owned by more than one farmer, are entrusted to herdsmen or women, known as *alpagistes*, who accompany them to the upper slopes. The animals move along at their own pace, grazing and browsing on flowers. The *alpagistes* stay in *chalets*, where they milk the cows twice a day and make cheese. The *chalets* are scattered all over the mountains and provide a kind of cheesemaking relay since the animals do not stop at a single place but keep on climbing. When all the grass in one area is eaten, the herd moves on upwards in search of new pastures. By the middle of August, the herd will have reached almost 3,000 m, just below the snowline. The first snows give the signal for the descent; stage by stage, the *alpagiste* takes the animals back down over the same slopes, which are rich and grassy again. On Saint-Michael's Day,

Mountain Milk
The rich and creamy milk produced by cattle grazing on the upper alpine slopes is used by the *alpagiste* to make cheese in *chalets* on the way up the mountain.

29 September, the herd returns to the village. The cows go back to their sheds to calve, and the production of winter cheeses begins.

In the Pyrénées a similar summer migration, known as *transhumance*, takes place, but here, the animals are sheep and goats tended by shepherds.

TOURMALET

Despite the imposing size of most Pyrenean cheeses, there are some of a size that is easier to sell and buy. The Tourmalet, named after a mountain in the region where it is produced, is an *artisanal* cheese made with ewe's milk. It has a solid, pleasantly rustic flavour and aroma, and easily holds its own against the bigger cheeses. Affinage takes one month.

Semi-hard pâte; uncooked, pressed

Hard, natural rind

⊖	10 cm diameter, 7 cm high
⚖	600 g
🗋	50%
✓	All year
⟁	Raw
♀	Jurançon *sec*

AQUITAINE
Pyrénées-
Atlantiques

LE PETIT PARDOU

This cheese is a cow's-milk version of the Tourmalet shown opposite. Both cow's and ewe's-milk versions are *artisanal* cheeses made in the town of Laruns.

Semi-hard pâte; uncooked, pressed

⊖	10 cm diameter, 7 cm high
⚖	600 g
⛾	50%
✓	All year
⌘	Not defined
♈	Madiran, Fronsac

AQUITAINE
Pyrénées-
Atlantiques

Hard,
natural, rind

Mountain sheep in the Pyrénées – their milk is used for Tourmalet, Matocq, Laruns, and many other regional cheeses

Brie

BRIE DE MEAUX (AOC)

Situated some 50 km east of Paris, the green region of Brie has a long history of cheesemaking. One reason for the rise in importance of the cheese was the proximity of the region to Paris, which was a great centre of consumption. The geographical separation between the places of production and affinage is a Brie tradition.

When a Brie de Meaux is sold, at least half the thickness of the cheese should be ripe. This is a refined cheese with a balanced appearance and smell, and the sweetness one would expect from a first-class dairy product. The cheese shown here is well-ripened, with a slight smell of mould. Its rind looks like white velvet and when the cheese is very ripe, the top and sides will redden. The pâte is compact, even-textured, and the colour of straw. It has a a slight scent of mould, and is full of sweet as well as smoky aromas, with a rich, condensed flavour.

Brie de Meaux is an *artisanal* or *industriel* cheese, and it must be cured within the AOC regions named below, as well as in parts of Haute-Seine, Seine-Saint-Denis, Val-de-Marne, and Paris.

During production of the cheese the curd is barely cut. Drainage is spontaneous and liquid evaporates from the large surface. If drainage is too quick, the cheese may split. Affinage normally takes eight weeks.

Rind of thin, white mould, with red patches and lines

Soft, even-textured, creamy pâte; unpressed, uncooked

⊖	36–37 cm diameter, 3–3.5 cm high
⚖	2.5–3 kg
🗋	Not defined
⁂	44 g min. per 100 g cheese
✓	All year
👁	Raw
🍷	St. Julien, Vosne Romanée, Hermitage

ÎLE-DE-FRANCE Seine-et-Marne
CENTRE Loiret
CHAMPAGNE-ARDENNE Aube, Marne, Haute-Marne
LORRAINE Meuse
BOURGOGNE Yonne

AOC Regulations: Brie de Meaux

1 The milk must be heated to a maximum of 37°C once and only at the renneting.
2 The cheese must be cast manually into its mould with a special *pelle à Brie* (Brie shovel).
3 The cheese must be salted with dry salt exclusively.

AOC GRANTED 1980

BRIE FERMIER

On her farm at Glandon, Mme Clein is the last cheesemaker to make the *fermier* Brie using traditional techniques. The development of the mould on the rind is encouraged by hot, ammonia-laden air from the cowshed. Her partner Mme Ganot ripens it, then sells it at the markets of Meaux and Melun. She says: "It's good with green apples and walnuts and perhaps a glass of champagne". It cannot be called a Brie de Meaux AOC because it is not the right size. The colour of the rind, with red marks from lying on straw, is that of a ripe Brie that is full of flavour and aroma. Affinage takes two months.

Soft pâte; uncooked, unpressed

Rind of white mould

⊖	32 cm diameter, 2 cm high
⚖	1.88 kg
🗓	Not defined
✓	From summer
♻	Raw
🍷	St. Julien, Vosne Romanée, Hermitage

ILE-DE-FRANCE
Seine-et-Marne

BRIE NOIR

The aged Brie shown on the right has had an affinage of about a year. It is thick and velvety. The locals soak it in their *café au lait* for breakfast.

Rind is crumbly

Dry pâte needs to be chewed

⊖	30 cm diameter, 2 cm high
⚖	1.45 kg
🗓	Not defined
✓	All year
♻	Raw
🍷	Château Chalon *jaune*, Arbois *jaune*

ÎLE-DE-FRANCE
Seine-et-Marne

BRIE DE MELUN
(AOC)

Brie de Melun and Brie de Meaux are both from the same region, but whereas the Meaux is refined and relaxed, Melun is strong, robust, and salty. This difference derives from the varying methods of production. Coagulation for Meaux takes less than 30 minutes thanks to renneting, while Melun depends on lactic fermentation, which takes at least 18 hours. The affinage also takes longer and cheeses are left to mature for a minimum of four weeks, but usually seven to ten. The *artisanal* cheese shown has a musty smell, and the pâte is creamy, sweet, and slightly salty.

Most Brie de Melun is eaten in the region and sold fresh or ripe at local markets. The fresh cheese is sour due to the lactic fermentation, and sweet, like good thick milk.

Rind of thin, white mould, with brown or red stains and lines

Soft, even-textured pâte of uniform cream colour; uncooked, unpressed

Affinage of ten weeks

Affinage of ten weeks

Fresh cheese

ILE-DE-FRANCE
Seine-et-Marne
CHAMPAGNE-
ARDENNES Aube
BOURGOGNE Yonne

⊖	27–28 cm diameter, 3.5–4 cm high
⚖	1.5–1.8 kg
🗋	45%
⁂	40 g for 100 g cheese
✓	All year
⟳	Raw
🍷	Bourgogne

AOC Regulations: Brie de Melun

1 The milk must be heated once only to a maximum of 30°C, but only at the renneting.
2 Coagulation must be caused mainly by lactic fermentation but also by renneting.
3 Coagulation must take at least 18 hours.
4 Drainage must be slow.
5 The curd must be cast manually.
6 The cheese must be salted exclusively with dry salt.

AOC GRANTED 1980

BRIE DE COULOMMIERS

It is said that Coulommiers is the ancestor of all Brie cheeses. Until 1989, a *fermier* version of the Brie de Coulommiers was produced by Mme Storme, who used to rear 50 cows. The cheeses were then taken to be ripened for four weeks by a family firm in the region, the Société Fromagère de la Brie.

The local people prefer the cheese when it is firm, not runny. Its sweet aroma and smell of mould spread in the mouth. Today, the *fermier* version is no longer made, and only an *artisanal* version is produced.

Soft pâte; uncooked, unpressed

Rind of white mould

⊖	21–25 cm diameter, 3 cm high
⚖	1.3 kg
🗅	45%
✓	Autumn to winter
⏀	Raw
🍷	Bourgogne, Bordeaux, Côtes du Rhône

ILE-DE-FRANCE
Seine-et-Marne

BRIE DE MONTEREAU

This *artisanal* cheese is close to Brie de Melun in taste. Its aftertaste and smell are strong for a Brie. The cheese shown is still quite young. Affinage takes five to six weeks.

Soft pâte, no elasticity; uncooked, unpressed

Rind of white mould, sometimes with red stains

⊖	18–20 cm diameter, 3 cm high
⚖	0.81 kg
🗅	40–45%
✓	Summer to winter
⏀	Raw
🍷	Bourgogne, Bordeaux, Côtes du Rhône

ILE-DE-FRANCE
Seine-et-Marne

COULOMMIERS

Brie cheeses come in three sizes: large, medium, and small. The Coulommiers is small but quite thick. The one shown here is at the point of affinage, which is how the local people prefer it. It has a small heart with the sourness of a fresh cheese, set in a pâte of pale yellow that has a sweet and melting taste. In this one single cheese, it is possible to see the different stages of affinage. Production may be *fermier*, *artisanal*, or *industriel*, with an affinage of eight weeks for the raw version and at least four weeks for the pasteurized version.

Small fresh heart

Soft pâte; uncooked, unpressed

Rind of white mould, with some red stains

⊖	12.5–15 cm diameter, 3–4 cm high
⚖	400–500 g
☘	140 g min. per cheese
⤳	40% min.
✓	End of summer (*fermier*); all year (pasteurized)
♻	Raw or pasteurized
♟	Bourgogne, Bordeaux, Côtes du Rhône

ILE-DE-FRANCE
Seine-et-Marne

LE FOUGERUS

This *artisanal* cheese belonging to the Brie group is slightly larger than a Coulommiers. Originally, it was made on a farm for family consumption, with the fern leaf serving as decoration and flavouring. It was commercially produced for the first time at the beginning of the 20th century. The scent of the fern blends with the smell of the mould. The pâte is supple and sweet and has a salty taste. Affinage takes four weeks.

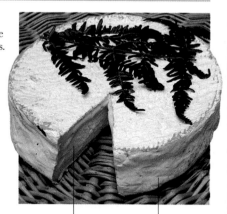

Soft pâte; uncooked, unpressed

Rind of white mould

⊖	16 cm diameter, 4 cm high
⚖	650 g
⤳	45–50%
✓	Spring to autumn
♻	Raw
♟	Bourgogne, Bordeaux, Côtes du Rhône

ILE-DE-FRANCE
Seine-et-Marne

BRIE DE NANGIS

This *artisanal* cheese was ousted by the Brie de Melun (*p. 82*) and disappeared from the market for some time. It was revived by a single maker but is no longer produced in the town of Nangis. The heart of the cheese shown here is barely ripe and would suit those who prefer their Brie young. Affinage takes four to five weeks.

Soft pâte; uncooked, unpressed

Rind of white mould

⊖	20–23 cm diameter, 4 cm high
⚖	1–1.2 kg
🗋	45%
✓	Summer to winter
🜪	Raw
🍷	Bourgogne, Bordeaux, Côtes du Rhône

ILE-DE-FRANCE
Seine-et-Marne

BRIE DE PROVINS

After a total, but short disappearance, the Provins has made a modest re-entry. The heart of the medium-sized Brie shown here is on the point of turning into a creamy pâte. It no longer rasps on the tongue nor the bottom of the mouth. Some people like young Brie, but it is best when ripened, as here, when the bouquet of the milk and a refined smell of mould are fully developed. This is an *artisanal* cheese with an affinage of four to five weeks.

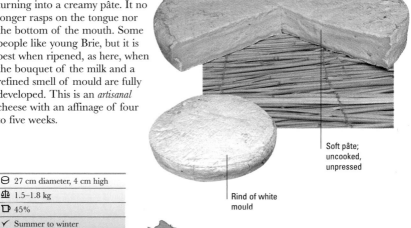

Soft pâte; uncooked, unpressed

Rind of white mould

⊖	27 cm diameter, 4 cm high
⚖	1.5–1.8 kg
🗋	45%
✓	Summer to winter
🜪	Raw
🍷	Bourgogne, Bordeaux, Côtes du Rhône

ILE-DE-FRANCE
Seine-et-Marne

FRENCH CHEESES

Cabécou/Rocamadour (AOC)

Made with raw goat's milk from the plains, these tiny but highly pleasing cheeses mature well, acquiring body and presence. Each year some 490 tonnes are produced in the triangle between Rocamadour, Gramat, and Carlucet. In the *langue d'Oc*, the old language of the south, a *cabécou* is a small goat's cheese. The fresh spring cheeses are well worth trying. The AOC "Rocamadour", reserved solely for goat's milk cheeses both raw and whole, was granted on 16 January, 1996.

CABÉCOU DE GRAMAT

This *fermier* cheese has an affinage of a minimum of ten days.

MIDI-PYRÉNÉES
Lot

Rind of natural mould

Cabécou de Gramat

Soft pâte; uncooked, unpressed

CABÉCOU

This is a *fermier* Cabécou from the region of Quercy.

PICADOU

This cheese is produced by wrapping a ripe Cabécou in walnut or plane leaves. It is then sprayed with *marc* of plums and preserved in an airtight container. The aroma of the *marc* permeates the cheese. The crushed pepper causes an almost crispy, pleasant sensation in the mouth, adding spice to an already piquant cheese, hence its name.

Cabécou

Rind of natural mould

Picadou

Soft pâte; uncooked, unpressed

⊖	4–5cm diameter, 1–1.5 cm high
⚖	30–40 g
🝧	45%
⅄	Spring to autumn
⟁	Raw
⚖	Raw
♀	Jurançon *sec*, Vouvray *sec*, Tursan (with Cabécou)
⎘	*Marc, Eau de vie* of plums (with Picadou)

◀ **The village of Camembert where Marie Harel, the alleged inventor of the famous cheese, once lived**

CABÉCOU DE ROCAMADOUR (AOC)

These small *fermier* and *artisanal* cheeses mature rapidly. They have a thin rind, and a tender, creamy pâte with a subtle scent reminiscent of milk and mould. The aftertaste is equally light, of sugar and hazelnuts. Affinage takes anything up to four weeks. The cheeses shown here have all had different periods of affinage. The AOC was granted in 1996.

Soft to hard pâte; uncooked, unpressed

Affinage of about one week

⊖	4–5 cm diameter, 1–1.5 cm high
⚖	30–40 g
🗋	45%
✓	Spring to autumn
🥄	Raw
🍷	Gaillac
🍷	Bergerac *sec*

Rind of thin, natural mould depending on affinage

MIDI-PYRÉNÉES
Lot

Affinage of about two weeks

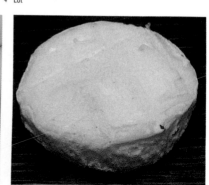

Affinage of about two weeks

Affinage of about four weeks

Affinage of about six weeks

HOW CAMEMBERT IS MADE

Camembert Fermier
This colourful sign advertising farmhouse Camembert marks the entrance to the farm where François Durand has made cheeses since 1981.

Normandie is a mild region in northern France where it tends to rain a lot. The gentle sun and humidity produce lush green grass on which the typical black-and-white Normande cows can feed. Their milk is of excellent quality, and has made Normandie famous for its butter and cream, as well as its traditional, noble cheeses such as Pont l'Evêque, Livarot, and Camembert.

Since 1981, François Durand, who was born in Paris in 1961, has produced Camembert *fermier* just outside the village of Camembert in Normandie. He makes at least 650 cheeses a week with the milk of 45 cows. Some 2.3 litres of milk are required in order to make just one Camembert of 250 g. Total production of the cheeses takes two days. Although it is of an excellent quality, his cheese has not been granted an AOC, which recognizes Camembert de Normandie only.

1 Normande Cows
The cows are milked once in the morning and once in the evening.

2 Milkings
The milk is transported from the milking place in refrigeration tanks (12°C).

3 The Starter
The day before production, the starter is added.

4 Skimming
Fat (20%) is skimmed off. The milk is heated to 32°C.

5 Warming the Milk
The milk is poured into buckets. The air is 30°C, with near 100% humidity.

6 Renneting
Liquid rennet from the fourth stomach of a calf is mixed in.

7 Coagulation
Coagulation occurs over a period of 90 minutes to 2 hours.

8 Preparing the Surface
A grooved, stainless-steel table is covered by a mat of boiled poplar wood.

9 Plastic Moulds
The moulds are 13 cm high and 11.5 cm in diameter. The sides are perforated.

10 Cleaning the Curd
A brush is used to remove any impurities that gather on the surface of the curd.

11 Cutting the Curd
The curd is cut four times vertically and horizontally with a 60-cm knife.

12 Ladling out the Curd
The curd is ladled out of the bucket and into the moulds.

13 Filling the Moulds
The ladle used has the same diameter as the moulds themselves.

14 Four Layers of Curd
Each mould is given on ladle full of curds, fou times round.

15 The Fifth Layer of Curd
One hour later, a fifth ladle of curds is added to the moulds.

16 Draining off the Whey
The whey drains naturally with the weight of the curd. It is fed to pigs.

17 Turning
Seven hours later, each mould is carefully turned by hand.

18 Covering
A metal plate (95 g) is laid on the white cheese which is left to rest for the night.

19 Removing the Mould
The moulds are removed. The metal plate helps the cheese to drain.

20 Removing the Plates
The metal plates are removed from each of the cheeses.

21 Adding the Mould
Three sorts of *Penicillium candidum* diluted in water are sprayed over.

22 Salting Top and Sides
After five days, fine dry salt is applied directly to the top and sides.

23 Salting Undersides
The cheeses are lined up and flipped over. The undersides are then lightly salted.

24 Adding Mould to the Tops
The new top of each cheese is sprayed with a diluted form of mould.

25 Resting
The cheeses are left to rest overnight before they are moved to the drying room.

26 Drying Room
The cheeses are kept at a temperature of 14°C, 85% humidity for two weeks.

27 Fifth Day
After five days, each cheese is still quite deep and developing a crust.

28 Eighth Day
The cheeses have shrunk by the eighth day. They are turned during drying.

29 Two Weeks
After two weeks the white mould characteristic of Camembert has developed.

30 Wrapping
After the cheeses have been drying or two weeks they are wrapped in wax paper ready for packing.

31 Packing
The cheeses are put in wooden boxes and sent to the *fromager* or cheese shop.

32 Ready to Eat
After two weeks ripening at a *fromager* the Camemberts are ready to eat.

CAMEMBERT DE NORMANDIE (AOC)

To many people, the name of Camembert is synonymous with French cheese. Even before Camembert was granted its AOC in 1983, it was the most copied cheese in the world. You should always choose a Camembert by eye: the shape should be intact, and the rind covered in white mould, with reddish stripes and stains. The pâte should be creamy yellow, supple, and give slightly to finger pressure. There should be a light smell of mould, and the taste is salty.

The locals prefer Camembert *moitié affiné* – half and half – when the *filet*, or heart, is still white and not yet creamy.

Coopérative and *industriel* versions of Camembert are produced, with an affinage of a minimum of 21 days from the date of manufacture within the AOC areas listed. Today, it is hard to find good Camembert: a young cheesemaker has taken up the production of Camembert *fermier (p. 90)*, but his cheese has yet to be granted an AOC.

⊖	10.5–11 cm diameter, 3 cm high
⚖	150 g min.
⁂	215 g per cheese
⫧	45% min.
✓	All year
⏃	Raw
⚑	St. Emilion, St. Estèphe

NORMANDIE Calvados, Manche, Orne, Eure, Seine-Maritime

Uncooked, unpressed, soft pâte; rind of white mould pierced by red stains ⎯

AOC Regulations: Camembert de Normandie

1 Concentrated or powdered milk, lactic proteins, or colouring may not be added to the milk.
2 The milk must not be heated above 37°C
3 Uncut curd to be sliced vertically.
4 The curd must be cast with a ladle whose diameter corresponds to that of the mould: the operation is undertaken in stages, with a

minimum of four successive fillings *(p. 90–92)*.
5 Salting must be carried out with dry salt exclusively.
6 After salting, the cheeses must be taken to the drying room, where the temperature is between 10°C and 14°C: they must be left in wooden boxes. Before this, they may be put on boards, in cellars at 8 or 9°C.

7 The words *Fabrication traditionnelle au lait cru avec moulage à la louche* may appear on the label of an AOC cheese. *Fabriqué en Normandie* indicates the place of production on the labels of cheeses not benefiting from the AOC.

AOC GRANTED 1983

CAMEMBERT AFFINÉ AU CIDRE DE LA MAISON

This cheese is a speciality of the *fromager* who makes it by soaking a young Camembert with its white rind on in cider for about 15 days. The cheese absorbs the taste of the cider and the aroma of the apple. Its smell stings the nose a little.

Marks from cloth used during affinage

CŒUR DE CAMEMBERT AU CALVADOS

This is a peeled Camembert, soaked in Calvados, a spirit distilled from cider; both the cheese and the Calvados are specialities of the region of Normandie.

| Beaujolais |
| Cider, Cidre-Jasnières |
| Calvados |

Decorated with a walnut

CANCOILLOTTE / METTON

A cheese called Metton, of which both *artisanal* and *industriel* versions are produced, is used to make Cancoillotte. The Metton is made from skimmed milk, which is coagulated, thinly cut, and heated to a maximum of 60°C, pressed, pounded, and then ripened for a few days. Cancoillotte is made by melting the Metton in a little water or milk over a low heat and adding salt and butter. Hot or cold, the Cancoillotte is spread on bread and eaten for breakfast or as a snack, sometimes with vegetables or meat. It is sold in containers, plain, or with butter, garlic, or wine. The taste is simple. La Cancoillotte is a popular food in the Franche-Comté.

Metton Metton comes in grains

FRANCHE-COMTÉ
Doubs

| Skimmed |
| Côtes du Jura, Bourgogne Passetoutgrains |

Cancoillotte Pale yellow, lightly salted, and creamy, with the consistency of liquid honey

Cantal, Salers, Laguiole, and Aligot

CANTAL / FOURME DU CANTAL (AOC)

Fermier, *coopérative*, and *industriel* versions of Cantal are produced. A piece of Cantal feels heavy and moist. The salt that is added to it brings out the full flavour of this cheese. A well-ripened Cantal has a strong taste, while a young cheese has the sweetness of raw milk. The AOC was granted in 1980.

⊖	36–42 cm diameter, 35–40 cm high
⚖	35–45 kg
⁂	57 g min. per 100 g matured cheese; 56 g min. for *fromage blanc* just after pressing
◫	45% min
✓	All year
⟳	Raw, pasteurized
♱	Côtes d'Auvergne, Châteaugay, Moulin-à-Vent SH

AUVERGNE Cantal, Haute-Loire, Puy-de-Dôme
MIDI-PYRÉNÉES Aveyron
LIMOUSIN Corrèze

Affinage of six months

Ivory, semi-hard, compact pâte; uncooked, pressed twice

Affinage of eight days

Aluminium ID tag: CA indicates Cantal; 15 is the department of production; EE is the maker's code

Affinage of six months

Dark yellow, natural rind with red and orange stains

HOW CANTAL IS MADE

Three different sizes of Cantal are produced:
a regular sized cheese at about 40 kg; small
at about 20 kg; and Cantalet at about 10 kg.

Renneting
The milk is heated to 32°C. The curd forms
approximately one hour after renneting.

Cutting the Curd
The curd is cut into cubes of 1 cm, then
brewed; the whey is removed.

First Pressing
Quantities of 80–100 kg at a time are wrapped in a
cloth and passed through the press (**1**). This results
in a thick slice called a *tome* (**2**), which is cut and
pressed several times to expel the whey.

Maturing of the Shape
After pressing, the *tome* is allowed to rest for eight
hours at 12–15°C. This encourages the natural development of lactic acids that protect and modify the physical
structure of the tome, necessary for its affinage. The
matured *tome* is broken into small pieces with the help
of a grinding machine. This process is commonly used
in other countries, but in France it is unique to Cantal.

Curing with Salt
The tome, reduced to nut-sized pieces, is salted, with
a minimum of 24 g salt per 1 kg of volume in summer,
21 g in winter, and then brewed. The salt dissolves and
mixes evenly with the *tome*. The next day, when the
tome has gathered, a handful is squeezed tightly and
then thrown. If the pieces come away from the hand
easily, curing is complete.

Casting and Pressing
A cloth-lined mould is filled with ground *tome* (**3**), closed
with a metal lid, and then passed through the press (**4**).
Over the next 48 hours, the cheese will be passed
through the press three or four times.

Affinage
Once the cheese is the shape of Cantal, it is removed
from the mould and transferred to the *cave d'affinage*,
a cool (10°C), damp (90% humidity), dark, and lightly
ventilated room. For at least 30 days from the date
of production, the cheese is rubbed and turned twice
a week. There are three stages of affinage: 30 days
gives a young, white, sweet cheese; two to six months
gives a golden, medium cheese (*entre-deux* or *doré*)
cheese; six months gives an old (*vieux*), reddish-
crushed cheese.

1 The curd is wrapped in a cloth and passed
through the *presse-tome*.

2 The *tome* is cut before being pressed
again to expel the whey.

3 The ground *tome* is placed in
a cloth-lined metal mould.

4 Each cheese is pressed three or four
times over 48 hours.

SALERS (AOC)

For 2,000 years, Salers and Cantal have been produced in the mountains of the Auvergne following traditional methods that have remained fundamentally the same. The AOC regulations stipulate that Salers must be made with milk from cows that graze on mountain pastures in summer; Cantal is made from the milk of the other seasons. Of the 36 AOC cheeses currently registered in France, Salers is the only entirely *fermier* cheese: its red aluminium tag states this. Affinage in the areas defined by the AOC is for a minimum of three months from the date of production. The cheese is ripened and preserved at a temperature below or equal to 12°C.

How Dry Matter Affects the Flavour

Salers and Cantal are not cooked-pâte cheeses, but they are pressed twice and the *tome* is ground between pressings, which is why they contain more than 58 g dry matter; a cooked and pressed cheese such as Beaufort (*p. 48*) contains even more. Usually, half of a cheese is composed of water, and it is rare that the percentage of dry matter should exceed 50 g per 100 g cheese. The high percentage of dry matter in Salers shows that it is a compact cheese with a firm pâte. As a result, it has volume, complexity, and an unequalled quality of flavour.

Period of Production

The mountains of Cantal are completely snowbound for half the year. It is only come late spring, in April or May, that the cows and herdspeople can leave for the higher summer pastures. Huts made of stone, called *burons*, serve not only as living quarters during the summer months, but also as dairies and ripening cellars. In the Savoie region of the Alps, these are called *chalets*. In 1948, there were 1,000 *burons* in the region, and the cheeses made there were called Salers *haute montagne*.

Affinage of ten months

Firm, yellow, semi-hard pâte; uncooked, pressed twice

Dry, natural rind

Dry Matter per 100 g Cheese				
Cantal	Salers	Laguiole	Beaufort	Brie
57 g min.	58 g min.	58 g min.	62 g min.	44 g min.

Fat Content per 100 g Cheese				
Cantal	Salers	Laguiole	Beaufort	Brie
25.6 g min.	26.1 g min.	26.1 g min.	29.7 g min.	19.8 g min.

Now there are only 20 *burons* left. In 1961, a law decreed that Salers *haute montagne* must be made between 20 May and 30 September but this period was extended from 1 May to 31 October.

Production
Salers is produced by about 90 farms. Each farm raises 35 to 50 cows. Every herd produces one Salers of approximately 40 kg per day, the equivalent of 350 to 400 litres of milk. The number of Salers made by all of the farms during the six months of the permitted season amounts to about 25,000 cheeses, or 1,000 tonnes (compared with 17,000 tonnes of Cantal).

The Salers Cows
Salers cows calve about once a year and give between 6.9 and 8.9 litres of milk per day or 3.3 tonnes of milk per year. The milk is of a high quality, with a 34% protein and 38% fat content. Equally appreciated for its meat, this breed of cow originates from the Massif Central. It is a robust and even-tempered animal, with a mahogany-coloured coat and lyre-shaped horns.

Affinage of 10 Months
The cheese shown opposite has had an affinage of ten months. The letters and numerals SA 15 HK on the red tag refer

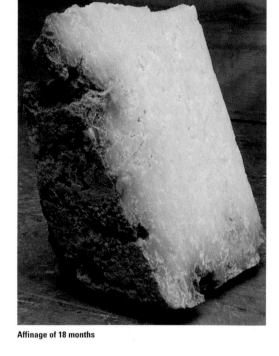

Affinage of 18 months

to the department and the maker. The brown crust resembles the surface of a dry rock. The crust is created by being repeatedly rubbed and left in a cool cellar at a temperature of 12°C. The thickness of the crust protects the pâte, which is the colour of egg yolk and gives off a strong, meaty smell. The pâte is firm yet surprisingly soft, and leaves a moist, fatty feeling on the tongue. In the mouth, the flavour opens up and has a full, sweet, nutty aroma of arnica, anemones, dandelions, gentians, and other mountain flowers that blossom in summer, as well as the tang and sourness of old salt. Salers is a strong cheese.

Affinage of 18 Months
The rind of the cheese shown above is fissured, and a bloom has formed after 18 months. This is caused by cheese mites that eat the rind and invade the pâte. Some people wait for this stage of the affinage: they grate the rind and taste the powder.

⊖	38–48 cm diameter (before affinage), 30–40 cm high
⚖	35–50 kg
⚫	58 g min. per 100 g ripened cheese
🝙	45% min. 26.1 g min. per 100 g cheese
✓	All year depending on affinage; a Salers made in May may be eaten in autumn
⟳	Raw, whole summer milk
❢	St. Pourçain, Touraine

AUVERGNE Cantal, Haute-Loire, Puy-de-Dôme
MIDI-PYRÉNÉES, LIMOUSIN

LAGUIOLE (AOC)

Laguiole derives its name from the village in the mountains of Aubrac. The name is pronounced laïyole – without the g. The cheese has a firm, golden pâte and a thick rind. Cantal (*p. 94*), Salers (*p. 96*), and Laguiole share the same method of production, their shapes are almost identical, and they all contain a high percentage of dry matter. Affinage takes at least four months from the date of production in the listed

areas. The temperature of affinage and conservation must be below 14°C. The AOC was granted in 1976.

The History of Laguiole

According to local history, Laguiole was first made at a monastery in the mountains of Aubrac during the 11th century. The monks taught their method of production to the *buronniers*, who still make cheese in their *burons*, or mountain huts. Production reached its peak in the early 20th century. At that time, the summer migration of herds and herdspeople lasted just 142 days, from 25 May to 13 October. A cow produced only 50 kg cheese – not only did the cows of the Aubrac breed give no more than a maximum of 3 to 4 litres of milk per day, but cheese production too was limited to the period of migration. Despite this, 1,200 *buronniers* would produce 770 tonnes of high-

Firm, yellow, semi-hard pâte;
uncooked, pressed twice

Natural, dry, light, orange
and white rind, which
darkens with affinage

MIDI-PYRÉNÉES
Aveyron;
AUVERGNE Cantal;
LANGUEDOC-
ROUSSILLON Lozère

⊖	40 cm diameter, 30–40 cm high
⚖	30–50 kg
⁂	58 g min. per 100 g cheese
⊓	45% min., 26.1 g min. per 100 g cheese
✓	All year, depending on affinage
⏝	Raw, whole
⏺	Côtes du Frontonnais

quality Laguiole each summer. Today, there are about 295 *burons* in existence.

An Association is Established

Towards the end of the 19th century, an association was formed to boost sales and the village of Laguiole became the centre of production for this cheese. In 1939, the association changed its role to protection of the cheese. Despite this, a sharp decrease in the workforce reduced the number of *burons* to 55. Annual production decreased. To put an end to this, the Coopérative Fromagère Jeune Montagne was created in 1960. In 1976, production was finally allowed throughout the year.

The Laguiole Cows

Sadly, there has been a marked decline in the quality of Laguiole cheeses since 1981, due to the introduction of Holstein cows. These cows, originally from Holland, produce a lot of milk but the protein content is inferior to that of the Aubrac breed. The Holsteins did not adapt well to their new environment, so studies were carried out to find a better breed that could adapt to the climate and soil of Aubrac. A Swiss breed, the Pie-Rouge-de-l'Est, was selected: these cows give 4,800 litres of milk in 300 days, with a protein content of 32.5%. Further studies are underway to reach a goal of 5,000 litres per year of milk, with a minimum of 32% protein.

Production

Laguiole is made in three different departments (*see map*). With nearly 50 villages producing about 750 tonnes annually, there is no comparison in terms of quantity with the Salers, nor even the Cantal. Although most of the production is *coopérative*, there are currently three *burons* that make Laguiole from raw milk produced on the plateau of Aubrac, but this cheese is sold to tourists without being ripened for the minimum of four months stipulated by the AOC.

HOW A LARGE, ROUND CHEESE IS CUT

When cutting a large, round cheese, some of which, like Laguiole, can weigh as much as 50 kg, great care must be taken to make straight, clean cuts through the pâte.

1 The first step is to stand the cheese firmly on one end ready to make the first vertical cut.

2 Using a strong cheese wire, the cheese is first cut from top to bottom in two equal halves.

3 Each half is then cut horizontally into two halves.

4 Each piece is then cut into triangles of various sizes which can vary in size.

Knives of Laguiole
In the past, the people of Laguiole worked in Spain over the winter. While there, they came across jackknives. When they returned to France, they began to make similar knives. These were so successful that they became known as knives of Laguiole.

ALIGOT / TOME FRAÎCHE

Uncooked, pressed, no rind

There are two possible origins for the name of this cheese. One theory says that *aligot* is a coruption in the local language of the Latin *aliquid*, meaning "something", which was the word used by pilgrims begging for money in the medieval monasteries. Monks gave them soup with bread and fresh *tome*, meaning a lump, of cheese. The second, and more likely, possible origin comes from the ancient French verb *alicoter*, which meant "to cut". In due course this was shortened to *aligot*.

Fermier, *coopérative*, and *industriel* versions of Aligot are produced. This cheese is used in many dishes and is often eaten with potatoes. A speciality of the region is Aligot with mashed potatoes.

Pieces of Aligot are mixed swiftly and melted in hot mashed potatoes, then seasoned with garlic, the juice of grilled sausages, salt, and pepper. Another local dish is Aligot with *tripoux*, or chestnut purée, accompanied by the favourite local red wine, St. Pourçain.

Fresh, white, spongy, elastic, non-salted pâte

⊕ Large hexagonal block	
⚖ 20 kg, also vacuum packs of 2.5 kg	AUVERGNE Cantal, MIDI-PYRÉNÉES Aveyron
🗗 45% min.	
✓ All year, especially spring to summer	
⚖ Raw or pasteurized	
🍷 St. Pourçain	

Cooking Cheese
Melted Aligot can stretch two or three metres when pulled with a spatula, and must be eaten piping hot.

.

CARRÉ DE L'EST

This cheese has a moist rind that sticks to the fingers and feels elastic. The pâte is evenly perforated and is soft, sticky, salty, and melts in the mouth. The cheese is easiest to eat when covered with mould. *Coopérative* and *industriel* versions are produced, with an affinage of three to four weeks.

Red, washed rind, sometimes covered with white mould

Soft pâte; uncooked, unpressed

◈ 11 cm square, 3 cm high	ALSACE, CHAMPAGNE-ARDENNE, LORRAINE
⚖ 300 g	
⬜ 45%	
✓ All year	
⟁ Pasteurized	
❢ Coteaux Champenois, Pinot Noir d'Alsace, Sancerre	

SAINT-RÉMY

This mild-flavoured cheese belongs to the same family as Carré de l'Est (*above*). It tastes similar to Camembert (*p. 92*) and is neither weak nor strong. It is ideal if you like just a small piece of washed-rind cheese. Production is *industriel*, with an affinage of two to three weeks.

Red, moist rind

Soft pâte; uncooked, unpressed

◈ 9 cm square, 3 cm high	LORRAINE Meuse
⚖ 250 g	
⬜ 45–50%	
✓ All year	
⟁ Pasteurized	
❢ Pinot Noir d'Alsace, Sancerre	

LE SAULXUROIS

This *artisanal* cheese, which comes from from Saulxures in the region of Bassigny in Champagne, also belongs to the same family as the Carré de l'Est (*above*). It tastes salty. Affinage takes at least three weeks, during which time the cheese is washed with brine.

Soft pâte; uncooked, unpressed

Red, moist rind

◈ 8–9 cm square, 2.5 cm high	CHAMPAGNE-ARDENNE Haute-Marne
⚖ 200 g	
⬜ 45%	
✓ All year	
⟁ Raw	
❢ Coteaux Champenois, Pinot Noir d'Alsace, Sancerre	

CHAOURCE (AOC)

Not all cheeses need to mature. The cheese shown is very young and melts in the mouth like light snow. Production is *artisanal* and *industriel* within specified areas of Bourgogne and Champagne. Affinage takes a minimum of two weeks, and usually at least one month.

Soft pâte; uncooked, unpressed

CHAMPAGNE-ARDENNE Aube;
BOURGOGNE
Yonne

White rind of *Penicillium candidum* mould

⊖	9 cm diameter, 6–7 cm high (small); 11 cm diameter, 5–6 cm high (large)
⚖	250 g min. (small); 450 g min. (large)
❖	215 g per cheese
⊓	50% min.
✓	All year; best summer to autumn
⟁	Not defined
❢	Coteaux Champenois
♀	Irancy, Sancerre
⚲	Champagne *rosé*

AOC Regulations: Chaource

1 Coagulation must be mainly lactic and last for at least 12 hours.
2 Drainage must be both spontaneous and slow.
AOC GRANTED 1977

CHAUMES

This *industriel* cheese is produced in Jurançon by the Fromageries des Chaumes, one of the biggest cheesemaking companies in France producing cheeses from cow and ewe's milk, low-fat cheeses, and blue cheeses. It is easy to eat, with practically no smell at first; some people may find it a little bland. Affinage takes four weeks.

Semi-hard pâte; uncooked, unpressed

Washed rind

⊖	20–23 cm diameter, 4 cm high
⚖	2 kg
❖	215 g per cheese
⊓	50% min.
✓	All year
⟁	Pasteurized
❢	Madiran, Côtes de Bourg

AQUITAINE
Pyrénées-Atlantiques

Chèvre de la Loire (AOC)

The River Loire, the longest river in France at 1,012 km long, rises in the Massif Central from where it flows into the Atlantic Ocean. It flows first to the north, then west. The soft plains flanking this giant curve form a region justly called the Garden of France, sprinkled with Renaissance castles and an abundance of wines and cheeses. In the 8th century, the Saracens were repelled at Poitiers. These people, of Arab descent, had been settled in the south of Spain for centuries and gradually moved north into France. When they were expelled from France, they left behind not only goats, but also the recipes for making cheese from their milk. The Loire Valley is therefore the starting point in the history of goat's-milk cheeses in France, and remains the most important area of production.

Villages on either side of the River Loire produce goat's-milk cheeses of different sizes and shapes. These cheeses have delicately varied flavours and include no fewer than six AOCs: in the eastern part of the area, there is Crottin de Chavignol (*p. 106*), shaped like a drum; to the west, Sainte-Maure de Touraine (*p. 108*), a thick stick covered with powdered oak charcoal; to the north of the central region, Selles-sur-Cher (*p. 110*), also covered with charcoal; and to the south, a small black pyramid, Valençay (*p. 111*), which was granted its own AOC in 1998; to the west is Pouligny-Saint-Pierre (*p. 107*), a slightly more slender pyramid; and southwest, Chabichou du Poitou (*opposite*). The goat's-milk cheeses of the Loire go well with white wines such as Sancerre.

HOW GOAT'S-MILK CHEESES ARE MADE

According to French tradition, goat's-milk cheeses should be on the table from Easter to All Saints' Day in November.

Coagulation of goat's milk is usually caused by lactic fermentation. The ferment (also called starter) is mixed into the milk. The milk rests for a night and turns sour. It is then heated to 18–20°C. A very small amount of rennet is introduced, and the milk rests for another 24 hours.

The curd is neither cut nor heated, mixed nor pressed: drainage is instant as the curd is ladled into the moulds, and the whey runs off through the fine holes in the sides and base.

The cheese is cured dry – *affiné à sec* – in a cool and well-ventilated room at 11°C and 80% humidity, which is relatively dry compared with cellars at 90 to 100%. The drying process of both rind and pâte must be balanced, otherwise the rind will wrinkle and the whey left in the pâte will stick to it from the inside. Although blue mould will appear naturally on the rind, a covering of powdered oak charcoal helps to create an environment that encourages its development.

Perforated Moulds
The holes in the moulds used to make Valençay (*above*), and Selles-sur-Cher (*right*) allow the whey to drain off quickly.

Coating
Covering the rind of this cheese with powdered charcoal encourages the blue mould to appear.

CHABICHOU DU POITOU (AOC)

Poitou is the main goat-breeding region in France. This goat's-milk cheese has a delicate and slightly sweet flavour with little salt and a faint acidity. Production can be *fermier*, *coopérative*, or *industriel*. The AOC was granted in 1990.

Thin rind of white, yellow, or blue mould

Soft, even-textured pâte becomes hard and brittle when mature; uncooked, unpressed

⊖	6 cm diameter base, 5 cm top, 6 cm high
⚖	100–150 g
♣	40 g min. per cheese
⌂	45% min.
✓	All year; spring to autum (*fermier*)
🐐	Whole
♀	Sancerre, Pouilly Fumé

POITOU-CHARENTES
Charente, Deux-Sèvres, Vienne

CHABICHOU / CHABIS

This *fermier*, *artisanal*, or *industriel* produced cheese has an affinage of 10 to 20 days. The cheeses shown here are all versions of Chabichou that were bought and photographed before the AOC was granted. The variety of sizes and shapes is interesting.

POITOU-CHARENTES
Charente

⊖	6.5 cm diameter base, 5 cm top, 5–7 cm high
⚖	120 g
♣	40 g min. per cheese
⌂	45% min.
✓	All year; spring to autum (*fermier*)
🐐	Raw, whole
♀	Sancerre, Menetou Salon

Chabis

Chabichou

Chabichou

Chabichou *fermier*

CROTTIN DE CHAVIGNOL (AOC)

This cheese is also known as Chavignol and should be hard, black, and knobbly on the surface.

A fresh, white Crottin weighs about 140 g and does not yet look like a true Crottin de Chavignol. After two weeks, it weighs only about 110 g. The rind begins to take on a bluish hue and the pâte becomes glossy. It is a little salty and the balance of sourness, sweetness, and the smell of milk enhance the taste. At this point, the cheese is ready to eat. After five weeks, the cheese is dry and has shrunk. The smell is strong and the pâte has a meaty texture, with a robust flavour. This is a ripe Crottin. After four months, it weighs only 40 g. The rind is rough and hard and should be removed by grating.

Annual production amounts to some 16 million cheeses, which may be *fermier*, *artisanal*, or *industriel*. Affinage must take place within AOC specified areas. It must last at least ten days from the date of production, but usually two to four weeks is allowed. The temperatures must be kept low and the room well ventilated. Hot Crottin on salad with wine vinegar makes a good starter.

Soft white or ivory-coloured pâte; uncooked, unpressed

Affinage of two weeks

Thin rind of blue or white mould; sometimes no mould

Affinage of four months

Affinage of one month

⊖	4–5 cm diameter, 3–4 cm high
⚖	60–110 g
♣	37 g min. per cheese
�𝇙	45% min.
✓	All year; spring to autumn (*fermier*)
⮂	Whole; frozen curd may be used
♀	Sancerre de Chavignol

AOC Regulations: Crottin de Chavignol

1 Coagulation must be mainly lactic with a small amount of rennet.
2 The curd must be drained in advance.

3 The words *fabrication fermière* or *fromage fermier* are forbidden for cheese made with frozen curd.

AOC GRANTED 1976

BOURGOGNE
Nièvre;
VAL-DE-LOIRE;
CENTRE
Cher, Loiret

POULIGNY-SAINT-PIERRE (AOC)

This cheese is nicknamed the Pyramid or the Eiffel Tower because of its cone shape. The cheese shown was ripened for four weeks until it was ready to be eaten. The rind is dry with a good, natural, blue mould. The pâte shows an amazing whiteness and is fine-textured, moist, soft, and crumbly. It smells of goat's milk and straw. On tasting, an exquisite sourness spreads in the mouth, followed by a salty taste, and then sweetness. A softer sourness dissolves at the end, although it leaves an aftertaste. After another six or seven days the rind is even more beautiful and complex: the colours are richer, the rind becomes knobbly, and the mould spreads.

Production may be *fermier* or *industriel*, and affinage takes two weeks from the date of production, usually four or five weeks. There are two labels: green for the Pouligny *fermier*; red for the *industriel* Pouligny *laitier* (dairy).

Rind of natural mould

Soft pâte; uncooked, unpressed

◈	6.5 cm square base, 8–9 cm high
⬗	250 g min.
⁂	90 g min. per cheese
⬠	45% min.
✓	All year; spring to autumn (*fermier*)
⬔	Whole
♈	Reuilly, Sancerre

AOC Regulations: Pouligny-Saint-Pierre

1 Coagulation must be mainly lactic with a small amount of rennet.
2 The words *fabrication fermière* or *fromage fermier* are forbidden for any cheeses made with frozen curd.

AOC GRANTED 1976

CENTRE
Indre

SAINTE-MAURE DE TOURAINE (AOC)

The method of production for this cheese is faithful to tradition (*p. 104*). The milk is heated to 18–20°C, then coagulated for 24 hours, cast in a long mould, and drained spontaneously. The cheese is then taken out of its mould and a long straw is inserted, the purpose of which is to hold the fragile cheese together and ventilate its interior. The cheese is then covered with salted powdered charcoal and laid on a board to complete drainage.

Production of this cheese may be *fermier*, *coopérative*, or *artisanal*. Affinage takes a minimum of ten days (usually, two to four weeks) after renneting, within AOC specified areas. The cheese is turned every day in a well-ventilated, cool cellar at 10–15°C with 90% humidity. On the tenth day, the rind is pale yellow, and has no mould. The pâte is still soft and has a sour smell. During the third week, a blue mould forms on the rind, which now appears dry. The pâte, too, changes from being moist to a dry, smooth, robust texture. After the fifth or sixth week, the surface of the cheese is dry and has shrunk. The mould is blue-grey and the pâte is fine-textured, smooth and firm. This cheese is mature, balanced, round, with salt, sourness, and an aroma of walnut.

Dried for 24 hours

White or ivory, fine-textured pâte; uncooked, unpressed

Affinage of three weeks

Rind of natural mould, sometimes covered with powdered charcoal

Affinage of six weeks

Long, truncated log

◇	3–4 cm diameter at one end, 4–5 cm diameter at other end, 14–16 cm long
⚖	250 g
⁂	100 g min. per cheese
🗋	45% min., 45 g min. per cheese
✓	All year; spring to autumn (*fermier*)
⊄	Frozen curd forbidden
❢	Chinon
⚲	Vouvray

CENTRE Indre, Indre-et-Loire, Loir-et-Cher; POITOU-CHARENTES Vienne

AOC Regulations: Sainte-Maure de Touraine

1 Coagulation must be mainly lactic with a small amount of rennet.
2 The fresh undrained curd (*p. 104*) is cast with a ladle or curd distributor.
3 Drainage must be natural.

AOC GRANTED 1990

▶ **Chèvre de la Loire cheeses are produced from the milk of goats that graze in the fertile region around the River Loire**

SELLES-SUR-CHER
(AOC)

A good goat's-milk cheese is defined by its lingering scent and aftertaste. The local people eat the rind: they are the ones who cultivate its mould and they consider that it contains the true taste of the cheese. About 1.3 litres of milk are needed to make a single cheese. The cheese shown here was made by the Moreau family, who run a goat farm called l'Elevage Caprin de Bellevue.

After an affinage of four weeks, the surface of the cheese is very knobbly and the rind is dry. It is covered completely with a blue-grey mould, under which is a layer of powdered charcoal. The pâte is characteristic of a true goat's-milk cheese. It is slightly hard at first, then moist, heavy, and clay-like as it blends and melts in the mouth. The taste is slightly sour and salty, with some sweetness. The aroma created by the goat's milk and the mould of a dark cellar remains.

Production of this cheese may be *fermier*, *coopérative*, or *industriel*. Affinage takes place within AOC stated areas over a period of at least ten days, usually three weeks.

Soft pâte; uncooked, unpressed

Rind of natural mould, covered with powdered and salted charcoal

Affinage of four weeks

CENTRE Cher, Indre, Loir-et-Cher

⊖	8 cm diameter base, 7 cm diameter top, 2–3 cm high
⚖	200 g min. when fresh, otherwise 150 g
⛿	45% min.
⁂	55 g min. per cheese
✓	All year; spring to autumn (*fermier*)
⚶	Whole
♀	Sancerre, Pouilly Fumé

AOC Regulations:
Sainte-Maure de Touraine

1 Coagulation must be mainly lactic with a small amount of rennet.
2 The curd must be cast with a ladle.

AOC GRANTED 1975

VALENÇAY (AOC)

The province of Berry has long been the source of famous cheeses, including Crottin de Chavignol (*p. 106*), Pouligny-Saint-Pierre (*p. 107*), and Selles-sur-Cher (*opposite*).

It is said that Valençay was originally shaped like a perfect pyramid. On his return from the disastrous campaign in Egypt, Napoléon stopped at the castle of Valençay and seeing the cheese that reminded him of the Egyptian pyramids, in rage chopped the top off with his sword.

When making a Valençay, the drained curd is cast in a mould, then it is removed, covered with salted charcoal ashes, and ripened in a well-ventilated room at 80% humidity. Production may be *fermier*, *artisanal*, or *industriel*. Affinage takes three weeks, after which a natural mould covers the surface. The AOC was granted in 1998.

Affinage of around three weeks

Soft, firm, moist pâte; uncooked, unpressed

Rind of natural mould, covered with salted, powdered charcoal

◈	6–7 cm square base, 3.5–4 cm square top, 6–7 cm high
⚖	200–250 g
🗋	45% min.
♣	90g min. per cheese
✓	Spring to autumn
🐄	Raw, whole
🍷	Quincy, Reuilly, Sancerre

CENTRE
Indre

Valencay Castle is where Napoléon is said to have cut the top off the local cheese

Chèvre de Coin

AMBERT / CROTTIN D'AMBERT

Goat's-milk cheeses are rare in the Auvergne.
The village of Saint-Just, in the suburbs of
Ambert where this cheese is made, lies at an
altitude of 840 m above sea-level. This is a
fermier cheese with an affinage of ten days.

Soft pâte;
uncooked,
unpressed

⊖	6 cm diameter, 3–3.5 cm high
⚖	130 g
🗋	Not defined
✓	April to November
🍶	Raw
🍷	Côtes du Forez, Beaujolais *primeur*

AUVERGNE
Puy-de-Dôme

Rind of
natural
mould

ANNEAU DU VIC-BILH

This *fermier* cheese looks hand-made and its
flavour has just the right balance of sourness and
salt. The cheesemaker says, "We southern people
like it young." Affinage takes at least ten days.

Soft, perfectly
white pâte;
uncooked,
unpressed

⊜	10 cm diameter, 3 cm hole, 2 cm high
⚖	200–250 g
🗋	45% min.
✓	Spring to autumn
🍶	Raw
🍷	Pacherenc du Vic-Bilh

MIDI-PYRÉNÉES
Hautes-Pyrénées

Rind of natural mould
powdered with charcoal

APÉROBIC

This mild *fermier* cheese is the smallest cheese in the
world. The word *bic* derives from *bicot*, a small goat.
It is made with cow's milk in winter, goat's milk
in spring and summer, and a mix of both in
autumn. It is ripened with care for 15 days.

Rind of
natural
mould

◈	1.5 cm diameter base, 2 cm high
⚖	3 g
🗋	Not defined
✓	All year
🍶	Raw, whole (spring to autumn)
🐄	Raw, whole (autumn to winter)
🍷	Bourgogne Aligoté

BOURGOGNE
Saône-et-Loire

Soft pâte;
uncooked,
unpressed

AUTUN

This *fermier* cheese has a fine texture. The flavour is rich, refined, and rounded, with a hint of acidity. Affinage takes at least three weeks.

Even-textured and compact soft, white pâte; uncooked, unpressed

Rind of natural mould

⊖	5-6 cm diameter, 8 cm high
⚖	270–300 g
⫪	45% min.
✓	Spring to autumn
⌘	Raw
⌂	Raw
♀	Mercurey, Rully

BOURGOGNE
Saône-et-Loire

BEAUJOLAIS PUR CHÈVRE (PETIT)

This *artisanal* cheese comes from the village of Saint-Georges-de-Reneins. Affinage usually takes four to five weeks until the pâte hardens. The cheese shown was ripened for six weeks by a *fromager* in the city of Lyon and is completely mature. It has a slightly sour taste.

Soft to hard pâte; uncooked, unpressed

Light brown rind, grey-blue natural mould

⊖	5 cm diameter, 2 cm high
⚖	45 g
⫪	45% min.
✓	April to October
⌘	Not defined
♀	Beaujolais, young and fruity

RHÔNE-ALPES
Rhône

BESACE DE PUR CHÈVRE

This *fermier* cheese is made by a woman on her small farm at the foot of Mont Tournier, in Savoie, at an altitude of 876 m. She shapes the cheeses by hand, squeezing each one in a cloth. The cheese is at its best after two weeks of affinage.

Rind of natural mould

Soft pâte; uncooked, unpressed

Affinage of two weeks

⊖	8 cm diameter, 4 cm high
⚖	170 g; 260 g fresh
⫪	45% min.
✓	Spring to autumn
⌘	Raw
♀	Crépy, Seyssel

RHÔNE-ALPES
Savoie

Fresh cheese

BIGOTON

This is a light and simple *fermier* cheese produced by a farm in the Orléanais region called La Chèvrerie d'Authon. Affinage takes at least 15 days.

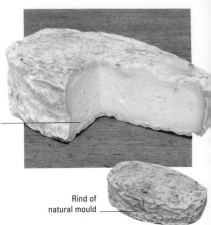

Soft pâte; uncooked, unpressed

⬙	5–6 cm wide, 12–13 cm long, 4 cm high
⚖	130–150 g
🗘	45%
✓	Spring to autumn
🐇	Raw
♟	Coteaux du Vendômois, young and fruity

CENTRE
Loir-et-Cher

Rind of natural mould

BILOU DU JURA (LE PETIT)

This goat's-milk cheese comes from the Franche-Comté region, where goat's-milk cheeses are quite scarce. It is made with high-quality milk, and is as good as the goat's-milk cheeses of the Loire. Affinage takes at least ten days.

Soft pâte; uncooked, unpressed

⊖	6–7 cm diameter, 3 cm high
⚖	100–150 g
🗘	45%
✓	Spring to autumn
🐇	Raw
♟	Côtes du Jura

FRANCHE-COMTÉ
Jura

Rind of natural mould

BONDE DE GÂTINE

This high-quality *fermier* cheese produced by the GAEC de la Fragnée comes from the marshy Gâtine area of Poitou. Affinage usually takes from four to ten weeks. The pâte has a pronounced acidity and saltiness and melts in the mouth, leaving a light but rich aroma.

Soft white pâte; uncooked, unpressed

⊖	5–6 cm diameter, 5–6 cm high
⚖	140–160 g
🗘	45%
✓	Spring to autumn
🐇	Raw
♟	Haut Poitou

POITOU-CHARENTES
Deux-Sèvres

Rind of white mould

LE BOUCA

In the local dialect, a *bouc* is a billy-goat.
This *fermier* cheese has a strong, milky aroma
and a perfect balance of acidity and saltiness.
The cut pâte of the cheese shown here has
a good degree of firmness. Affinage takes
at least ten days.

Soft pâte;
uncooked,
unpressed

⬨	5–6 cm wide, 12–13 cm long, 4 cm high
⚖	130–150 g
🗋	45%
✓	Spring to autumn
🥛	Raw
🍷	Touraine

CENTRE
Indre-et-Loire

Rind of natural mould,
covered with
charcoal powder

BOUGON

This cheese is made by a *coopérative* from
raw milk. It looks like a Camembert and
is packaged in a thin wooden box. The
pâte is firm, and both rind and pâte taste
the same. Affinage takes two to
three weeks.

Soft pâte;
uncooked,
unpressed

⊖	10 cm diameter, 2.5 cm high
⚖	180 g
🗋	50%
✓	All year
🥛	Raw; pasteurized for export
🐄	Raw; pasteurized for export
🍷	Haut Poitou

POITOU-CHARENTES
Deux-Sèvres

Affinage of ten days

Rind of
white mould

BOUTON DE CULOTTE

These little cheeses are eaten by the locals
as they pick grapes in autumn. They may be
made using goat or cow's milk, or a mixture of
both. Production is either *fermier* or *artisanal*.
A blue mould appears on the rind after two
weeks of affinage. After a month, the pâte
turns yellow and tingles on the tongue.

⊖	3–4 cm diameter, 3–4 cm high
⚖	180 g
🗋	50%
✓	All year
🥛	Raw
🍷	Bourgogne Aligoté

BOURGOGNE
Saône-et-Loire

**From left to
right, affinage of
ten days, two weeks,
and one month**

Rind of natural
mould, covered
with powdered and
salted charcoal

BOUTON D'OC

These unusual, pear-shaped, *fermier* cheeses are sold by the dozen and make a good accompaniment to an apéritif. The pâte has a very fine texture and a pleasant flavour. Because of their small size, the cheeses ripen quickly. Affinage takes ten days.

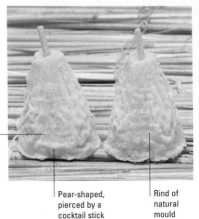

Soft pâte; uncooked, unpressed

◈ 3 cm diameter base, 1 cm diameter top, 3.5 cm high

⚖ 15 g

🗋 45%

✓ Spring to autumn

🍶 Raw

🍷 Gaillac *perlé* or *mousseux*

MIDI-PYRÉNÉES
Tarn

Pear-shaped, pierced by a cocktail stick

Rind of natural mould

BRESSAN

Although this *fermier* cheese is made with goat's milk, cow's milk may be added depending on the season and maker. In the province of Bresse, it is eaten for breakfast with jam. Affinage takes at least one week.

Soft to hard pâte; uncooked, unpressed

⊖ 5 cm diameter base, 4 cm diameter top, 4 cm high

⚖ 100 g

🗋 45%

✓ Spring to autumn

🍶 Raw

🐄 Raw

🍷 Bugey, Seyssel, Roussette de Savoie

RHÔNE-ALPES Ain;
BOURGOGNE
Saône-et-Loire

Affinage of one week

Rind of natural mould

BRIQUE ARDÉCHOISE

This elegant *fermier* cheese is the product of a successful combination of talented cheesemaker, high-quality milk, and a careful affinage of three to four weeks. It is slightly pungent and goes well with a robust white wine.

Soft pâte; uncooked, unpressed

⬧ 4–5 cm wide, 11–12 cm long, 3 cm high

⚖ 150 g

🗋 Not defined

✓ Spring to autumn

🍶 Raw

🍷 Hermitage, St. Joseph, St. Péray

RHÔNE-ALPES
Ardèche

Affinage of four weeks

Rind of natural mould

BRIQUE DU FOREZ

The cheese shown here was made from a
mixture of goat and cow's milk. Production
may be *fermier* or *artisanal*, with an affinage
of two to three weeks.

Soft pâte;
uncooked,
unpressed

⬦	5–6 cm wide, 13 cm long, 3.5 cm high
⚖	350–400 g
🗌	40–45%
✓	All year; spring to autumn for pure goat's-milk cheeses
🧀	Raw, whole
🐄	Raw, whole
🍷	Beaujolais, Côtes Roannaises

AUVERGNE
Puy-de-Dôme;
RHÔNE-ALPES
Loire

Affinage of three weeks

Rind of natural
white mould

BRIQUETTE DE COUBON

This *fermier* cheese, which comes from
Velay in the Auvergne, looks like a small
brick, or *briquette*. Many *briquettes* made
from various milks are currently being
produced all over France; this one is
made from cow's milk. Affinage takes
at least eight days.

Soft pâte;
uncooked,
slightly pressed

⬦	5 cm wide, 12 cm long, 3 cm high
⚖	240 g
🗌	Not defined
✓	All year
🐄	Raw
🍷	St. Pourçain

AUVERGNE
Haute-Loire

Affinage of ten days

Rind of
natural mould

BÛCHETTE D'ANJOU

This *artisanal* cheese was modelled on
Sainte-Maure (*p. 108*). It is a young,
almost fresh cheese, with a faint smell
of milk and slightly acid taste. The rind,
which is covered in charcoal powder,
may be eaten, but the cheese tastes better
without it. Affinage takes two weeks.

Rind of
natural mould

⬦	3–4 cm diameter, 9 cm long
⚖	85–100 g
🗌	45%
✓	Spring to autumn
🧀	Raw
🍷	Saumur, Anjou Villages

PAYS DE LA LOIRE
Maine-et-Loire

Soft pâte,
uncooked and
unpressed

BÛCHETTE DE BANON

The light sourness of this fresh *fermier* cheese blends with the aroma of the savory, giving it the typical taste of Provence. This is a cheese to eat fresh under a shady tree on a warm summer's day, preferably at the start of a meal. It can be eaten fresh or allowed to ripen for a maximum of a week.

No rind | Sprig of savory for decoration

◇ 3 cm diameter, 14 cm long	PROVENCE-ALPES-CÔTE-D'AZUR
⚖ 120 g	Alpes-de-Haute-Provence
🏷 45%	
✓ Spring to autumn	
🥛 Raw	
🍷 Coteaux d'Aix *rosé*	

CAPRI LEZÉEN

Each of these *fermier* cheeses produced by the GAEC du Capri Lezéen is wrapped in a chestnut leaf and packaged in a thin wooden box. The sticky, pale gold rind has a very light blue mould. The distinctive flavour comes from the creamy, slightly runny pâte. Affinage takes eight to 15 days at 100% humidity, which is high for a goat's cheese.

Very soft pâte; uncooked, unpressed | Chestnut-leaf wrapper

Natural rind

⊖ 8–9 cm diameter, 1.5 cm high	POITOU-CHARENTES
⚖ 120 g	Deux-Sèvres
🏷 50%	
✓ All year	
🥛 Raw	
🍷 Haut Poitou	

CAPRICORNE DE JARJAT

This *fermier* cheese, made by R. Gribaldi, belongs to the same family as Picodon (*p. 206*). It has a strong-tasting mould and tingles in the mouth, which makes it a good accompaniment to wine. Affinage takes up to three or four months, at 90% humidity; the cheese can be eaten fresh.

Soft pâte; uncooked, unpressed

Rind of natural white and blue mould

Affinage of one month

⊖ 10 cm diameter, 3.5 cm high	RHÔNE-ALPES
⚖ 250 g	Ardèche
🏷 45%	
✓ All year	
🥛 Raw	
🍷 St. Péray, Crozes Hermitage	

LE CATHELAIN

The word *cathelain* means goat in the old dialect of Savoie. The cheese shown is very young and has a smooth, slightly sour pâte that melts in the mouth. Affinage of this *fermier* cheese takes 15 days.

Natural rind

Soft pâte; uncooked, unpressed

⊖ 7 cm diameter, 4 cm high	
⚖ 170 g	
🗋 45%	RHÔNE-ALPES
✓ April to December	Savoie
⌇ Raw	
⚲ Crépy	

CHAROLAIS / CHAROLLES

This *fermier* or *artisanal* cheese comes from the granite plains of the Charolais region of Bourgogne. It enhances the flavours of the milk – the saltiness, acidity, and sweetness of its aroma open up in the mouth. The colours and texture of the mould give a lingering aftertaste. Affinage lasts two to six weeks.

Soft, refined pâte; uncooked, unpressed

Rind of blue or white, natural mould

⊖ 5–6 cm diameter, 7–8 cm high	
⚖ 200 g	
🗋 45%	BOURGOGNE
✓ Spring to autumn	Saône-et-
⌇ Raw	Loire
⌇ Raw	
⚲ Mercurey, Rully, Montagny	

CHEF-BOUTONNE

This cheese should suit modern tastes for young cheeses that are light and simple, without strong flavours. In addition to this flat-topped pyramid, there are round and square versions of Chef-Boutonne. This is a *fermier* or *coopérative* cheese with an affinage of two weeks.

Rind of natural mould

Soft pâte; uncooked, unpressed

◈ 7–8 cm square base, 4 cm square top, 6–7 cm high	
⚖ 250 g	POITOU-
🗋 45%	CHARENTES
✓ Spring to autumn	Deux-Sèvres
⌇ Raw	
⚲ Haut Poitou	

CHÈVRE FERMIER

This *fermier* goat's-milk cheese is produced
by the Marchal farm near the town of
Le Thillot. The cheese shown is still
slightly moist, with a blue and brown
mould, and the beginnings of a dry rind.
It has a good, balanced flavour of salt and
acidity. Affinage takes two to four weeks.

Soft pâte;
uncooked,
unpressed

| ⊖ 6 cm diameter, 3–4 cm high |
| ⚖ 100–130 g |
| 🗋 45% |
| ✓ Spring to end of autumn |
| 🜛 Raw |
| ♀ Vin gris des Côtes de Toul (*rosé*) |

LORRAINE
Vosges

Rind of
natural
mould

CHÈVRE FERMIER ALPILLES

This young *fermier* cheese is produced by
a farm at the foot of the Alpilles, a range
of small mountains in Provence. It has
a delicate yet robust flavour, which
improves with age. Affinage usually
takes a minimum of ten days.

| ⊖ 6 cm diameter, 2 cm high |
| ⚖ 60 g |
| 🗋 45% |
| ✓ All summer |
| 🜛 Raw |
| ♀ Bellet, Côtes de Provence |

PROVENCE-ALPES-
CÔTE D'AZUR
Bouches-du-Rhône

Soft pâte;
uncooked,
unpressed

Rind of
natural
mould

CHÈVRE FERMIER DU CHÂTEAU-VERT

This *fermier* cheese comes from the slopes
of Mont Ventoux in Provence. Its rind
is covered in charcoal powder with a
coating of white-grey mould. The pâte
is smooth, slightly sour, and sweet.
Affinage takes at least two weeks.

| ⊖ 6 cm diameter, 2 cm high |
| ⚖ 70 g |
| 🗋 45% |
| ✓ Spring to autumn |
| 🜛 Raw |
| ♀ Côtes du Ventoux *blanc* and *rosé* |

PROVENCE-
ALPES-CÔTE
D'AZUR
Vaucluse

Rind of natural
mould, covered
with charcoal
powder

Soft pâte;
uncooked,
unpressed

CIVRAY

From the same family as Chabichou (*p. 105*), this soft, *fermier* goat's-milk cheese is made on the plains around the town of Civray. The natural mould gives it a pleasant flavour, and it has a fine pâte, with pronounced acidity and little sugar. Affinage takes a minimum of two weeks.

Rind of natural mould

Soft pâte; uncooked, unpressed

⊖	5–6 cm diameter base, 5 cm top, 5 cm high
⚖	110–150 g
🗘	45%
✓	Spring to autumn
🍶	Raw
🍷	Haut Poitou

POITOU-CHARENTES
Vienne

CLACBITOU

Like the Charolais (*p. 119*), which it resembles, this recently created *fermier* cheese comes from the Charolais region of Bourgogne. It tastes best when it is still quite young. Affinage takes two to three weeks.

Soft pâte; uncooked, unpressed

Rind of natural mould

⊖	5 cm diameter, 7–8 cm high
⚖	150 g
🗘	45%
✓	Spring to autumn
🍶	Raw
🍷	Bourgogne Aligoté de Bouzeron

BOURGOGNE
Saône-et-Loire

CLOCHETTE

This *fermier* cheese has a pleasant aroma, which is a combination of both the mould and the cellar in which the cheese was ripened. Affinage takes at least two weeks.

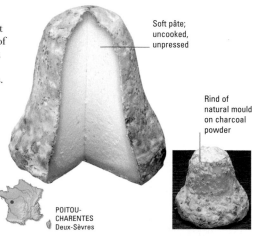

Soft pâte; uncooked, unpressed

Rind of natural mould on charcoal powder

◈	8–9 cm diameter base, 9 cm high
⚖	250 g
🗘	45%
✓	Spring to autumn
🍶	Raw
🍷	Haut Poitou

POITOU-CHARENTES
Deux-Sèvres

CŒUR DU BERRY

This *artisanal* cheese belongs to the same family as Selles-sur-Cher (*p. 110*) but it is heart-shaped. Affinage takes at least two weeks, and the rind is covered with charcoal powder.

Soft pâte; uncooked, unpressed

⊖	9–10 cm wide, 10 cm long, 3 cm high
⚖	150 g
🝙	45%
✓	Spring to autumn
🥛	Raw
♀	Quincy, Reuilly

CENTRE
Indre

Rind of natural mould on charcoal powder

LE CORNILLY

These three *artisanal* cheeses from the province of Berry show different stages in the affinage, which usually takes three to four weeks – although sometimes there is none at all. They have a nutty flavour and very little smell.

Rather soft to hard pâte; uncooked, unpressed

⊖	5–8 cm diameter base, 5 cm diameter top, 7–9 cm high
⚖	150–250 g
🝙	45%
✓	All year
🥛	Raw
♀	Quincy, Reuilly

CENTRE
Indre

Rind of natural mould   Fresh cheese   Ripe cheese   Dry cheese

COUHÉ-VÉRAC

This *fermier* or *artisanal* cheese blends the flavours of the leaf in which it is wrapped, with those of its mould. Affinage takes three to four weeks.

Rind of natural mould

Soft pâte; uncooked, unpressed

◇	9 cm square, 3 cm high
⚖	250–280 g
🝙	45%
✓	Spring to autumn
🥛	Raw
♀	Haut Poitou

POITOU-CHARENTES
Vienne

Plane or chestnut leaf

CROTTIN DE PAYS

This sweet, soft *fermier* cheese from the Albigeois region of Languedoc is made with mountain goat's milk. It is completely organic, and no chemical fertilizers are used on the pastures. Affinage takes around two weeks.

Soft pâte; uncooked, unpressed

⊖	5 cm diameter, 3 cm high
⚖	50–60 g
🄳	45%
✔	All year except in January; best from spring to autumn
🐄	Raw
♀	Gaillac

MIDI-PYRÉNÉES
Tarn

Rind of natural mould

FIGUE

During its affinage, which lasts for at least two weeks, this *artisanal* cheese is squeezed, and moulded in a cloth. It is about the size of an adult fist and crumbles easily. Occasionally it is covered with charcoal powder. It is made in a similar way to Besace de Pur Chèvre (*p. 113*).

Soft pâte; uncooked, unpressed

Rind of natural mould

◈	7–8 cm diameter base, 5 cm high
⚖	160–200 g
🄳	45%
✔	All year
🐄	Raw
♀	Bergerac *sec*

AQUITAINE
Dordogne

FOURME DE CHÈVRE ARDÈCHE

This slightly sour *fermier* cheese needs an affinage of six weeks.

Rind of natural, blue and brown mould

Affinage of one month

⊖ 9-10 cm diameter, 15 cm high

⚖ 1 kg

📁 45%

✓ Spring to autumn

🐄 Raw

🍷 St. Péray

RHÔNE-ALPS
Ardèche

Soft pâte; uncooked, unpressed

FROMAGE DE CHÈVRE ARIÈGE

Acidity and sweetness are pronounced in this *fermier* cheese, which is made at a farm on a mountainside close to the town of Foix in the Central Pyrénées. Affinage takes at least ten days.

⊖ 10 cm diameter, 3 cm high

⚖ 250 g

📁 40%

✓ Spring to autumn

🐄 Raw

🍷 Limoux, Vouvray *sec*

MIDI-PYRÉNÉES
Ariège

Soft pâte; uncooked, unpressed

Rind of white mould

FROMAGE DE CHÈVRE DE COIN

The people of the village of Glénat used to make *fermier* goat's-milk cheeses for themselves. Gradually, the cheeses started to be commercialized, although they retain their homemade appearance. Affinage takes at least ten days.

⊖ 6 cm diameter, 2 cm high

⚖ 50 g

📁 45%

✓ Spring to autumn

🐄 Raw

🍷 St. Pourçain

AUVERGNE
Cantal

Rind of natural mould

Soft pâte; uncooked, unpressed

The ancient town of Foix in the Central Pyrénées ▶

FROMAGE DE CHÈVRE FERMIER (1)

The *fermier* cheese shown here was made on a farm at Cierp-Gaud in the Pyrénées. It is small but well made, and smells slightly of goat. It can be eaten after the fourth day of affinage.

Soft pâte; uncooked, unpressed

⊖ 5–6 cm diameter, 3 cm high	
⚖ 100 g; 200 g (fresh)	
🗋 45%	
✔ February to November	
🥄 Raw	
🍷 Limoux, Vouvray *sec*	

MIDI-PYRÉNÉES
Haute-Garonne

Affinage of one month

Rind of natural mould

FROMAGE DE CHÈVRE FERMIER (2)

This is a barely ripened, pleasantly sour *fermier* cheese that reflects its high quality of milk. In the town of Marciac in Gascogne, where it is produced, it is often eaten for breakfast, seasoned with ground pepper. Although it can be eaten fresh, affinage may take up to two weeks.

Soft pâte; uncooked, unpressed

⊖ 6 cm diameter, 3–4 cm high	
⚖ 120 g	
🗋 45%	
✔ Spring to autumn	
🥄 Raw	
🍷 Gaillac	

MIDI-PYRÉNÉES
Gers

Affinage of ten days

Rind of natural mould

FROMAGE DE CHÈVRE LARZAC

This is a very fresh *fermier* cheese, even after a week of affinage. It has a sweet smell of good-quality milk and comes from the Causse du Larzac in the region of Roquefort, which is traditionally an area of sheep's-milk cheeses. Affinage takes at least one week.

Soft pâte; uncooked, unpressed

⊖ 5–6 cm diameter, 2 cm high	
⚖ 50–60 g	
🗋 45%	
✔ Spring to autumn	
🥄 Raw	
🍷 Coteaux du Languedoc	

MIDI-PYRÉNÉES
Aveyron

Rind of natural mould

FROMAGE FERMIER

This slightly spicy *fermier* cheese is produced
in the village of Granges-sur-Volognes in
the mountainous region of the Vosges. The
cheese shown here has been ripened for
four weeks and is dry, hard, and covered
with a white, brown, and pale blue
mould. Affinage takes at least ten days.

Soft pâte;
uncooked,
unpressed

⊖ 5–6 cm diam., 2.5–3 cm high	
⚖ 70 g	
🗋 Not defined	LORRAINE Vosges
✓ Spring to end of autumn	
🥛 Raw	
♀ Vin gris des Côtes de Toul (*rosé*)	

FROMAGE DU JAS

This *fermier* cheese is made on a farm called
the Domaine Le Jas at La Roque-sur-Pernes
in the Vaucluse. In old Provençal dialect
a *jas* is a sheepfold. The cheese has a mildly
sweet and sour flavour. Affinage takes one
to three weeks.

Soft pâte;
uncooked,
unpressed

Rind of
natural
mould

⊖ 6 cm diameter, 2 cm high	
⚖ 60 g	
🗋 45%	PROVENCE-ALPES-CÔTE-D'AZUR Vaucluse
✓ All year, especially spring to autumn	
🥛 Raw	
♀ Côtes de Provence	

FROMAGE AU LAIT DE CHÈVRE / CHÈVRE DE PAYS

The village of Saint-Jean-de-Chapteuil,
where the main industries are lace and
shoemaking, has a population of just 1,700.
A local farmer, J-A. Garnier, made the
drum-shaped cheese shown here at the
Domaine de Villeneuve. Affinage
takes at least 15 days.

Soft pâte;
uncooked,
unpressed

Rind of
natural
mould

⊖ 5 cm diameter, 4 cm high	
⚖ 100–120 g	
🗋 Not defined	AUVERGNE Haute-Loire
✓ April to October	
🥛 Raw	
♀ St. Pourçain	

GALET DE BIGORRE

This *fermier* cheese is a subtle combination of flavours – salt, then sourness, and finally sweetness open in the mouth. A local cheesemaker said that this cheese is best on the young side, and suggested trying it with ripe apricots. Affinage takes two weeks.

Soft pâte; uncooked, unpressed

Rind of natural mould

⊖	9 cm diameter base, 8 cm diameter top, 3–4 cm high
⚖	200–220 g
🗗	45%
✓	Spring to autumn
⌔	Raw
♀	Jurançon *moelleux*

MIDI-PYRÉNÉES
Hautes-Pyrénées

GALET SOLOGNOT

This *fermier* cheese has a strong-smelling mould and a balanced sweet-and-sour flavour. The mould is attractive and influences both the smell and taste of the pâte. (An unattractive mould does little to whet the appetite and gives cheese an unpleasant aftertaste, even if the rind is removed.) Affinage takes two weeks.

Soft pâte; uncooked, unpressed

Rind of natural mould covered with charcoal powder

⊖	7 cm diameter base, 6 cm diameter top, 3 cm high
⚖	120 g
🗗	45%
✓	Spring to autumn
⌔	Raw
♀	Reuilly

CENTRE
Loiret

GRAND COLOMBIER DES AILLONS

This *fermier* cheese is produced in the mountains of the Massif des Bauges in Savoie. It is usually made with goat's milk or a mixture of goat and cow's milk. The flavour increases as it matures. Affinage usually takes at least four weeks.

Soft pâte; uncooked, unpressed

Dry, washed rind

⊖	20 cm diameter, 3 cm high
⚖	800–900 g
🗗	45%
✓	Spring to autumn
⌔	Raw
⌔	Raw
♀	Vin de Savoie

RHÔNE-ALPES
Savoie

MONT D'OR DU LYONNAIS

This characteriestics of this small *fermier* or *artisanal* goat's-milk cheese from Lyon are a blue mould and reddish rind, which appear after a long and very humid affinage of two to four weeks. The cheese has a strong taste of salt, and no acidity.

⊖	10 cm diameter, 1–1.5 cm high
⚖	120–140 g
🗋	45%
✓	Spring to autumn
🐐	Raw
🥛	Raw
🍷	Beaujolais, Mâcon

RHÔNE-ALPES
Rhône

Soft pâte; uncooked, unpressed — Rind of natural mould

GALETTE DES MONTS DU LYONNAIS

This *artisanal* cheese has a soft, gentle flavour, more like milk than cheese. The consistency is so runny that it is eaten with a spoon, and it is difficult to transport without its thin wooden container. It is made by only one cheesemaker in the Monts du Lyonnais. Affinage takes two to three weeks.

⊖	10 cm diameter, 1.5 cm high
⚖	100–140 g
🗋	45%
✓	All year
🥛	Raw
🍷	Coteaux du Lyonnais

RHÔNE-ALPES
Rhône

Runny pâte; uncooked, unpressed — Rind of natural mould

MÂCONNAIS

This *fermier* or *artisanal* cheese, also called Chevreton de Mâcon, is made either solely from goat or cow's milk, or a mixture of the two. The cheese shown is hard enough to make *fromage fort* (*p. 173*). A faint smell of spring herbs comes from the dense pâte. Affinage takes at least two weeks.

⊖	4–5 cm diameter, 3–4 cm high
⚖	50–60 g
🗋	45%
✓	All year
🐐	Raw
🥛	Raw
🍷	Bourgogne Aligoté

BOURGOGNE
Saône-et-Loire

Soft to hard pâte; uncooked, unpressed

Rind of natural mould

PAVÉ BLÉSOIS

Both square and rectangular versions
of this *artisanal* cheese are produced
in the Blésois region near the town
of Blois on the River Loire. The rind
has a dry surface covered with a silvery
blue mould. When cut, the pâte is clean,
fine-textured, and tingles on the tongue.
Affinage takes two to four weeks.

Rind of
natural mould on
charcoal powder

Silvery blue mould

◈	8 cm square, 3–4 cm high (square);
◈	11–12 cm long, 6–7 cm wide, 3.5 cm high (rectangle)
⚖	250 g (square); 300 g (rectangle)
🍼	45%
✓	Spring to autumn
🥛	Raw
🍷	Sancerre, Pouilly Fumé

CENTRE
Loir-et-Cher

Soft pâte; uncooked,
unpressed

LE PAVÉ

Although some people may find this
fermier cheese rather dry and overripe,
the pâte is firm to the bite and slightly
sticky and the taste has a perfect
balance of acidity, sweetness, and salt.
The mould is a beautiful pale blue.
Affinage takes at least four weeks.

◈	7 cm square, 2 cm high
⚖	110–130 g
🍼	45%
✓	Spring to autumn
🥛	Raw
🍷	St. Péray

RHÔNE-ALPES
Ardèche

Soft pâte;
uncooked, unpressed

Rind of
natural mould

PAVÉ DE LA GINESTARIÉ

This is an organic mountain goat's-milk cheese. It has an affinage of at least two weeks, but the production method is a secret. There are traces of straw on the rind as well as in the flavour. The straw absorbs the water, and its bacteria play a role in the ripening.

Soft pâte; uncooked, unpressed

MIDI-PYRÉNÉES
Tarn

Rind of spots of natural mould

◈	8 cm square, 2–2.5 cm high
⚖	150–200 g
🗋	45%
✓	All year except January; best from spring to autumn
🧀	Raw
🍷	Coteaux du Languedoc, Collioure

POURLY

This *artisanal* cheese is produced in the limestone plateaux of the Auxerrois regions of Bourgogne. It is ideal for those who like a light goat's-milk cheese. Affinage usually takes two to four weeks, although the cheese may be eaten almost fresh, after the fifth day.

BOURGOGNE
Yonne

Soft pâte; uncooked, unpressed

Rind of natural mould

⊖	7 cm diameter base, 6 cm diameter top, 6–7 cm high
⚖	250–300 g
🗋	45%
✓	Spring to autumn
🧀	Raw
🍷	Sauvignon de St. Bris

QUATRE-VENTS

This *fermier* cheese is made without chemical rennet since this would impair the taste. The name, which means four winds, was chosen because of the location of the farm where it is made, which is on top of a hill exposed to wind from all directions. Affinage takes 12 to 15 days.

RHÔNE-ALPES
Isère

Soft pâte; uncooked, unpressed

Rind of natural mould

⊖	5–6 cm diameter, 2.5 cm high
⚖	60 g
🗋	45%
✓	Spring to autumn
🧀	Raw
🍷	St. Péray

PETIT QUERCY

This light, *fermier* goat's-milk cheese takes its name from the province of Quercy in which it is produced. The rind is attractively decorated with wild mulberry leaves. Affinage takes at least two weeks.

Mulberry leaf

⊖	7 cm diameter, 2 cm high
⚖	100 g
🗂	Not defined
✓	Spring to autumn
🥛	Raw
🍷	Cotes de Roussillon

QUERCY

Soft pate; uncooked, unpressed | Unripe heart

Rind of natural mould

ROGERET DE LAMASTRE

A red mould appears during the ripening of this *fermier* or *artisanal* cheese, which accounts for its other name: Fromage de Lamastre Rouge (red). The pâte is creamy and delicate. The cheese is produced in the town of Lamastre. Affinage takes two to four weeks.

⊖	7–8 cm diameter base, 2 cm high
⚖	100–120 g
🗂	Not defined
✓	All year
🥛	Raw
🍷	St. Peray

RHÔNE-ALPES
Ardèche

Soft pâte; uncooked, unpressed

Rind of natural mould

SAINT-FÉLICIEN DE LAMASTRE

The crust, pâte, and flavour of this *fermier* cheese are soft due to the method of production, using soft curd, or *caillé doux*. Affinage takes at least two weeks.

⊖	8–10 cm diameter, 1–1.5 cm high
⚖	90–120 g
🗂	45%
✓	Spring to autumn
🥛	Raw
🍷	St. Péray, St. Joseph

RHÔNE-ALPES
Ardèche

Soft pâte; uncooked, unpressed | Rind of natural yellow mould

SAINT-PANCRACE

The goats on the farm where this *fermier* cheese is made graze on the slopes of the Saint-Pancrace mountain. Spots of blue mould appear on the rind as it starts to dry. The pâte is firm, smooth, and melts in the mouth, revealing a light sweetness and a mild flavour. Affinage takes two to three weeks.

⊖ 11 cm diameter, 2 cm high	
⚖ 200–220 g	RHÔNE-ALPES
🗋 45%	Rhône
✓ Spring to autumn	
🧀 Raw	
⚲ Condrieu, Château Grillet	

Soft pâte; uncooked, unpressed

Rind of spots of blue natural mould

SANTRANGES

Halfway down the River Loire lies the region of Sancerrois, with three *fermier* cheeses bearing village names: Chavignol (*p. 106*), Crézancy, and Santranges. Chavignol is the most famous, but Santranges is also good. It is produced in small numbers and is a robust cheese to be eaten with wine. Affinage takes four weeks.

⊖ 6 cm diameter, 3 cm high	
⚖ 120–150 g	CENTRE
🗋 45%	Cher
✓ Spring to autumn	
🧀 Raw	
⚲ Sancerre, Pouilly Fumé	

Runny pâte; uncooked, unpressed

Rind of natural mould

SÉCHON DE CHÈVRE DRÔMOIS

This *fermier* cheese is called a *séchon*, which means a small, dry cheese. It is named after the River Drôme in the immense Dauphiné region of southeast France where it is produced. The flavour is rather salty as well as sweet. Affinage takes at least three weeks.

⊖ 5 cm diameter, 2 cm high	
⚖ 50 g	RHÔNE-ALPES
🗋 45%	Drôme
✓ All year	
🧀 Raw	
⚲ St. Péray	

Soft to hard pâte; uncooked, unpressed

Rind of natural mould

TARENTAIS

This *fermier* cheese comes from the Tarentaise region of Savoie. After four weeks of ripening, a slight blue mould covers the rind. After another week, a red and blue mould develops. Affinage takes from 15 days to three months; the cheese may also be eaten fresh.

Rind of natural mould

Soft pâte; uncooked, unpressed

⊖ 6–7 cm diameter, 7 cm high	RHÔNE-ALPES
⚖ 250 g	Savoie
🗋 45%	
✓ Spring to autumn	
🥛 Raw	
♀ Crépy	

LA TAUPINIÈRE

This *fermier* cheese from St. Estèphe is similar in shape to Gaperon (*p. 183*) and is made with highly concentrated milk. It is produced by M. Jousseaume at his farm in the province of Angoumois. During the two-week period of affinage, the cheese absorbs natural mould in the cellar, which gives it a good flavour.

Rind of natural mould on charcoal powder

Soft pâte; uncooked, unpressed

⊖ 9 cm diameter base, 5 cm high	POITOU-CHARENTES
⚖ 100–120 g	Charente
🗋 45%	
✓ All year	
🥛 Raw	
♀ Haut Poitou	

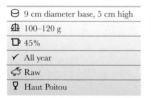

TOUCY

This goat's-milk cheese is made in the Auxerrois region in northern Bourgogne. It is light and easy to eat. Both *fermier* and *artisanal* versions are produced, with an affinage of at least ten days.

Washed rind of natural mould

Soft pâte; uncooked, unpressed

⊖ 6 cm diameter base, 5 cm diameter top, 4–5 cm high	BOURGOGNE
⚖ 170–200 g	Yonne
🗋 45%	
✓ Spring to autumn	
🥛 Raw	
♀ Sauvignon de St. Bris	

Goats in the Tarentaise region of Savoie ▶

VENDÔMOIS

This *fermier* goat's-milk cheese is produced
on farms in the Vendômois region north of
the town of Vendôme. Although the rind
of the cheese shown here would suggest
that it is fully ripe, the cut pâte is clearly
rather young. It is fine and slightly sour.
Affinage takes a minimum of ten days.

⊖ 6–7 cm diameter, 3 cm high	
⚖ 90–100 g	CENTRE
🝱 45%	Loir-et-Cher
✓ Spring to autumn	
🐄 Raw	
🍷 Coteaux du Vendômois	

Rind of natural
mould on
charcoal powder

Soft pâte;
uncooked,
unpressed

CROTTIN DU BERRY
À L'HUILE D'OLIVE

To make this Provençal speciality, small
goat's-milk cheeses with a mild soft pâte
are soaked in olive oil flavoured with
pepper, thyme, rosemary, laurel, juniper
berries, and garlic. They are usually served
with bread or salad and tomatoes.

PROVENCE-
ALPES-CÔTE-
D'AZUR

🐄 Not defined
🍷 Tavel *rosé*, Sancerre *rosé*

Cheese soaked
in oil and Provençal herbs
absorbs their flavours

CHÈVRE À L'HUILE
D'OLIVE ET À LA
SARRIETTE

Small, young Provençal goat's-milk cheeses
are soaked in olive oil with berries and
savory leaves to make this local speciality.
The cheese should have no mould, which
would discolour the mixture. The savory
must be quite dry.

PROVENCE-ALPES-
CÔTE-D'AZUR
Alpes-de-Haute-
Provence

🐄 Not defined
🍷 Bandol *rosé*

Olive oil flavoured with
dried savory and berries

SEASONAL GOAT'S-MILK CHEESES

Jean-Pierre Moreau is the owner of Bellevue, the goat farm where he, his wife, and two employees raise 200 goats and eight billy-goats. All the goats belong to the pedigree white Saanen (*right*) and brown Alpine breeds, whose quality is reflected in his cheeses. M. Moreau himself takes the cheeses to Paris twice a week.

The flavour of a goat's-milk cheese varies according to a number of factors: the breed of goat, what the animals are fed on, the way they are raised, the protein and fat content of the milk, the shape of the cheese, and the methods of coagulation and drainage, to name but a few. The goats first give birth at a year old, and subsequently once a year, between January and mid-March. Two or three kids are born to each goat; surplus kids are sold off immediately since their value diminishes as they grow. At the age of two, goats begin to give more milk, and continue to produce it for about five years. Around 200 goats give some 700 litres of milk, which is used to make 12 different cheeses.

Seasonal cheeses are made by traditional methods using milk produced after the birth of the kid in spring. Fresh spring milk, from goats grazing on lush grass outdoors, is used to make spring cheeses from April to May. Modern goat's-milk cheeses are made using milk from animals kept in sheds and fed on hay. Thanks to artificial insemination and frozen curd, goat's-milk cheeses can be made and sold even in winter, but they lack the flavour of the seasonal cheeses.

White Saanen goats at Bellevue

Ready for milking

Farms in Provence produce many fine foods, including the goat's-milk speciality Crottin du Berry à l'Huile d'Olive

CHEVRETTE DES BAUGES

In the mountain region of Savoie, a cheese made from a blend of goat and cow's milk is called a *chevrette*, while a pure goat's-milk cheese is a *chevrotin*. Today, this *fermier* cheese is made only by older producers, on two or three farms, and is in danger of dying out. The top picture shows a cheese made from three-quarters goat's milk and one-quarter cow's milk and was photographed at a cheese shop in Thonon, near Lake Geneva.

The cheese in the lower picture was made with equal proportions of the same milks; it was found in a shop in Chambéry. The owners of both cheese shops are well known for their Savoie cheeses and they also ripen them according to their own methods. Both claim that the mould that forms on a *chevrette* depends on the type of food the animals eat, their exact location on the mountainsides, and even on whether they are milked in the morning or evening. This explains why each of these cheeses has such an individual taste. Affinage takes one to three months.

Rind of natural mould

Semi-hard pâte; uncooked, pressed

Cheese made with three-quarters goat's milk, and one-quarter cow's milk

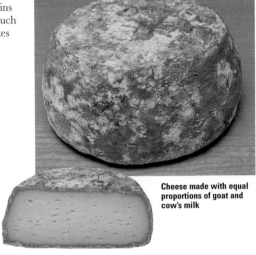

Cheese made with equal proportions of goat and cow's milk

⊖	10–15 cm diameter, 5 cm high
⚖	500 g–1 kg
⛉	Not defined
✓	Early spring to early winter
🥛	Raw
🥛	Raw
♉	Seyssel

RHÔNE-ALPES
Savoie, Haute-Savoie

CHEVROTIN D'ALPAGE, VALLÉE DE MORZINE

The *fermier* goat's-milk cheese shown here was made in a *chalet* in the Vallée de Morzine in Savoie. Its moist surface still shows traces of the cloth used to wrap it during affinage, which can take up to four months. The milk used to make this cheese comes from goats grazing on flower meadows in the Alps, which gives the pale yellow pâte a sugary smell and a taste of honey. There are small holes in the pâte, which is characteristic of a pressed cheese. Chevrotin *d'alpage* was inspired by another great cheese, Reblochon (*p. 213*).

Semi-hard pâte sinks under finger pressure; uncooked, pressed

Affinage of 14 weeks

Moist rind of natural white and reddish-brown, waxed mould

⊖	17–20 cm diam., 4 cm high
⚖	1–1.3 kg
ⅅ	Not defined
✓	Autumn to winter
⌔	Raw
♚	Vin de Savoie

RHÔNE-ALPES
Haute-Savoie

CHEVROTIN DES ARAVIS

This *fermier* goat's-milk cheese is made in a *chalet* in the Chaîne des Aravis in Savoie. Its appearance and flavour are quite different from those of the goat's-milk cheeses of the Loire. It has a moist, yellowish-orange rind stained with white mould. The pâte is rounded, mild, fine-textured, and melting at the edges – rather like Reblochon (*p. 213*), which is made using very similar methods of production. Affinage requires 95% humidity and takes three to six weeks, during which time the cheese is washed in brine, turned, and lightly pressed by hand.

Soft pâte; uncooked, slightly pressed by hand

Moist, washed, yellowish-orange rind, with a flowery natural mould

⊖	8–10 cm diam., 3–4 cm high
⚖	250–350 g
ⅅ	45%
✓	Summer to autumn
⌔	Raw
⌔	Raw
♚	Vin de Savoie

RHÔNE-ALPES
Savoie, Haute-Savoie

CHEVROTIN DE MACÔT

One of the prime requirements of a good
fromagerie is the *cave d'affinage*, since this is
where the cheese is "finished". This
cheese is made in an adapted bomb
shelter from World War II. This space of
around 300 square metres cut into the
mountainside offers the ideal cool, dark,
damp conditions. When it leaves the farm
where it is made in the Tarentaise region
of Savoie, this *fermier* cheese is white.
It is taken to be ripened by a *fromager*.
Affinage takes between one and three
months. The cheese is left to rest
for a month, during which time
the yellow and pink mould
opens up on the surface.
The pâte ripens slowly.

Rind of
natural mould

Affinage of one month

⊖	10–11 cm diameter, 6 cm high
⚖	500–600 g
🗁	45%
✓	June to December
🐄	Raw
🍷	Vin de Savoie

RHÔNE-ALPES
Savoie

Semi-hard pâte;
uncooked, pressed

CHEVROTIN DU MONT CENIS

This *fermier* goat's-milk cheese comes
from the area around Mont Cenis.
Because of its relatively large size, it
requires a long affinage of up to six
months. The rind, which is washed in
brine, is regularly rubbed with a cloth
soaked in liquid *morge* (*p. 41*). As the
rind develops, it protects the cheese
against bad mould but allows contact
between the inside of the cheese
and the natural environment
in the cellar. The cheese
shown has been ripened for
a full six months. The rind
is still smooth and the elastic
pâte begins to turn sticky.

Semi-hard
pâte;
uncooked,
pressed

Washed rind

⊖	45 cm diameter, 8 cm high
⚖	8 kg
🗁	45%
✓	Best from autumn onwards
🐄	Raw
🍷	Crépy

RHÔNE-ALPES
Savoie

CHEVROTIN DE MONTVALEZAN

This *fermier* cheese was discovered by a *fromager* who then helped the cheesemaker to produce it in the Tarentaise region of Savoie. Its appearance reflects the enthusiasm and quality of their work together. It has a compact, fine, ivory pâte, which is sticky and smells of mould. Affinage takes from four to five weeks.

Semi-hard pâte; uncooked, pressed

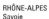

Rind of natural mould

⊖	10–12 cm diameter, 6 cm high
⚖	500–600 g
🗋	45%
✓	Spring to autumn
🐇	Raw
♀	Roussette de Savoie

RHÔNE-ALPES
Savoie

CHEVROTIN DE PEISEY-NANCROIX

At an altitude of 1,300 m, the tiny villages of Peisey and Nancroix in Savoie have a total of only 481 inhabitants between the two of them. Their local goat's-milk cheese is *fermier* produced with an affinage of up to six months, which is a long time considering its small size. After affinage, the change in the crust is impressive; the pâte is rather sticky. This is a goat's-milk cheese of quality, with a mature taste.

Semi-hard pâte; uncooked, pressed

Rind of natural mould

⊖	10–12 cm diameter, 6–7 cm high
⚖	550–600 g
🗋	Not defined
✓	Spring to autumn
🐇	Raw
♀	Roussette de Savoie

RHÔNE-ALPES
Savoie

COMTÉ (AOC)

Also called Gruyère de Comté, this is the richest and most popular cheese in France, along with Beaufort. Traditionally, it is produced in the mountains of the Jura, where farmers bring their milk down to the *fruitières*, which are cooperatives. It takes 530 litres of milk – the daily production of 30 cows – to make one Comté cheese weighing 45 kg.

Firm, slightly elastic, ivory to pale-yellow pâte; cooked below 53°C, pressed

Natural, stippled, golden-yellow to brown rind

Affinage of approximately one year

Appearance and Flavour

The surface of the cheese shown here is broad and flat with a moist, cool, grey, yellow, and ochre rind. When it is cut, it reveals a firm and supple pâte that melts in the mouth, leaving a sweet taste. The salt is strong but balanced and the flavour has a nutty tang. Comté is a nourishing and versatile cheese: it is a good accompaniment to an apéritif, or may be eaten in a salad, with fruit, in a sandwich, or cooked in a croque-monsieur or a fondue.

Production and Affinage

Consumed by 40% of the French population, Comté has the highest production figures of all French cheeses. The AOC restricts production to the Franche-Comté, eastern Bourgogne, and parts of Lorraine, Champagne, and the Rhône-Alpes. Quality is strictly controlled, and each year 5% of cheeses fail to pass the AOC tests. Affinage must take place within the AOC specified areas and needs 90 days from the date of production at below 19°C with a minimum humidity level of 92%. The cheeses are regularly wiped and rubbed with brine. The rind must be moist and treated with *morge*.

Eye

Eyes
The "eyes" in the pâte of a Comté are the result of careful affinage. They vary from the size of a pea to that of a small cherry. If the affinage is prolonged at low temperatures, no eyes form.

⊖	40–70 cm diameter, 9–13 cm high
⚖	35–55 kg
⁂	62 g per 100 g cheese
⬡	45%; 27.9 g min. per 100 g cheese
✓	All year
🜂	Raw
⚱	Côtes du Jura (*jaune*), Vin de Paille *doux*

FRANCHE-COMTÉ Jura, Haute-Saône, Territoire de Belfort; RHÔNE-ALPES Ain; BOURGOGNE Côte d'Or, Saône-et-Loire; CHAMPAGNE-ARDENNE Haute-Marne; LORRAINE Vosges

HOW TO CUT A COMTÉ

To cut a whole Comté in two or four, first use a cutting wire. Thereafter, it may be cut with a kitchen knife.

1 The cheese is first cut in half.

2 Each half is then halved.

3 A right-angle is cut off each quarter.

4 A wedge is then cut off the side of each quarter.

5 A slice is cut off the end of the quarter.

6 A second slice is cut parallel to the last.

7 The remaining quarter is cut into wedges.

8 Each quarter is cut to the same pattern.

AOC Regulations: Comté

1 The milk must be transported immediately after milking to the place of production. If the milk is refrigerated and kept at 14–18°C, renneting must be carried out within 14 hours. If the milk is kept at 4°C, renneting must occur within 24 hours, 36 hours in winter.
2 The milk may be heated once to a maximum of 40°C, but only at the renneting. Systems or machinery that would allow the rapid heating to above 40°C before renneting may not be kept on the premises.
3 The salt must be applied to the surface of the cheese directly or with brine.
4 The green *casein* label must be applied to the side of the cheese, bearing the date of production.
5 Grated cheese may not be sold as Comté.

AOC GRANTED 1976

THE GRADING OF COMTÉ

Comté is graded on a scale of 1 to 20. The minimum score for a pass is an average above 12. Cheeses with marks of 15 to 20 have green *casein* labels; those with 12 to 15 show brick-red *casein* labels. The minimum score for taste is 3 out of 9. A score of 0 in the following areas leads to elimination: shape, rind, holes, and pâte. Rejected cheeses are sold as Gruyère.

Aspect	Marks	Ideal Conditions for Reference
Overall appearance	1/20	Rounded sides; clear-cut form: no joint between sides, top, and bottom; well-proportioned; no bulging, no stretching.
Quality of rind on top, bottom, and sides	1.5/20	Treated with *morge*; stippled (with cloth marks); solid (not crumbly); clean (dry, smooth, not stained or coated); even (light orange to ochre); no defects, no cracks.
Appearance of the cut and eyes	3.5/20	Holes should be present: 10 to 20 eyes on a half cheese; round, clear, cherry sized, well spread, no grooves or other defects.
Quality of pâte	5/20	Even colour (creamy to light orange-yellow); supple (slightly elastic); smooth (not too moist or oily); medium resistance to deformation; fine pâte (no little particles when the cheese is reduced in the mouth); should not stick to the palate.
Quality of taste	9/20	Simple (no defects); nutty (walnut); fruity (apricot, dried fruits); "lactic" (milk, butter); lightly roasted (caramel); grassy (hay); balanced (sour, salty, sweet, bitter); no tingling, lingering taste.

Corse

The island of Corsica, which is called Corse in French, lies in the Mediterranean 170 km south of France's Côte d'Azur and 83 km west of Piombino on the Italian coast. The highest point on the island is Monte Cinto, which is covered in snow for much of the year. The Corsican people see themselves as independent and some even refer to France as "the Continent". The language is closer to Italian than French and the independence movement is active.

Due to its strategic position and commercial potential, the island has been coveted, invaded, and dominated by different powers throughout history – Greece, Rome, the Saracens, Pisa, Genoa, and for the last 200 years France. The Greeks introduced sheep, wine, and olives to the island, and the Saracens their goats. Most of Corsica has a Mediterranean climate, but above 1,500 m, it gets colder and more alpine. The range of climates has permitted around 2,000 species of plant to become established, all of which are resistant to fierce heat, arid conditions, strong winds, and intense cold. Of these species, 78 are unknown elsewhere. The *maquis*, which is the rocky landscape where many of these bushy and herby plants grow wild, shows an explosion of colours in spring, and provides excellent grazing for goats and sheep. The mixed climate, varied terrain, robust vegetation, and near-wild sheep and goats are ideal ingredients for a rich variety of cheeses that are quite different from those of the mainland.

Corsican cheeses are generally small or medium-sized and marked by the *faisselle* (colander) when moulded. They tend to be salty and highly flavoured, with a pronounced smell. Due to a long affinage, many of them are strong-tasting and are best eaten with local red wines.

MAP OF CORSICA

Aerial View of the Plateau du Niolo
The mountainous Niolo region in the centre of Haute-Corse is home to many herds of semi-wild goats and sheep whose milk is used for making a vast range of Corsican cheeses.

FROMAGE CORSE

M. Manenti's home and cheese-making *atelier*, where this *fermier* cheese is made, lie some 360 m up Col San Bastiano in Calcatoggio, which is itself 411 m high. The herds of ewes and goats are taken into the mountains at the end of June or beginning of July, and come down again in October. The ewes stay outdoors all year round. The rennet that makes the milk coagulate is homemade from an enzyme called chymosin that is found in the stomach of a young goat. The stomach is dried indoors for at least 40 days, thinly cut, and soaked in a litre of warm water for two days. In the past, the reed colander used to strain the cheese was also made at home. After 100 days, the cheese is covered with mould. It is salty, with a fine texture. Affinage takes at least two months.

Soft pâte, slightly elastic to finger pressure; uncooked, unpressed

Affinage of four months

Affinage of ten hours

Dried kid's stomach containing cheese

Affinage of eight days

Washed rind

CORSE
Corse-du-Sud

⊖	11–13 cm diameter, 3–4 cm high
⚖	500 g
⛴	48%
✓	Spring to autumn
🐄	Raw
🐐	Raw
❦	Patrimonio

Affinage of five months

BROCCIU / FROMAGE DE LACTOSÉRUM (AOC)

The Corsican name for this cheese is Brocciu, while in French it is called Broccio. The origin of the name may be *brousse*, which is another word for *fromage frais* made from goat or ewe's milk. Brocciu is an unusual cheese since it is the first AOC cheese to be made from *lactosérum*, or whey, which is usually discarded during cheese production. Because some proteins and other nutritional elements remain in it, whey makes a useful by-product. Brocciu, which is similar to Italian ricotta, is popular with Corsicans and is sold at local markets in returnable baskets.

Production

First the whey is heated to 35°C and salted, then whole milk (10 to 15% of its volume) is added. This blend is mixed while being further heated to 90°C. Solid white particles floating on the surface are skimmed, transferred to a colander, and drained. Production may be *fermier*, *artisanal*, or *coopérative*.

How to Eat Brocciu

Brocciu is usually eaten fresh, hot or cold, within 48 hours of production, although if drained and salted it can be ripened like other cheeses. The pâte is soft and sweet; it smells of milk and feels liquid in the throat. Brocciu is excellent eaten for breakfast with jam or salt and pepper. It can also be served with local *marc* poured on it, or used as a filling for omelettes or cannelloni. *Fiadone* is a tasty, lemon-flavoured sponge cake made with Brocciu, eggs, sugar, and grated lemon rind. The AOC was granted in 1988.

Fresh, white pâte

Very fresh Brocciu, still hot and steaming

⊖	Colander-shaped, in different formats
⚖	Generally 500 g (as shown) to 1 kg
🍶	40–51%
✓	Spring to autumn (fresh goat's cheeses); winter to early summer (fresh ewe's cheeses); all year, if matured
🐄	Raw
🐐	Raw
⬚	*Marc* de Corse

CORSE

The mountains of Corsica

DIFFERENT TYPES OF BROCCIU

1 Brocciu in its traditional Corsican basket, from the Domaine de la Porette, near Corte.

2 Brocciu from a Parisian *fromager*.

3 Brocciu from Ajaccio market.

4 Brocciu from Lyon market.

5 Brocciu *poivré* – pepper Brocciu from a market at Sainte-Maure.

CALENZANA
(LE NIOLO)

This is a well-known *fermier* cheese from the Niolo plateau in the northern part of Corsica. It has an affinage of at least three months. The cheese shown here is rather white. The rind is wet, and the pâte is heavy and crumbles like clay, and has a strong taste.

Soft pâte; uncooked, unpressed

Natural rind

◇	10 cm square, 4–5 cm high
⚖	600 g
🗂	Not defined
✓	Spring to autumn
🐑	Raw
🐐	Raw
♟	Patrimonio

CORSE
Haute-Corse

LE FIUM'ORBO

This *artisanal* cheese, named after a small river in the north of Corsica, has a sticky rind, marked by the colander in which it was moulded. It has a concentrated flavour, and the pâte sinks under light finger pressure, with no elasticity. Affinage takes at least two months, during which time the cheese is turned every two days.

Soft pâte with no elasticity; uncooked, unpressed

Natural mould rind

◖	10–12 cm diameter, 4 cm high
⚖	400–450 g
🗂	50%
✓	November to end June (ewe's); January to end June (goat's)
🐑	Raw
🐐	Raw
♟	Vin de Corse

CORSE
Haute-Corse

FLEUR DU MAQUIS

This *artisanal* cheese is called the "flower of the *maquis*" which is the French name for the scrubby Corsican landscape.

Fleur du Maquis

Chillis, juniper berries, savory, and rosemary

Natural rind, covered with savory and rosemary

BRIN D'AMOUR

Both this cheese and the Fleur du Maquis have a strong scent of dried herbs that bites on the tongue. Their pâte is fine-textured and ivory in colour, and tastes slightly sour. Both types are occasionally made in France, where they are more popular than in their native Corsica. They are both *artisanal* cheeses with an affinage of at least one month.

Brin d'Amour

Soft pâte, with no elasticity; uncooked, unpressed

◈	10–12 cm square, 5–6 cm high
⚖	600–700 g
🗇	Fleur du Maquis: 45%; Brin d'Amour: not defined
✓	Winter to summer
⌬	Raw
♈	Vin de Corse, Côtes de Provence

CORSE
Haute-Corse

A FILETTA (LA FOUGÈRE)

A filetta means "the fern" in Corsican. This *artisanal* cheese, decorated with a sprig of fern, comes from Isolaccio, which lies 45 km south of the town of Bastia. It has a faint smell of the cellar and fern leaves. Young cheeses may be exported to the mainland. Affinage takes three to four weeks, during which time the cheese is turned.

Soft pâte with no elasticity; uncooked, unpressed

Rind of natural mould with colander marks and decorated with fern

⊖	10 cm diameter, 3–4 cm high
⚖	300–350 g
⏇	45%
✓	December to June (ewe's-milk); March to November (goat's-milk)
◈	Raw
◈	Raw
♀	Patrimonio

CORSE
Haute-Corse

FROMAGE DE BREBIS

The *fermier* cheese shown here was made in November in Santa-Maria-Siché with milk from the farm of M. Cianfarani. This photograph was taken only a week later. The white rind looks fresh, but the pâte is elastic. The first milk from the morning's milking makes it slightly bitter. Affinage usually takes at least three months.

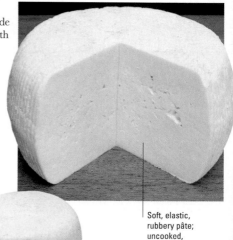

Washed rind

Soft, elastic, rubbery pâte; uncooked, unpressed

⊖	11–13 cm diameter, 7 cm high
⚖	1 kg
⏇	50%
✓	Spring to autumn
◈	Raw
♀	Patrimonio

CORSE
Corse-du-Sud

FROMAGE FERMIER BREBIS

This *fermier* sheep's milk cheese has a wet rind and sticky pâte and belongs to the same family as Venaco (*p. 161*). It is best eaten from spring to autumn. Production starts at the beginning of winter and continues until summer. Cheesemaking commences as soon as the ewes on the farm begin to produce milk on 7 December. Every day of the 45 days of affinage, the cheeses are all washed with a little water and turned. At the beginning of affinage, the cheese has almost no smell.

Soft pâte, with no elasticity; uncooked, unpressed

Washed rind

Fresh cheese

Handmade Cheeses
Although this might look like a washed-rind cheese, it is only rubbed with a moistened hand and turned several times.

⊖	9–11 cm diameter, 4 cm high
⚖	350–400 g
🗗	45%
✓	Best from spring to autumn
🐄	Raw
♀	Patrimonio

CORSE
Haute-Corse

FROMAGE AU PUR LAIT DE BREBIS

The four *fermier* cheeses shown here are all of the same type, but the length of affinage – from two months to a year – gives them each a very different character.

Rind and pâte reveal the quality of the milk

Pâte sinks under finger pressure and is so moist that it crumbles

Young cheese, around two months old

Colander marks on rind

Patches of white, green, and straw-coloured mould cover the light brown rind

Pâte is riddled with holes and slightly elastic

Mature cheese

Holes made by the cheesemite, *le ciron*

Brittle pâte with spicy taste

Old, hard cheese

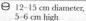

⊖	12–15 cm diameter, 5–6 cm high
⚖	500–700 g
▶	Not defined
✓	Winter to summer
⇔	Raw
♀	Vin de Corse

CORSE
Corse-du-Sud

Affinage of one year

FROMAGE CORSE

There are hardly any cheese shops in Corsica, so people buy cheese at the morning market. Cheesemakers also sell their own cheeses, which become known by the maker's name – for example, Mme Nicole's cheese. The *fermier* cheese shown is so young that it is still exuding whey; pâte and salt are not yet integrated. It was bought at the supermarket in Calacuccia.

Fresh,
unripened pâte

⬙ 11 cm square, 5 cm high	
⚖ 570 g	CORSE
🏷 Not defined	Haute-Corse
✓ Winter to early summer	
🐄 Raw	
🍷 Ajaccio	

FROMAGE CORSE NIOLO

The *fermier* cheese shown was bought at a market in Lyon. It was sold under the name of "Niolo" but according to Corsican cheese experts it is of the *bastelicaccia* type made in the Ajaccio area. The mould is blue and reddish-brown and the rind is moist. The pâte sinks a little under finger pressure. It is a little young for a Corsican cheese, but it has flavour. Affinage takes at least three months.

Soft pâte;
uncooked, unpressed

Washed rind, marked
by colander

⊖ 11–12 cm diameter, 4.5 cm high	
⚖ 450 g	CORSE
🏷 45%	Haute-Corse
✓ Winter to early summer	
🐄 Raw	
🍷 Patrimonio *rosé*	

FROMAGE FERMIER DE CHÈVRE DE LA TAVAGNA

The Giancoli family's house lies on the coast in a mountainous area south of Bastia. For eight months of the year they make some 70 *fermier* cheeses per day. A pungent smell fills the air when this cheese is unwrapped, and the paper wrapper bears the marks of the colander. The cheese itself looks moist and is hard, like soap. It has been ripened for seven months. Affinage usually takes two months, during which time the cheese is regularly wiped with a moist cloth.

Soft pâte; uncooked, unpressed

Natural rind

⬙	9–10 cm wide, 11 cm long, 4 cm high
⚖	300–400 g
🗁	45%
✓	All year
🐄	Raw
🍷	Château Chalon (*jaune*), Arbois *jaune*
🍶	*Marc* de Corse

CORSE
Haute-Corse

LE NIOLO

The Corsican village of Casamaccioli has only 140 inhabitants. It is here, deep in the mountains, that the Santini brothers produce Le Niolo cheese. It is a *fermier* cheese with a strong smell, a sticky consistency, and a taste that tingles on the tongue. The smell grows and never disappears. In Paris, when people think of Corsican cheeses, this is what comes to their minds. Affinage takes at least three months.

Soft, sticky pâte; uncooked, unpressed

Washed rind, marked by colander

⬙	10–13 cm square, 4 cm high
⚖	400–500 g
🗁	50%
✓	Winter to summer
🐄	Raw
🍷	Château Chalon (*jaune*), Arbois *jaune*
🍶	*Marc* de Corse

CORSE
Haute-Corse

LE MOUFLON

This *fermier* cheese is made from raw goat's milk in Cargèse in southern Corsica. Affinage, which usually lasts for three months, takes place in the mountain town of Calacuccia in the north of Corsica.

Washed rind

Pâte breaks like hard clay, with no elasticity; uncooked, unpressed

The Mouflon

Although cheesemakers think of it as a goat, the *mouflon* is a wild mountain sheep, the ancestor of domestic European sheep, with curved horns, but no beard. They are still found today, mainly in Sardinia and Corsica, where they are known as *muflone* and *mufoli*. Although *mouflons* are now an endangered species, they used to be eaten roasted or stewed in much the same way as mutton or venison.

◈	12 cm square, 3 cm high
⚖	400–500 g
🜨	50%
✓	Best in summer
◁	Raw
♀	Patrimonio

CORSE
Corse-du-Sud

PÂTE DE FROMAGE

Pâte de fromage, meaning cheese paste, is a Corsican speciality. Ripened cheese is milled, put into a container, and ripened again. Some locals say that it is best when it is infested with the *ciron*, or cheese mite. This is an *artisanal* cheese with an affinage of five to six months in vats.

🏺	In a pot
⚖️	200 g net
🗄️	50%
🐄	Raw
🐐	Raw
✓	All year
🍷	Château Chalon (*jaune*), Arbois *jaune*
🥃	*Marc* de Corse

CORSE
Haute-Corse

A FILETTA

It is said that this cheese – a *pâte de fromage* (cheese paste) – was formerly made in all Corsican homes. The smell of A Filetta is so strong that it stings the eyes. It is an *artisanal* cheese with an affinage of five to six months

🏺	In a pot
⚖️	230 g net
🗄️	45%
✓	Spring to autumn
🐐	Raw
🍷	Château Chalon (*jaune*), Arbois *jaune*
🥃	*Marc* de Corse

CORSE
Haute-Corse

Mountain village, Corsica ▶

SAN PETRONE

This is another *pâte de fromage* made from mature milled cheese, shaped without including further additives, and ripened for seven to eight months. There is no rind. The pâte looks like dough that has been lightly kneaded. It is sticky, with a strong salty, sharp, and tingling taste, which resembles that of *fromage fort*. Production is *artisanal*.

Dough-like pâte
Washed rind

◈	10–11 cm square, 5 cm high
⚖	500 g
🗅	45%
✓	Produced from December to end of June; available all year
⟶	Raw
♀	Château Chalon (*jaune*), Arbois *jaune*
⬚	*Marc* de Corse

CORSE
Haute-Corse

LE VIEUX CORSE

This *pâte de fromage* is wrapped in three layers of wax paper. The pâte is stained with blue mould. It is salty, spicy, and tasty. The Corsicans eat it thickly spread on bread like butter. This is an *artisanal* cheese with an affinage of at least three months.

Pâte is stained
with blue mould

◈	10 cm square, 2–3 cm high
⚖	500 g
🗅	50%
✓	All year
⟶	Raw
♀	Château Chalon (*jaune*), Arbois *jaune*
⬚	*Marc* de Corse

CORSE
Haute-Corse

TOME CHÈVRE

This is an excellent *fermier* cheese
made by M. Andreani from the
village of Piaggiola near Sartène.
This cheese is very different from
the goat's-milk cheeses of the
mainland. The mould looks like
a dry stone covered with reddish
lichen, and the pâte is so shiny
that it resembles candle wax and
has to be broken with a hammer.
It smells slightly of the cellar in
which it is matured. Affinage
takes at least three months. This
cheese is probably related to a
Sardinian cheese called Fleur de
Sardaigne (flower of Sardinia),
which is said to date from
Roman times.

Dough-like pâte

⊖	17–18 cm diameter, 8–9 cm high
⚖	2 kg
🗋	Undefined
✓	Summer to winter
🐄	Raw
⚲	Patrimonio

CORSE
Corse-du-Sud

TOME DE CHÈVRE

This very dry *fermier* cheese smells
of hay. Perhaps it is the smell of
the flowers that grow in the *maquis*
(mountain scrub) on which the
goats feed. It has an affinage of
at least three months. The
precise origin of the cheese
shown here is unknown.

Pâte is stained
with blue mould

⊖	16 cm diameter, 6 cm high
⚖	1.5 kg
🗋	Undefined
🐄	Raw
✓	All year
⚲	Patrimonio

CORSE

TOMME CORSE (1)

Bite into the hard pâte of this *artisanal* cheese and an almost coppery flavour of salt, sweetness, red pepper, and sourness explodes in the mouth. It goes particularly well with a vintage Corsican wine. Compare Ossau *fermier* (*p. 77*) or Salers (*p. 96*) with this Corsican cheese. Affinage takes three months to one year.

Semi-hard pate;
uncooked, pressed

Rind of
natural mould

◯	20 cm diameter, 8 cm high
⚖	2 kg
🗋	47%
✓	All year
🐄	Raw
🍷	Vin de Corse (vintage)

CORSE
Haute-Corse

TOMME CORSE (2)

The *coopérative* A Pecurella, where this cheese is made, was founded in 1975. A *pecurella* is the Corsican name for the young ewe that produces the rich, strongly aromatic milk used to make this cheese. The piece shown below is a year old and very crumbly. Tomme Corse has an affinage of three months to one year at 12°C and 85% humidity. The locals are very partial to it.

Semi-hard pâte
becomes granular with
age; uncooked, pressed

Rind of
natural mould

Affinage of one year

◯	20 cm diameter, 8–10 cm high
⚖	2.5 kg
🗋	48%
✓	All year
🐄	Raw
🍷	Vin de Corse (vintage)

CORSE
Corse-du-Sud

U RUSTINU

Corsican cheeses do not usually have specific names and are simply called cheese or *brocciu*. Sometimes the wholesaler will name them himself. This one was made by Joseph Guidicelli. His cheeses are known by two names: U Rustinu, which is a geographical name, and U Muntanacciu, which is Corsican for a mountain. U Rustinu is an *artisanal* cheese with an affinage of at least three months, during which time it is turned regularly.

Soft pâte; uncooked, unpressed

Moist red rind of white and red mould

○	10 cm diameter, 5 cm high
⚖	450 g
ⅅ	45%
✓	Produced from December to late June; best in spring
⅏	Raw
♀	Patrimonio

CORSE
Haute-Corse

LE VENACO

With Niolo *(p. 154)*, Calenzana *(p. 148)*, and Brocciu *(p. 146)*, Venaco is one of the most typical Corsican cheeses. The name originally derived from the place of production, Venaco, a town in the centre of Corsica, but it is no longer made there. It is a *fermier* cheese made from ewe's milk, with an affinage of at least two months.

Soft, sticky pate; uncooked, unpressed

Washed rind

○	9 cm diameter, 3–4 cm high
⚖	350 g
ⅅ	45%
⅏	Raw, whole
✓	Produced from winter to early summer; best from spring to autumn
♀	Ajaccio

CORSE
Haute-Corse

French Cheeses
D–G

DREUX À LA FEUILLE / FEUILLE DE DREUX

The ancient town of Dreux lies in a cereal-producing region to the north of Chartres, some 80 km from Paris. The flat, thin cheeses produced there ripen gently under the cover of chestnut leaves, which stop them from sticking to each other.
A faint smell of the chestnut leaf mingles with a pleasant scent of mould. The patchy white mould turns to a reddish-brown late in the cheese's affinage, which lasts two to three weeks. This *artisanal* cheese used to be eaten as a snack by workers in the fields.

Soft pâte; uncooked, unpressed

Rind of white mould decorated with chestnut leaf

⊖	14–16 cm diameter, 2–3 cm high
⚖	300–350 g
🗋	30–40%
✓	All year
⌓	Raw or pasteurized
❢	Touraine

CENTRE
Eure-et-Loir

EMMENTAL

This *industriel* cheese is almost identical to Emmental Grand Cru (*opposite*) but is made with pasteurized milk.

Hard, ivory to pale yellow pâte, with cherry- to walnut-sized holes; cooked, pressed

Hard, dry ochre to light-brown rind

⊖	70 cm–1 m diameter, 13–25 cm high
⚖	60–130 kg
⚭	60 g per 100 g cheese
🗋	45% min., 27 g per 100 g cheese
✓	All year
⌓	Pasteurized
❢	Vin de Savoie, Givry, Rully, Mercurey

ALL REGIONS
OF FRANCE

◀ **Cows grazing in front of a château in the village of Castillon-en-Auge, near Livarot**

EMMENTAL GRAND CRU

This cheese has a red *casein* label, which is a kind of guarantee of its quality. This label gives details of the place of production, fat content, and licence number of the maker. Emmental Grand Cru is a large *coopérative* or *industriel* cheese with a cooked and pressed pâte like that of Beaufort (*p. 48*) and Comté (*p. 142*). It is produced using raw milk in the regions listed below. The pâte is smooth; its aroma and taste are sweet.
Affinage takes at least ten weeks.

Dry, natural, washed and brushed, ochre rind

Firm ivory to pale yellow pâte; cooked, pressed

Holes should be 1.5–3 cm in diameter

⊖	70 cm–1 m diameter, 13–25 cm high
⚖	60–130 kg
⣶	62 g min. per 100 g cheese
⬜	45% min., 27.9 g per 100 g cheese
✓	All year
⌓	Raw
❢	Vin de Savoie, Givry, Rully, Mercurey

RHÔNE-ALPES Ain, Rhône, Savoie, Haute-Savoie; BOURGOGNE Côte d'Or, Saône-et-Loire; LORRAINE Vosges; CHAMPAGNE-ARDENNE Haute-Marne

HOW EMMENTAL GRAND CRU IS MADE

The whole process of making this Emmental takes at least six weeks.

Coagulation
It takes 800 to 900 litres of milk to make a 70-kg Emmental. The milk is heated to 33°C at the renneting stage and coagulates within 30 minutes. The curd is milled to help the whey separate, and then heated and cooked for 90 minutes at a maximum of 53°C.

Moulding
The curd is put into moulds and pressed for 24 hours. The *fromage blanc* is then floated in brine for 48 hours. The brine salts the cheese and forms the rind.

Affinage
The cheese rests in a cellar at 10–13°C for four to five days, then the temperature is raised to 16–18°C. After a week, the cheese is transferred to a cellar, at 21–25°C and 60% humidity, where it stays for a month. Natural bacteria in the cheese transform oxygen into CO_2 to form holes, while the pâte becomes more elastic, fine-textured, and tasty. When the surface of the cheese bulges, it is moved back to a cellar at 16–18°C, then to another cellar at 10–13°C.

Fromage blanc floats in brine to salt cheese and form rind

M. Boujon, the *fromager*, guillotines his giant cheese

EPOISSES DE BOURGOGNE (AOC)

Napoléon is said to have been partial to this cheese and ate it with Chambertin wine. It was very popular at the beginning of the 20th century, but production did not survive World War II. M. Berthaut of the village of Epoisses revived it in 1956. A single farm in Bourgogne currently makes all the *fermier* cheeses. There are also *artisanal*, and large and small versions.

This is a strong-smelling, washed-rind cheese, with an aroma of *marc*. The fine-textured pâte melts in the mouth, with a mixture of salt, sweet, metallic, and milky flavours. Affinage takes place in specified areas and lasts for at least four weeks; the cheese is first washed in water or brine, to which *marc* has been added. The cheese is washed one to three times a week, with gradually increasing quantities of *marc*.

Cheese ripens from outside in

Supple, soft, light beige pâte; uncooked, unpressed

Smooth, washed rind sometimes wrinkled; ivory, orange to brick-red colour, depending on age

⊖	16.5–19 cm diameter, 3–4.5 cm high (large); 9.5–11.5 cm diameter, 3–4.5 cm high (small)
⚖	700–1100 g; 250–350 g
☘	50% min.
⚭	40 g min. per 100 g cheese
✓	All year
⊘	Whole
♀	Pouilly-Fuissé, Sauternes (*moelleux*)
⎕	*Marc* de Bourgogne

BOURGOGNE
Côte d'Or, Yonne;
CHAMPAGNE-ARDENNE
Haute-Marne

AOC Regulations: Epoisses de Bourgogne

1 The coagulation of the milk for a period of 16 hours must be caused mainly by lactic acid.
2 The curd should be roughly cut. It must not be broken.
3 After drainage, the cheese must be salted with dry salt.

AOC GRANTED 1991

L'AMI DU CHAMBERTIN

This *artisanal* cheese is made in the village of Gevrey-Chambertin in Bourgogne. Affinage takes at least four weeks.

Uncooked, unpressed soft pâte

Moist, red rind, washed with water and *marc* de Bourgogne

⊖	9 cm diameter, 4 cm high
⚖	250 g
☘	50%
✓	All year
⊘	Pasteurized
⎕	*Marc* de Chambertin

BOURGOGNE
Côte d'Or

FOURME D'AMBERT AND FOURME DE MONTBRISON (AOC)

These two cheeses are made in two regions around the towns of Ambert and Montbrison, now joined by the AOC, which has streamlined methods of production. The word *fourme* comes from the Latin *forma*, meaning form or shape; it is thought that the word *fromage* may have the same roots.

As with Roquefort (*p. 216*), the blue mould is introduced first, then air is injected into the pâte through syringes to help it develop (*p. 218*). This is one of the mildest of all the blue cheeses. Its rind is rather dry, the pâte creamy and firm, with a smell of the cellar. Production is *coopérative* or *artisanal*; there is no *fermier* version. Affinage within AOC specified areas takes a minimum of 28 days from the date of production, but is more usually about two months. The AOC was granted in 1976.

Fourme d'Ambert

Natural rind of red or white mould

Soft pâte with veins of blue mould; uncooked, unpressed

Fourme de Montbrison

⊖	13 cm diameter, 19 cm high
⚖	1.5–2 kg
⁂	50 g min. per 100 g cheese
▯	50% min., 25 g min. per 100 g cheese
✓	All year
⌇	Raw
♀	Sauternes *moelleux*, Rivesaltes (VDN)

RHÔNE-ALPES Loire; AUVERGNE Cantal, Puy-de-Dôme

FRINAULT

In any good ashed cheese, the pâte dries slowly under its extra coating and compacts without growing hard. The ancient method of applying ashes to the moist surface of cheese to protect it comes from the Orléanais region of Central France. Originally, only the ash of vine shoots was used. The cut cheese shown here is less ripe than the uncut cheese. Frinault reveals its quality in the mouth and has a mild aftertaste. It is an *industriel* cheese, with an affinage of three to four weeks.

Soft pâte; uncooked, unpressed

Natural rind covered with ashes

⊖	9–10 cm diameter, 2 cm high
⚖	120–150 g
🗋	50%
✓	Summer to autumn
⟁	Pasteurized
�령	Touraine

CENTRE
Cher, Loiret

Fromage Allégé

Allégé, meaning light, is a fashionable term used to refer to foods that are low in fat, such as certain kinds of yoghurt, butter, margarine, and *fromage blanc*. A cheese may be described as *allégé* when the fat content shown on the label is between 20–30%. The classification for the fat content of cheeses is as follows:

- *Maigre* – less than 20%
- *Allégé* – 20 to 30%
- *Normal* – 40 to 50%
- *Double crème* – 60 to 75%
- *Triple crème* – more than 75%
- Some *fermier* cheeses have no clearly defined fat content. This is due to the slight daily variations in their milk.
- Processed cheese (*fromage fondu, p. 21*) has a minimum 40% fat content; light processed cheese (*fromage fondu allégé*) has 20 to 30% fat.

According to the regulations of the *Journal Officiel* governing cheese production, a product must contain more than 23 g dry matter per 100 g to qualify as cheese; 43 g for processed cheese; and 31 g for light processed cheese.

There is a close link between fat content and taste. Cheeses with a fat content of 40–50% are generally firm, with a rounded flavour. High-fat cheeses tend to be soft and spread easily on bread, rather like butter. Low-fat cheeses have neither the flavour of a cheese with a *normal* fat content, nor do they have the melting, smooth texture of the latter. They do, however, offer an alternative for people who may be following a low-fat diet or watching their cholesterol intake, but who do not wish totally to forgo the pleasure of eating cheese.

BERGUES

The town of Bergues in Flandres lies 12 km from the Belgian border. The cheese shown is untypically thin and may have lost its shape during transportation. Bergues is a *fermier* or *artisanal* cheese with an affinage of three weeks to two months, sometimes longer, during which the cheese is repeatedly washed with brine or beer.

Washed rind

Soft pâte; uncooked, unpressed

The town of Bergues

NORD-PAS-DE-CALAIS Nord

⊖	12 cm diameter, 4 cm high
⚖	320–350 g
⏛	15–20%
✓	All year
⏃	Skimmed
⚷	Local beer
❦	Beaujolais

LE BOURRICOT

This cheese from Cantal in the Auvergne is produced in an *industriel* dairy. Affinage takes eight weeks on straw, and the cheese has a slight smell of the straw.

Natural rind   Semi-hard pâte; uncooked, unpressed

⊖	12 cm diameter, 4 cm high
⚖	500 g
🗋	30%
✓	All year
⌀	Skimmed
❦	St. Pourçain

AUVERGNE
Cantal

FROMAGE CENDRÉ

Locally, this *artisanal* cheese is also known as Cendré de Champagne and is a speciality of the time of the grape harvest. The white wood ash on the rind keeps the flies away out in the vineyards, but is removed with a wet brush before the cheese is eaten. The smell is musty, of the cellar. During affinage the cheeses are left to cure in ashes for more than two months.

Soft pâte; uncooked, unpressed

Rind of ashes

⊖	12–14 cm diameter, 3 cm high
⚖	300–400 g
🗋	20–30%
✓	All year
⌀	Skimmed
❦	Bouzy, Coteaux Champenois

CHAMPAGNE-ARDENNE
Marne

LOU MAGRÉ

This *artisanal* cheese comes from the village of Terraube in the Lomagne region in southwest France. It has a slight smell of the cellar. Affinage takes three to ten weeks.

Natural rind with traces of mould

Slightly elastic, semi-hard pâte; uncooked, pressed

⊖	20 cm diameter, 5 cm high
⚖	1.8–2 kg
▯	25%
✓	All year
⏣	Raw, skimmed
♟	Madiran

MIDI-PYRÉNÉES
Gers

SOURIRE LOZÉRIEN

This is an *artisanal* cheese from the village of Luc in the Cévennes region of Languedoc. It has a slight smell, a faint blend of the musty cellar in which it was ripened, and mould. Affinage takes at least ten days.

Natural rind

Semi-soft, elastic pâte; uncooked, unpressed

⊖	11 cm diameter, 4–5 cm high
⚖	380–450 g
▯	25%
✓	All year
⏣	Skimmed
♟	Corbiéres, Fitou

LANGUEDOC-ROUSSILLON
Lozère

TOMME DE LOMAGNE

This *artisanal* cheese, with a slight
smell of the cellar, is produced in
the Lomagne region of Gascogne.
Affinage takes two months.

Semi-hard
pâte;
uncooked,
pressed

Natural
rind, with
traces of
mould

⊖	18–20 cm diameter, 6–7 cm high
⚖	2 kg
🗗	30%
✓	All year
🗁	Raw, skimmed
🍷	Madiran

MIDI-PYRÉNÉES
Gers

LE VACHARD

This slightly musty-smelling *artisanal*
cheese comes from the village of
Saint-Bonnet-le-Courreau in the
hilly Forez region of the Auvergne.
Affinage takes one month.

Semi-hard
pâte;
uncooked,
pressed

Rind of
natural
mould

⊖	12–13 cm diameter, 3 cm high
⚖	600 g
🗗	30%
✓	All year
🗁	Raw, skimmed
🍷	Côtes d'Auvergne, Châteaugay

RHÔNE-ALPES
Loire

Fromage Fort

Originally, *fromage fort* was made at home by grating and breaking leftover bits of cheese, and mixing them with, and letting them ferment in, one or more liquids such as whey, milk, or vegetable broth. Oil, *eau-de-vie*, or wine was added to stabilize the mixture, and herbs, spices, salt, and wine or cider, to season it. It was then left for months, to be served when finished with wine.

Fromage fort is a local product, especially in wine-producing regions where each area has its own tradition. The names too are individual – for example, Cachat or Cacheilla, from areas of goat's-milk or half-goat's-milk cheeses. The Lyonnais, Mâconnais, Beaujolais, Dauphiné, and the Massif du Ventoux are the main areas where *fromage fort* continues to be made.

M. Voy, chief *fromager* and proprietor of the Ferme Saint-Hubert cheese-mongers in Paris says: "Our *fromage fort* is strong. We put it in a covered stoneware pot. If the pot did not have its lid on and you took it down the Metro, people would avoid you like the plague".

Cheeses with a strong smell and taste, such as Epoisses (*p. 166*), Langres (*p. 186*), and Maroilles (*p. 188*) are used to make the *fromage fort du Lyonnais* sold in the Ferme Saint-Hubert. The mixture is soaked in *marc* de Bourgogne until the pâte is completely smooth. Depending on the season, if the smell of cheese in the shop is not strong enough, the pot is stirred every now and then and left open to "scent" the air.

Fromage fort is sold by the ladleful. It tingles on the tongue and is good on toasted garlic bread or as an accompaniment to an apéritif. On tasting, a variety of flavours opens in the mouth, leaving a complex aftertaste. The cheese goes well with *marc* de Bourgogne.

FROMAGE FORT DU LYONNAIS

This is a Lyonnais speciality made with hardened cow or goat's-milk cheeses left to ferment in a covered stoneware pot at home or in a cheese shop. The strong, piquant smell and flavour go better with *marc* than with wine.

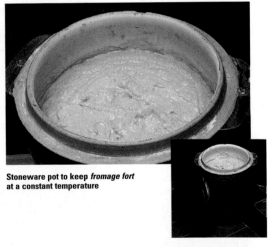

Stoneware pot to keep *fromage fort* at a constant temperature

🥮 Not defined	
🥐 Not defined	
🍷 Château Chalon (*jaune*) or Arbois Jaune	
🍶 *Marc*	

RHÔNE-ALPES
Rhône

CACHAT

Both Cachat and the Confit d'Epoisses shown below are made by Georges Carbonel and his wife at their Restaurant in Aix-en-Provence. Cachat is made with young goat's-milk cheeses (Banon, *p. 46*) soaked in *marc*. The cheese turns creamy from the fifteenth day onwards.

Cachat in an earthenware dish

 Not defined
 Arbois jaune

 PROVENCE-ALPES-CÔTE D'AZUR
Bouches-du-Rhône

CONFIT D'EPOISSES

Originally from the village of Epoisses, the Confit is made with a young Epoisses cheese (*p. 166*). This is soaked in white Burgundy and a little *marc* for a week; then the liquid is discarded and replaced with more white wine. After a week in *marc*, it tingles on the tongue, and tastes sharp and copperish. Two weeks later, it turns creamy. The salt appears to be well integrated and there is a sweetness that might be called metallic. It should be eaten with bread.

M. Carbonel (*see above*) says that in the past there were many flavoured cheeses made with salt, pepper, saffron, garlic, rosemary, thyme, and mustard. Meat was expensive, so people would eat a lot of bread with a small amount of strong flavoured cheese.

Confit d'Epoisses

 Not defined
 Marc de Bourgogne

 PROVENCE-ALPES-CÔTE D'AZUR
Bouches-du-Rhône

CACHAILLE

This *fromage fort* comes from the village of Puimichel. It is made by grating dry cheese into an earthenware pot, and adding *eau-de-vie*, pepper, olive oil, and fresh cheese up to three days old. Affinage takes two to three months. It must be stirred well. Cachaille will keep for up to 20 years, if periodically topped up with new cheese.

🍯 Sold in a pot	PROVENCE-ALPES-CÔTE D'AZUR
⚖️ 200 g net	Alpes-de-Haute-Provence
🗆 Not defined	
✓ All year	
🐄 Raw	
🐐 Raw	
🍷 Coteaux Varois *rosé*	

FROMAGÉE DU LARZAC

Like Roquefort (*p. 216*) this sweet-tasting *fromage fort* comes from the Causse du Larzac in Rouergue. It is an *artisanal* cheese, made in an earthenware pot.

🍯 Sold in an earthenware pot	
⚖️ 160 g net	
🗆 50%	MIDI-PYRÉNÉES
✓ All year	Aveyron
🐄 Not defined	
🍷 Sainte Croix du Mont *moelleux*, Rivesaltes (VDN)	

PATEFINE FORT

This *artisanal* cheese from Saint-Georges-d'Espéranche in the department of Isère is sold in a plastic pot. The ingredients are 90% cow's-milk cheese, white wine, spices, salt, and pepper. The cheese is served spread on country bread and toast. Its flavour is sour.

🍯 Sold in a plastic pot	
⚖️ 200 g net	RHÔNE-ALPES
🗆 Not defined	Isère
✓ All year	
🐄 Not defined	
🍷 St. Joseph	

Fromage Frais

Fromage frais (fresh cheese) has to be made in the following way:
- It must be unripened and made from milk coagulated by lactic fermentation.
- Bacteria, such as lactic ferment, must be active in the cheese when sold.
- It must contain 10 to 15 g dry matter per 100 g of cheese.
- It should be eaten soon after production. The consume-by date must be clearly indicated.
- Pasteurized milk is usually used. There are some *fermier*, raw-milk *fromages frais*.

- Depending on the fat content, *maigre*, *allégé*, *double-crème*, and *triple-crème* versions (*p. 256*) are produced.

Composition of *Fromage Frais* and Other Cheeses per 100g

	Water	Dry Matter	Fat Content
Fromage Frais	85 g	15 g	45% (c.7 g)
Camembert	55 g	45 g	45% (c.20 g)
Cantal	43 g	57 g	45% (c.25 g)
Comté	38 g	62 g	45% (c.28 g)
Roquefort	44 g	56 g	52% (c.29 g)

BROUSSE DU ROVE

The word *brousser* means to beat or stir in Provençal. This *artisanal* cheese is called Brousse because its curd is beaten before being drained. It was also known as *fromage frais de corne*, meaning fresh cheese in a horn, because it used to be poured into sheep's horns. It is liquid, light, sweet, and mild, with a slight smell of milk.

Sold in 9-cm-high plastic cones	PROVENCE-ALPES-CÔTE D' AZUR
45%	Bouches-du-Rhône
All year; December to June (ewe's-milk cheese)	
Not defined	
Not defined	
Côtes de Provence *blanc* or *rosé*	

CERVELLE DE CANUT / CLAQUERET LYONNAIS

This is the traditional way of eating *fromage frais* in the Lyonnais region. Shallots, garlic, parsley, chervil, chives, and other herbs are mixed with well-drained, fresh, white *fromage blanc* (*p. 178*). The cool, sour flavour goes well with toasted bread. The cheese is occasionally served chilled at the end of a meal.

Not defined	
St. Véran, Mâcon	RHÔNE-ALPES Rhône

CHÈVRE FRAIS

This artisanal cheese is made in the same region as Selles-sur-Cher AOC (*p. 110*) in the province of Berry. It has a gentle, sweet smell of goat's milk.

⊖	5–6 cm diameter 4 cm high
⚖	125 g
🍶	45%
✓	All year
🐇	Not defined
♀	Quincy

CENTRE
Loir-et-Cher

FAISSELLE DE CHÈVRE

The name of this *fermier* cheese from Rouergue comes from the word *faisselle*, meaning the basket in which the curd is drained. The *industriel* version of Faisselle, made with cow's milk, can be found anywhere in France. It is sold in plastic pots and is usually eaten with a spoon.

⊖	Sold in a pot
🍶	Not defined
✓	Spring to autumn
🐇	Raw
♀	Côtes d'Auvergne

MIDI-PYRÉNÉES
Aveyron

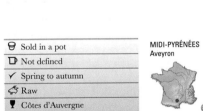

FONTAINEBLEAU

This creamy *fromage frais* is thought to originate from a village near the Forêt de Fontainebleau. It is an *artisanal* blend of whipped cream and *fromage frais* that may be made by the *fromager*. The flavour is mild, sweet, and light, more like a cream cake than a cheese. Try it with crystallized fruit.

Shaped in a gauze-lined container

🍶	60%
✓	All year
🐄	Pasteurized
♀	Maury, Banyuls (VDN)
♀	Bordeaux (with crystallized fruit)

ILE-DE-FRANCE
Seine-et-Marne

FROMAGE BLANC

There are two kinds of *fromage blanc*. One
is young cheese that has been drained and
shaped in a mould. The other (shown here)
has undergone lactic fermentation only.
It is slightly drained and sold by weight.
Fromage blanc makes a refreshing, milky
dish with a slightly sweet-and-sour taste.

🏺 Sold in a pot	
🥛 40%	
✓ All year	THROUGHOUT FRANCE
🦠 Pasteurized	
🍷 Beaujolais	
🍷 Coteaux du Layon *moelleux*, Vouvray *moelleux* (dessert)	

Creamy consistency goes well with
salt, pepper, and chives, or as a
dessert with jam, honey or fruit

FROMAGE BLANC FERMIER

This *fromage blanc* is a *fermier* cheese
made in the small town of Marciac in
the department of Gers in Gascogne.
Like the Fromage Blanc shown above,
it makes a refreshing, milky dish and
has a slightly sweet-and-sour taste.

🧀 9 cm wide, 10 cm long, 3.5 cm high	
⚖️ 200 g	MIDI-PYRÉNÉES Gers
🥛 Not defined	
✓ Spring to autumn	
🦠 Raw	
🍷 Tursan	

FROMAGE FRAIS DE NÎMES

This *artisanal*-produced *fromage frais* comes
from Languedoc. It is decorated with a
bay leaf, the aroma of which blends with
the milk of the cheese. It has a smooth
texture and a mildly acidic flavour with
a hint of sweetness.

🧀 8 cm diameter, less than 2 cm high	
⚖️ 150 g	LANGUEDOC-ROUSSILLON Gard
🥛 Not defined	
✓ All year	
🦠 Raw	
🍷 Faugères	

Bay leaf
decorates and
flavours cheese

GARDIAN

These little *fromages frais* are produced
in the Pravençal department of Bouches
du Rhône. They are made with cow or
ewe's milk, sprinkled with pepper and
herbes de Provence, and decorated with bay
leaves. Production is solely *fermier*.

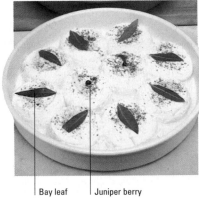

Bay leaf | Juniper berry

🧀	6–7 cm diameter, 3 cm high
⚖️	250 g
🥛	45%
✓	December to summer (ewe's-milk cheese); all year (cow's-milk cheese)
🗓	Not defined
✂️	Not defined
🍷	Côtes de Provence *rosé*

PROVENCE-ALPES-
CÔTE D' AZUR
Bouches-du-Rhône

GASTANBERRA

Gastanberra means coagulated ewe's milk
in the Pays Basque, which is where this
fermier cheese is produced by one woman.
The buyer must return the earthenware
pot in which the cheese is sold. It tastes
like solidified milk.

🧀	Sold in an earthenware pot
🥛	45–50%
✓	December to June
🗓	Raw
🍷	Irouléguy

AQUITAINE
Pyrénées-
Atlantiques

GOURNAY FRAIS

This is an *artisanal* cheese from Pays
de Bray in Normandie. It has a sweet
smell of milk and a light flavour.

🧀	10 cm wide, 10 cm long, 3.5 cm high
⚖️	250 g
🥛	45%
✓	All year
✂️	Not defined
🍷	Bordeaux, Bourgogne, Côtes du Rhône

HAUTE-
NORMANDIE
Seine-Maritime

PETIT-SUISSE

These popular *artisanal* and *industriel* cheeses were invented in about 1850 by a Swiss worker in a cheese dairy in Normandie. Sold by the half-dozen, they have a sweet-and-sour flavour, with a very soft pâte. These little cheeses are often served with jam or coffee.

⊖ 3 cm diameter, 4 cm high	
⚖ 30 g	
⚬⚬ 23% min.	
🌡 40% min.	THROUGHOUT FRANCE
✓ All year	
🍶 Pasteurized, with cream	
🍷 Bordeaux, Bourgogne, Côtes du Rhône	

Very soft, fresh, even-textured pâte

SÉGALOU

The name of this *fermier* cheese derives from the area of production, called Ségala, in the south of the Quercy. Ségala is a poor region in the Tarn, where only rye (*seigle*) can be grown. Although fresh, the cheese shown here has already begun to ripen. It is supple and made from good milk, and has a lingering aftertaste.

⬭ 4 cm diameter in the middle, 15 cm long	
⚖ 250 g	MIDI-PYRÉNÉES Tarn
🌡 45%	
✓ All year	
🍶 Raw	
🍷 Gaillac, Cahors	

VACHE FRAIS

This unsalted *fermier* cheese is produced in the Béarn by M. A. Penen. Rennet is added to the milk from the evening milking, and one hour later the curd is moulded and left to drain overnight. The fresh cheese is taken to market on the following day.

⊖ 8 cm diameter, 4 cm high	AQUITAINE Pyrénées-Atlantiques
⚖ 280 g	
✓ All year	
🍶 Raw	
🍷 Tursan	

Fromage de Lactosérum

Fromages de lactosérum are obtained by the coagulation or precipitation of *lactosérum*, or whey. These low-fat cheeses may be concentrated, and other dairy products may be added. One of the most famous whey cheeses is Brocciu (*p. 146*) from Corsica, which is the only whey cheese to have been granted AOC status.

Whey is the liquid extracted when the milk coagulates during cheesemaking. Most of the protein and fat remains in the curd and becomes the main consti-tuent of the cheese, but some of it is lost in the thin, milky whey, which is commonly called *petit-lait*. This liquid still contains a number of nutritious elements, such as protein, fat, and minerals.

Fromage de lactosérum is made from a secondary coagulation (usually by heat) to recoup the residual protein and fat before the whey is finally discarded. It is a profitable by-product of cheese. Whey cheeses should have a sweet, mild, milky flavour and may be spread on bread as a savoury snack, or eaten as a dessert on their own or with jam.

BREBIS FRAIS DU CAUSSEDOU

This *fermier* cheese from the Poux Del Mas farm in the department of the Lot is neither salty nor acid, but mildly sweet. The flavour and strength of the milk produced by ewes grazing on the plateaux of Quercy is pronounced.

⊖	9–10 cm diameter, 4.5 cm high
⚖	360 g
⤬	Not defined
✓	All year
⟐	Whey of raw milk
♀	Bergerac, Gaillac

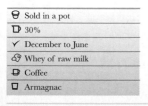

MIDI-PYRÉNÉES
Lot

Fresh, soft pâte – whey is heated, coagulated, and drained

BREUIL / CENBERONA

This low-fat *fermier* cheese from the Pays Basque is called Breuil in French, and Cenberona in Basque. It has a mild, milky smell and supple texture. Traditionally it is served as a breakfast dish, with strong coffee spooned over it. For dessert, it is eaten with sugar and Armagnac.

⊖	Sold in a pot
⤬	30%
✓	December to June
⟐	Whey of raw milk
☕	Coffee
⚱	Armagnac

AQUITAINE
Pyrénées-
Atlantiques

Cheese is shaped by container

Fresh, soft pâte – whey is heated, coagulated, and drained

GREUILH

This is a *fermier* cheese from the Vallée d'Ossau in Béarn. Greuilh may be eaten by itself or as a dessert with jam. It is light and refreshing and goes especially well with quince jam. Sold in vacuum-packs, this cheese should be consumed within 21 days.

Fresh, soft pâte – whey is heated, coagulated, and drained

⚖	Sold in vacuum-packs of 2 to 3 kg; also sold by weight
⚐	Not defined
✓	December to end of June
◔	Raw whey
♟	Tursan

AQUITAINE
Pyrénées-Atlantiques

SÉRAC

This *fermier* cheese from Savoie is delicious by itself or on toast with herbs and olive oil. A version of this cheese is made with whey from Beaufort cheese (*p. 48*).

Fresh, soft pâte – whey is heated, coagulated, and drained

⚖	Size varies according to size of container
⚐	Not defined
✓	Spring to autumn (goat's-milk cheese); all year (cow's-milk)
◔	Raw whey
◔	Raw whey
♟	Roussette de Savoie

RHÔNE-ALPES
Savoie

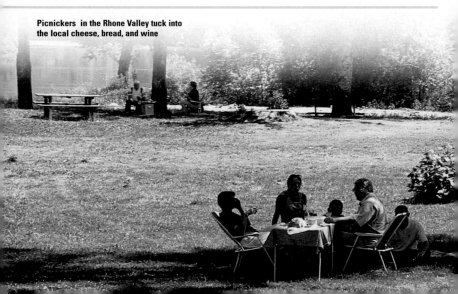

Picnickers in the Rhone Valley tuck into the local cheese, bread, and wine

GAPERON

The name Gaperon may derive from the word *gap* or *gape*, which means buttermilk in the dialect of the Auvergne. In the past, when butter was made in a churn, the liquid left in the churn called *lait de beurre* (buttermilk), or *lait battu* (beaten milk), was mixed with fresh milk to make Gaperon.

This *artisanal* cheese has a hard, dry rind, while the pâte, which contains garlic and ground pepper, is elastic. The flavour is tingling and rough. This is a low-fat cheese, cured on a hook by the fire, which explains the tang of smoke. Affinage takes one to two months.

Semi-hard pâte; uncooked, pressed

Rind of natural mould

⊖	8–9 cm diam. base, 8–9 cm high, suspended from yellow string
⚖	250–350 g
⮃	30–45%
✓	All year
⌇	Raw, pasteurized, whole, partly skimmed
❢	Côtes d'Auvergne

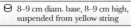

AUVERGNE
Puy-de-Dôme

GRATARON D'ARÈCHES

The *fermier* cheese shown here was ripened for four weeks and is salty and sticky. It was made from strong milk in a *chalet* in the Beaufort region of Savoie. During the affinage of four weeks, this cheese is rubbed with brine and turned.

Washed rind

Soft pâte; uncooked, slightly pressed

⊖	9–11 cm diameter, 3–4 cm high
⚖	300–400 g
⮃	45%
✓	Spring to autumn
⌇	Raw
❢	Crépy, Seyssel

RHÔNE-ALPES
Savoie

FRENCH CHEESES
L–N

LANGRES (AOC)

As the name indicates, this *artisanal* cheese originates from the high plains of Langres, in Champagne. It is shaped like a short, fat cylinder and has a 5-mm deep well on top called a *fontaine*, a kind of basin into which Champagne or *marc* may be poured. This is a pleasant way to eat this cheese and is typical of wine-producing areas.

The surface of the cheese is sticky, wet, and shiny, and has a pronounced smell. The pâte is firm and supple, and melts in the mouth, releasing a complex mixture of aromas. The salt too is strong, yet Langres is a milder cheese than Epoisses de Bourgogne (*p. 166*). The cheeses shown are completely ripe.

Langres is produced in both a large and a small version. Affinage usually takes five to six weeks within the areas specified by the AOC. The cheeses are placed in a cellar at a humidity of 95%, where they are rubbed with brine regularly, either using a damp cloth or by hand. The minimum permitted affinage is 21 days for large cheeses and 15 days for small ones. A red dye extracted from the seeds of the American annatto treeis applied to colour the rind. This is called *rocou* in French and is also added to other cheeses and butter.

White to light-beige pâte, becomes softer towards centre; uncooked, unpressed

Smooth, fine-textured, washed rind, brick-red to light brown

⊖	16–20 cm diameter, 5–7 cm high (large); 7.5–9 cm diam., 4–6 cm high (small)
⚖	800 g min. (large); 150 g min. (small)
⁂	42 g min. per 100 g cheese
⬚	50% min., 21 g min. per 100 g cheese
✓	All year
⟁	Pasteurized
☐	*Marc* de Champagne

CHAMPAGNE-ARDENNE Haute-Marne; LORRAINE Vosges; BOURGOGNE Côte d'Or

AOC Regulations: Langres

1 The sliced curd must be neither washed nor kneaded. (Concentrated or reconstituted milk is not allowed.)
2 It is permitted to add annatto to the brine, applied when rubbing the cheese, in order to impart a red colouring to the rind.

AOC GRANTED 1975

◀ **Sheep grazing in the Pays d'Auge in the Calvados *département* of Normandie**

LIVAROT (AOC)

This *artisanal or industriel* cheese is named after a village in Normandie. Its nickname is the Colonel because it is bound with straps of rush or paper reminiscent of a colonel's stripes.

Both the smell and taste of Livarot have lessened over the years, but it is still very strong tasting. It should be very ripe when chosen – a finger should sink into the pâte. A smell of ammonia, however, can indicate that the cheese is past its best. The rind is washed and coloured with annatto, and sticks to the fingers. The ripe pâte has no elasticity and feels heavy and moist on the tongue. It dissolves in the mouth, with a spicy flavour, close to that of hung meat. Affinage takes at least three weeks, during which time the cheese is washed in water or light brine and turned regularly.

Moist, washed rind

Soft pâte, uncooked, unpressed

⊖ 12 cm diameter of mould, 4–5 cm high	
⚖ 450 g	
❖ 230 g min. per cheese	
🗋 40% min., 92 g min. per cheese	BASSE-NORMANDIE Calvados, Orne
✓ All year	
♻ Raw or pasteurized	
❢ Pomerol *jeune*	
♀ Tokay, Pinot Gris d'Alsace *vendange tardive*	

AOC Regulations: Livarot

1 The curd must be divided and kneaded to enforce drainage.
2 Three small formats are allowed:
Trois-quarts Livarot: (three-quarters size): minimum internal diameter of the mould 10.6 cm, 135 g minimum dry matter per cheese.
Petit-Livarot (small size): minimum internal diameter of the mould 9 cm, 120 g minimum dry matter per cheese.
Quart-Livarot (quarter size): minimum internal diameter of the mould 7 cm, 60 g minimum dry matter per cheese.

AOC GRANTED 1975

MAMIROLLE

The flavour of this brick-shaped cheese from the village of Mamirolle is sweet; the consistency of the pâte is elastic and fine. It is a washed-rind cheese made by students of the École Nationale d'Industrie Laitière. The cheese is also made by the Union Agricole Comtoise at Besançon. Affinage takes at least 15 days, during which time the cheese is washed in brine with annatto.

⬨ 15 cm long, 6–7 cm wide, 4 cm high	
⚖ 500–650 g	FRANCHE-COMTÉ Doubs
🗋 45%	
✓ All year	
♻ Pasteurized	
❢ Arbois	

Moist, brick-red, rubbed, washed, and waxed rind

Semi-hard, elastic pâte; uncooked, pressed

Maroilles

MAROILLES (AOC)

This cheese is said to have been created in AD 962 by a monk. Maroilles, also called Marolles, is a powerful *fermier or industriel* cheese. The pâte is golden, soft, and oily. The sweet taste lingers in the mouth. Affinage takes at least five weeks within the specified areas, although two to four months are more usual. During this time, the cheese is regularly turned and brushed and its rind changes from yellow, to orange, and finally red. Repeated turnings and washings eliminate the natural white mould and promote the development of bacteria (red ferments) that form the distinctive red rind.

Moist, brick red, washed rind

Soft pâte; uncooked, unpressed

◈	12.5–13 cm square, 6 cm high
⚖	700 g
⁂	360 g min. per cheese
⅁	45% min., 162 g min. per cheese
✓	All year
⟳	Raw or pasteurized
♀	Châteauneuf-du-Pape

PICARDIE Aisne;
NORD-PAS-DE-
CALAIS Nord

Mignon – the small version of Maroilles

AOC Regulations: Maroilles

1 The divided curd must not be washed.
2 Use of fungicides is forbidden.
3 Three sizes are permitted:
Sorbais: 12–12.5 cm square, 4 cm high, weight 550 g with a minimum of 270 g dry matter. Affinage of at least four weeks.
Mignon: 11–11.5 cm square, 3 cm high, weight 350 g with

a minimum of 180 g dry matter. Affinage of at least three weeks.
Quart: 8–8.5 cm square, 3 cm high, weight 180 g with a minimum of 90 g dry matter. Affinage of at least two weeks.

AOC GRANTED 1976

BAGUETTE LAONNAISE

This is an *industriel* cheese from the city of
Laon. It is usually brick-shaped, but baguette-
shaped versions also exist in the Avesnois
and Thiérache areas. They are all strong
and of the same family as Maroilles.
No-one seems to know whether production
of this cheese started after World War I
or II. Affinage takes two months.

Small format baguette of 250 g

◇ 6 cm wide & high, 15 cm long	
◫ 500 g	PICARDIE Aisne
☐ 45%	
✓ All year	
⌛ Pasteurized	
♥ Coteaux Champenois, Bouzy	

Soft pâte;
uncooked,
unpressed

Moist, red,
washed rind

BOULETTE D'AVESNES

This *fermier* or *industriel* cheese is named
after Avesnes, near the Belgian border.
It is made from buttermilk or Maroilles
fromage blanc flavoured with parsley, pepper,
tarragon, and cloves, shaped by hand and
dyed with annatto or covered with paprika.
Affinage takes two to three months; the
fermier version is washed with beer.

Moist, dark red-coloured
washed rind with annatto
or covered with paprika

Soft-flavoured
pâte; uncooked,
unpressed

◈ 6–8 cm at base, 10 cm high	
◫ 180–250 g	NORD-PAS-DE-CALAIS Nord
☐ 45%	
✓ All year	
⌛ Raw or pasteurized	
♥ Bourgogne Passetoutgrains	

BOULETTE DE CAMBRAI

The region of Cambrai produces cereals
and sugar beet, and is known for its
andouillettes (tripe sausages). Boulette de
Cambrai is made by hand from *fromage
frais*, to which salt, pepper, tarragon,
parsley, and chives are added. It is only
eaten fresh. Production may be *fermier*
or *artisanal*, with no affinage.

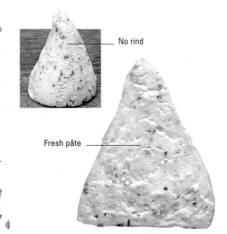

No rind

Fresh pâte

◈ 7–8 cm base, 8 cm high	
◫ 200 g	NORD-PAS-DE-CALAIS Nord
☐ 45%	
✓ All year	
⌛ Raw or pasteurized	
♥ Bourgogne Passetoutgrains, Beaujolais	

CŒUR D'ARRAS

Do not be put off by the pungent smell of this *artisanal* cheese from the Maroilles family. It has a strong flavour, and the weight of the cheese melts slowly and heavily on the tongue, leaving a sweet, lingering aftertaste. Affinage takes three to four weeks, during which time the cheese is washed.

Soft pâte; uncooked, unpressed

Washed, humid rind

🗇	10 cm wide 7–8 cm long 3 cm high
⚖	200 g
🗔	45%
✓	All year
🝙	Pasteurized
♈	Châteauneuf-du-Pape, Collioure

NORD-PAS-DE-CALAIS
Pas-de-Calais

CŒUR D'AVESNES

This *artisanal* cheese is a good introduction to washed-rind cheeses. It has a light smell and flavour, with a lingering sweetness. The pâte is yellow and slightly elastic, with a few small holes. The slightly moist, orange rind sticks to the fingers. Affinage takes three to four weeks, during which time the cheese is washed regularly.

Soft pâte; uncooked, unpressed

Washed, slightly moist, orange rind

🗇	10 cm x 8 cm x 3.5 cm
⚖	200 g
🗔	45%
✓	All year
🝙	Pasteurized
♈	Bordeaux *supérieur*

NORD-PAS-DE-CALAIS Nord

DAUPHIN

Legend has it that Louis XIV so enjoyed this cheese that he allowed it to be named after the Crown Prince. It is made with Maroilles and flavoured with tarragon, parsley, pepper, and cloves before affinage, which takes two to four months. Both *artisanal* and *industriel* versions are produced.

Washed, brick-red, humid rind

Soft, slightly sticky pâte; uncooked, unpressed

🗇	Less than 5 cm high
⚖	300–500 g
🗔	45%
✓	Spring to autumn
🝙	Raw or pasteurized
♈	Côtes du Rhône

NORD-PAS-DE-CALAIS Nord;
PICARDIE Aisne

GRIS DE LILLE

Also known as Puant de Lille, Puant Macéré, and Vieux Lille, this cheese is a ripened Maroilles soaked for three months in brine. *Puant* means strong smelling, and this cheese does have a putrefied smell – but the stronger it grows, the more the locals like it. It is said that northern miners ate this *artisanal* or *industriel* cheese down the pit.

Soft, slightly elastic pâte; uncooked, unpressed

Grey, sweaty, sticky surface – no real rind

◈ 13 cm square, 5–6 cm high		
⚖ 700 g–1 kg	NORD-PAS-DE-CALAIS	
🗋 45%	Pas-de-Calais	
✓ All year		
⏀ Raw or pasteurized		
ⵜ Local beer		
ⵗ Champagne		

GUERBIGNY

This is an *artisanal* cheese produced in the village of the same name in the northern province of Picardie. It has a strong smell and flavour and a moist pâte that sticks to the tongue. It may be a cousin of the heart-shaped Rollot. Affinage takes five weeks.

Soft pâte; uncooked, unpressed

Moist, washed, red rind

◗ 11 cm wide, 8–9 cm long, 2.5 cm high		
⚖ 250 g	PICARDIE	
🗋 45%	Somme	
✓ Spring to autumn		
⏀ Raw, whole		
ⵗ Sancerre, Coteaux Champenois		

ROLLOT

The first Rollot was a *fermier* cheese produced in the village of Rollot. It has a salty flavour with a lingering bitterness. The cheese shown here is young and mild but will be very strong when it ripens. There is also a heart-shaped *industriel* version. Affinage takes four weeks.

◖ 7–8 cm diameter, 3.5 cm high		
⚖ 280–300 g	PICARDIE	
🗋 45%	Somme	
✓ Spring to autumn		
⏀ Raw or pasteurized		
ⵗ Sancerre, Coteaux Champenois		

Soft, sticky pâte; uncooked, unpressed

Washed, brick-red, moist rind

Heart-shaped *industriel* version

MUNSTER / MUNSTER-GÉROMÉ (AOC)

This cheese is made under different names on either side of the Vosges mountains, in Alsace to the east, and Lorraine to the west. In Alsace it is called Munster, while in Lorraine it is known as Géromé. In 1978, the AOC Munster-Géromé united these two cheeses.

Appearance and Flavour

The chief characteristics of this cheese are firstly the pungent smell, and secondly the soft, smooth pâte, with the consistency of melting chocolate. The rind is brick-red, and the pâte is fine-textured and golden, slightly sticky, and sweet, with the flavour of rich milk, as long as the cheese has been properly matured. When this cheese is young, the rind is orange-yellow, while the pâte is pale cream with the consistency of brittle soap. A ripe Munster smells very strong. Locally, the cheese is eaten with cumin or potatoes boiled with their skins on. Cumin-flavoured Munster may be bought ready-made.

Affinage of three weeks

Washed rind _____

Fresh, non-AOC cheese

AOC Regulations: Munster

1 The divided curd must be neither washed nor kneaded before moulding.
2 If the cheese is ripened in a region other than the place of production, the label must indicate the place of production and the place of affinage.

AOC GRANTED 1978

The Munster Cows

The milk used to make Munster comes from Vosgiennes cows, a breed that was imported from Scandinavia in the 18th century. The animals are strong and yield good-quality milk that is high in protein.

Production and Affinage

Fermier, industriel, and *coopérative* versions of this cheese are produced. Concentrated or reconstituted milk is not permitted. Affinage must take place within the areas specified by the AOC and needs a minimum of three weeks (two weeks for Petit-Munster), although two to three months are more usual. During affinage, the cheeses are stored in a cellar at 11–15°C and 95–96% humidity, where they are rubbed with a light brine by cloth or by hand every two to three days. This causes the characteristic yellow to reddish-orange rind to develop.

Munster flavoured with cumin

Rind is a yellow to reddish-orange in colour due to red ferments *(Bacterium linens)*

Reddish-orange rind beginning to develop

Soft pâte, uncooked, unpressed

⊖ 13–19 cm diameter, 2.4–8 cm high; 7–12 cm diameter, 2–6 cm high (Petit-Munster)

⚖ 450 g min; 120 g min. (Petit-Munster)

♣ 44 g per 100 g cheese

◗ 45% min., 19.8 g per 100 g cheese

✓ All year; summer to winter *(fermier)*

⟳ Raw or pasteurized

♀ Gewürztraminer, Tokay, Pinot Gris d'Alsace

ALSACE Bas-Rhine, Haut-Rhine; LORRAINE Meurthe-et-Moselle, Moselle, Vosges; FRANCHE-COMTÉ Haute-Saône, Territoire de Belfort

Affinage of one week

MORBIER (AOC)

The rind of Morbier is natural and rubbed, and the mild pâte is supple and sweet. Originally made by the cheesemakers of Comté, it has bulging sides and a horizontal black furrow through the middle. In the past, soot was sprinkled on the fresh curd to prevent a rind from forming and keep insects away, as it rested for the night at the bottom of a barrel. Today, the black layer is a vegetable product and purely decorative. Production may be *artisanal*, *fermier*, *coopérative*, or *industriel*. Affinage takes at least 30 days, usually two months. The AOC was granted in 2000.

Natural, moist, beige rind

Semi-hard, ivory to pale yellow pâte; uncooked, pressed

⊖	30–40 cm diameter, 6–8 cm high
⚖	5–9 kg
⚬⚬	50 g min. per 100 g cheese
⛁	45% min.
✓	All year
⚗	Raw or pasteurized
♀	Crépy, Seyssel

FRANCHE-COMTÉ
Doubs, Jura

MOTHAIS À LA FEUILLE

This *fermier* goat's cheese has a sticky rind and a melting pâte with a soft flavour. Goat's cheeses are usually ripened in drier and better ventilated cellars than other cheeses. This one, however, has an affinage of three to four weeks in a cellar at almost 100% humidity, with no ventilation. The cheese rests on a chestnut or plane leaf to retain as much moisture as possible, and is turned every four to five days.

Moist affinage

Rind of natural mould

⊖	10 cm diameter, 3 cm high
⚖	250 g
⛁	45%
✓	Spring to autumn
⟆	Raw
♀	Fleurie
⚱	Champagne *rosé*
⛾	Coffee

POITOU-
CHARENTES
Deux-Sèvres

Normal affinage

Chestnut leaf

Soft pâte; uncooked, unpressed

MUROL

Traces of cloth are visible on the rind of this *industriel* cheese. The pâte is yellow when ripe, fine-textured, and very elastic. Its smell and flavour are mild. Murol is a Saint-Nectaire cheese (*p. 224*) with a hole in the middle. Affinage takes one month.

☺	12 cm diameter, 4–5 cm high
⚖	450–500 g
🗗	45%
✓	All year
🗘	Pasteurized
❢	Fleurie
♀	Champagne *rosé*

Semi-hard, elastic pâte; uncooked, pressed

Washed, rubbed, waxed, orange-red, humid rind

MUROLAIT

This cheese was made from the centre piece cut out of the Murol above.

Red paraffin wax

AUVERGNE
Puy-de-Dôme

☺	3.5 cm diameter, 4.5 cm high
⚖	0 g

NANTAIS / CURÉ

This is a cheese with many names, including Curé Nantais and Fromage du Pays Nantais dit du Curé. Originally round, and made by the *curé*, or curate of Vendée, it was brought into this region, which previously lacked cheeses, by a monk who was fleeing from the French Revolution. The rind is smooth and wet, the pâte golden and supple, with a few small holes. This is a strong, small-scale *industriel* cheese. Affinage takes one month.

◈	8–9 cm square, 2.5–3 cm high
⚖	170–200 g
🗗	40%
✓	All year
🗘	Pasteurized
♀	Muscadet, Gros Plant

PAYS DE LA LOIRE
Loire-Atlantique

Soft, slightly elastic pâte; uncooked, unpressed

Washed, wet, orange-pink rind

NEUFCHÂTEL (AOC)

This *fermier*, *industriel*, or *artisanal* cheese
comes from the town of Neufchâtel in
the Pays de Bray in northern Normandie.
It may date from as far back as AD 1035,
when Hugues I of Gournay, a town close
to Neufchâtel, offered it as a donation
to the Abbey of Sigy. Parisians discovered
it through the famous food guide of the
time, *Almanach des Gourmands*,
(1803–1812). Neufchâtel lies
only 132 km from Paris and the
proximity boosted the popularity
of the cheese in the capital.

Soft, firm,
smooth pâte
with no holes;
uncooked,
slightly pressed

The rind of the cheese is
dry and velvety and crumbles
when pinched, while the firm
but supple pâte sinks under
finger pressure.

Six versions of Neufchâtel
are produced: *bonde* and *double
bonde*, which are a small and
large cylinder; *carré*, which is
square; *briquette*, which is a small
brick shape; and *cœur* and *grand cœur*,
which are a small and large heart.

***Bonde,* or cylinder-shaped version**

Following a good affinage of at
least ten days, usually three weeks,
after renneting the cheese develops
a covering of fine white mould. The
mould flavours the cheese and gives it
a pronounced mouldy smell. The flavour
goes well with a good, crusty bread.

Rind *"fleurie"*,
meaning covered
in a "bloom" of
white mould

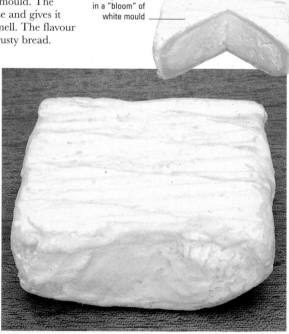

***Carré,* or square-
shaped version**

HAUTE-NORMANDIE
Seine-Maritime;
PICARDIE Oise

Rind of white
mould

◇ *Bonde*: 4.5 cm diameter,
6.5 cm high (100 g)
Double bonde: 5.8 cm diameter,
8 cm high (200 g)

◇ *Carré*: 6.5 cm square,
2.4 cm high (100 g)

◇ *Briquette*: 5 cm wide, 7 cm
long, 3 cm high (100 g)

◗ *Cœur*: 10 cm wide, 8.5 cm
long, 3.2 cm high (200 g)
Grand cœur: 14 cm wide,
10.5 cm long, 5 cm high

♣ 40 g min. per 100 g cheese

◻ 45% min., 18 g min. per
100 g cheese

✓ Summer to winter (raw);
all year (pasteurized)

♨ Raw or pasteurized

❢ Pomerol, St. Emilion

Cœur, or small,
heart-shaped version

Firm, young,
heart

AOC Regulations: Neufchâtel

1 The drained curd must be kneaded until it
becomes uniform.
2 Pieces of mature, blooming Neufchâtel are
added to the curd.

AOC GRANTED 1977

NEUFCHÂTEL BONDARD / BONDE / BONDON

The point of affinage reached by the cheese
shown here is just right. It has a white, velvety
mould that forms a thick rind. The fat content
is high and the pâte melting. When eaten with
the rind, it tingles on the tongue and is rather
salty. Production may be *fermier or artisanal*, with
an affinage of two weeks to two months.

Rind of white,
velvety mould

◇ 5 cm diameter, 8 cm high

⚖ 200 g

◻ 50–60%

✓ Summer to winter

♨ Enriched with cream

❢ Jasnières

HAUTE-NORMANDIE
Seine-Maritime

Soft pâte;
uncooked,
unpressed

FRENCH CHEESES
O–P

OLIVET CENDRÉ

This *artisanal* cheese is made in Olivet, a town on the River Loire. In May and June, the milk produced by cows grazing on the lush pastures is very rich and the cheeses made during this period are kept for the harvesting season, when there will be a lot of people to feed as they work in the fields and vineyards. Olivet ripens slowly and used to be preserved in vine ashes. The pâte is slightly resistant to the bite and has a slight scent of mould. Affinage in ashes takes at least one month.

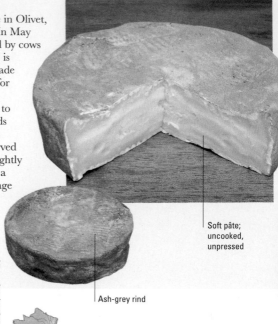

Soft pâte; uncooked, unpressed

Ash-grey rind

⊖	10–12 cm diameter, 3 cm high
⚖	250–300 g
🗋	40–45%
✓	All year
♺	Pasteurized
🍷	Sancerre

CENTRE
Loiret

OLIVET AU FOIN

This recently introduced cheese is a variation on the Olivet Cendré shown above. The white mould contains a few strands of hay. There is also a version covered in crushed pepper.

Soft pâte; uncooked, unpressed

Rind of white mould with a few strands of hay

⊖	10 cm diameter, 2 cm high
⚖	250 g
🗋	45%
✓	All year
♺	Pasteurized
🍷	Sancerre

CENTRE
Loiret

◄ A delicatessen in Chamonix, Mont Blanc, selling fresh cheeses, meats and bottles of wine

PALOUSE DES ARAVIS
(PUR CHÈVRE D'ALPAGE)

This is a *fermier* cheese from the town of Grand-Bornand in the chain of mountains called the Aravis on the edge of the Alps. In the local dialect, *palouse* means a dry disc, which aptly describes this cheese. The cheeses are made in a *chalet* during the summer, and cured over a long period. The pâte is drained under pressure and the rind is washed at the beginning of the affinage, then left for the mould to expand naturally, and dry out. Affinage takes between five and ten months. The rind is as hard as a rock, and the pâte is dry and rough with a concentrated flavour.

Semi-hard pâte; uncooked, pressed

Rind of natural mould

⊖	16–19 cm diameter, 3 cm high
⚖	800 g
🏷	Not defined
✓	Summer to winter
🥛	Raw
🍷	Vin Jaune du Jura, Alsace

RHÔNE-ALPES
Haute-Savoie

PAVÉ D'AUGE

In the centre of most old towns in France is a church square with rough paving stones, called *pavés*. This *fermier or artisanal* cheese is shaped like one of those stones. It has a mild and supple pâte, with a relatively high fat content. The dry or washed rind resembles Pont l'Evêque (*p. 208*). If you can find a Pavé d'Auge *fermier* that has rested long enough in a cellar, you will be able to taste the quality of the Normandie milk used in production. Affinage takes two to three months.

Soft pâte; uncooked, unpressed

Dry or washed rind

◈	11 cm square, 5–6 cm high
⚖	600–800 g
🏷	50%
✓	Summer to winter
🥛	Raw or pasteurized
🍷	Cidre du pays d'Auge
🍾	Champagne

BASSE-NORMANDIE
Calvados

LE PAVÉ DU PLESSIS

The pâte of this cheese bounces slightly
under finger pressure because it is full
of small holes. Its taste is soft, with a
flavour of sweet salt. Le Pavé is an
artisanal cheese from the Fromagerie
du Plessis in Normandie, with an
affinage of two to three months.

Soft, yellow pâte;
uncooked,
unpressed

Rind of natural, dry, white
or orange-red mould

◈	11–12 cm square, 5 cm high
⚖	500 g
⛊	50%
✓	All year
⌂	Raw
⚲	Haut Médoc, Margaux

HAUTE-
NORMANDIE
Eure

PAVÉ DE ROUBAIX

Roubaix is a town in the north of France,
which grew with the expansion of the
textile industry. It is said that this cheese
was a permanent fixture on the tables
of the weavers and a symbol of
wealth. Pavé de Roubaix has a dry,
rock-hard rind, and the pâte is of the
same carrot-orange colour as that of
Mimolette (*p. 58*). It is an *artisanal*
cheese, with an affinage at 15°C of one
or even two years, during which time
it is turned and brushed once a month.
Sadly, there are only two or three people
making this cheese, and it is in danger
of disappearing altogether.

Semi-hard pâte;
half-cooked,
pressed

Natural, hard,
dry rind

◈	13 cm wide, 27 cm long, 8 cm high
⚖	3.3 kg
⛊	45%
✓	All year
⌂	Pasteurized
⚲	Banyuls (VDN)

NORD-PAS-
DE-CALAIS
Nord

PÉLARDON DES CÉVENNES (AOC)

This young goat's-milk cheese comes from the Cévennes region near Alès in Languedoc, where all small goat's-milk cheeses are called *pélardon*. It has almost no rind and a compact, nutty pâte. The balance of acidity and salt is just right and there is a full, rich, milky flavour with a lingering aftertaste. Both *fermier* and *artisanal* versions are produced, with an affinage of two to three weeks. The cheese was granted AOC status in 2000.

Soft pâte; uncooked, unpressed

Rind of natural mould

Affinage of two to three weeks

⊖	6–7 cm diameter, 2–3 cm high
⚖	60–100 g
ᴰ	45%
✓	Spring to autumn
⌘	Raw
♀	Clairette du Languedoc

LANGUEDOC-ROUSSILLON
Gard, Lozère

PÉLARDON DES CORBIÈRES

This *fermier* goat's-milk cheese, another *pélardon*, comes from Lagrasse in the Corbières region on the Mediterranean coast. After one week of ripening, the rind shows a bloom of natural mould, and the pâte is supple. The flavour is slightly acidic, with no sweetness. This is a *fermier* cheese, with an affinage that lasts from one week onwards.

Soft pâte; uncooked, unpressed

Rind of natural mould

Affinage of more than three weeks

⊖	6–7 cm diameter, 2 cm high
⚖	70–80 g
ᴰ	45%
✓	All year
⌘	Raw
♀	Côtes du Roussillon

LANGUEDOC-ROUSSILLON Aude

Persillé

Blue goat's-milk cheeses from the mountainous Savoie region are called *persillés*. The blue comes from a very subtle natural mould that only becomes visible after a minimum affinage of three months. These cheeses may be made with pure goat's milk, or from a mixture of different milks. Cow's-milk cheeses with internal blue moulds are most commonly known as *bleus*, but may sometimes be called *persillés*, depending on the way the mould is distributed through the pâte. Cheeses in which the pâte is delicately marbled with the blue mould are described as *marbré*. If there are definite veins of blue mould, the cheese is described as *veiné* or *veineux*.

PERSILLÉ DE LA TARENTAISE

This *fermier* cheese from the Tarentaise area of Savoie has the typically acid tang of a young goat's-milk cheese. It has a white, fine-textured pâte with a blue mould that is not yet apparent in the cheese shown here. Affinage usually takes one-and-a-half months, but may be shorter than that.

⊖	6–8 cm diameter, 6–8 cm high
⚖	250–550 g
🡇	45%
✔	Best in early summer
🐐	Raw
♀	Crépy

RHÔNE-ALPES
Savoie

Rind of natural mould

Soft pâte; uncooked, unpressed – veins of blue mould will develop over time

PERSILLÉ DE LA HAUTE-TARENTAISE

The Haute-Tarentaise, where this *fermier* cheese is made, lies at the source of the River Isère, which rises just one kilometre away from the Swiss border. The cheese has an affinage of two to three months.

⊖	9–10 cm diameter, 8 cm high
⚖	500–600 g
🡇	Not defined
✔	April to December
🐐	Raw
♀	Crépy

RHÔNE-ALPES
Savoie

Rind of natural mould

Soft pâte; uncooked, unpressed, will turn blue

PERSILLÉ DE TIGNES

The original village of Tignes in Savoie, where this cheese was first made, was submerged in 1952 by an artificial lake. This cheese comes from the new village that was built to replace it. The younger cheese (shown top right), has a raw, salty taste. As the cheese ripens, the crust hardens, and the pâte dries, becomes spicy, and breaks easily. It is said that the mustard-coloured crust is a sign that the goats were fed on grass growing on sulphurous soil. This *fermier* cheese has an affinage of at least one-and-a-half months.

Affinage of one-and-a-half months

White, blue, natural mould is not visible

Soft pâte; uncooked, unpressed

Affinage of six months

Slightly bluish pâte

⊖	9.5–11 cm diameter, 9–10 cm high
⚖	680–975 g
🗓	Not defined
✓	Best in summer
🐐	Raw
🍷	Crépy

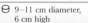

RHÔNE-ALPES
Savoie

PERSILLÉ DU SEMNOZ

The rock-hard crust on this *fermier* cheese is formed by a light brown mould. The pâte is greyish-yellow, with a blue mould that is not yet visible in the cheese shown here. The sticky consistency is evidence of the quality of the milks used in its production – usually equal parts of goat and cow's milk. Affinage takes one to two months.

Rind of natural mould

Semi-hard pâte; uncooked, pressed

⊖	9–11 cm diameter, 6 cm high
⚖	400–450 g
🗓	45%
✓	April to December
🐐	Raw
🐄	Raw
🍷	Crépy

RHÔNE-ALPES
Haute-Savoie

Picodon

PICODON (AOC)

The region of Picodon straddles the River Rhône. The department of the Drôme lies to the east of the river, and the Ardèche to the west. The name of this cheese derives from the ancient language, Langue d'Oc, and means spicy.

The climate of the lower Rhône is dry. Mountain grass and shrubs, with strong aromas and flavours, grow short and thick there. The goats that feed on the mountain devour everything, including the shoots and leaves of trees. Their milk is the basis of this spicy cheese. Its pâte is so dry that the best way of getting all the taste out of it is to suck it.

Pélardon (*p. 203*) is often mistaken for Picodon. This is unsurprising, given the similarity of their names and the fact that both are southern mountain cheeses that look like stones and weigh less than 100 g. Production may be *fermier*, *artisanal*, or *industriel*, with an affinage of at least twelve days from the day of renneting, although three to four weeks is more usual. AOC regulations forbid the addition of powdered or concentrated milk, lactic protein, and frozen curd.

⊖	5–8 cm diameter, 1–3 cm high
⚖	50–100 g
⋆	40 g min. per 100 g cheese
⛫	45% min., 18 g min. per 100 g cheese
✓	All year; spring to autumn (*fermier*)
⌔	Whole
♀	Rivesaltes (VDN)

Dry, thin rind of natural moulds; sometimes no mould

Soft, white pâte cuts cleanly

Ripe Picodon de l'Ardèche

Smooth, fine-textured pâte

Well-matured Picodon de l'Ardèche

Uncooked, unpressed pâte

Young Picodon de l'Ardèche

Picodon de la Drôme

RHÔNE-ALPES Ardèche, Drôme; PROVENCE-ALPES-CÔTE D'AZUR Vaucluse; LANGUEDOC-ROUSILLON Gard

The Picodons on these pages demonstrate some of the variations that may be found.

1 Picodon de l'Ardèche
This cheese weighs 55 g.
2 Picodon de l'Ardèche
After an affinage of four weeks, this cheese weighs just 40 g. It has a sticky pâte that smells of dry mould and has good acidity.
3 Picodon de l'Ardèche
This 60-g cheese has an acid, salty flavour. It needs another week of affinage.
4 Picodon de la Drôme
This cheese weighs 45 g. The saltiness and sweetness have blended and there is little acidity.
5 Picodon de Crest
This cheese is made with rich, high-quality milk, and its flavour has a good blend of salt, sweetness, and acidity. It weighs 60 g.
6 Picodon de Dieulefit
This young cheese weighs 90 g and has a white mould and a soft pâte.
7 Picodon de Dieulefit
This cheese has shrunk to half its original size and weighs 40 g. The rind is hard and coloured by the mould. On tasting, the sun of Provence and the aroma of herbs and grass open up in the mouth as the cheese slowly melts.
8 Picodon du Dauphiné
This cheese is well ripened.
9 Picodon à l'huile d'olive
This cheese is marinated in olive oil flavoured with bay leaves.

Picodon de Crest

Soft, young cheese

Young Picodon de Dieulefit

Pâte becomes hard and brittle as it ripens

Well-ripened Picodon de Dieulefit

Picodon du Dauphiné

AOC Regulations: Picodon

1 The milk must be coagulated with a low quantity of rennet. (Concentrated or powdered milk, lactic protein, and frozen curd are not allowed.)
2 The cheese must be salted with dry (fine or semi-coarse) salt.
3 The label may say *affinage méthode Dieulefit*. This method

of affinage consists of rubbing the surface of the cheese by hand and with water, after which the cheese is left to mature and soften for more than a month in covered earthenware jars.

AOC GRANTED 1983

Picodon *à l'huile d'olive*

PONT-L'EVÊQUE (AOC)

This washed-rind cheese
is probably the oldest
Norman cheese still in
production. Some people
say that Pont-l'Evêque
originated in an abbey, but
this story has never been
substantiated. A document
from the 12th century says that
"a good table always finishes with
a *dessert d'angelot*", which may be the
old name for Pont-l'Evêque. During
the 17th century, cheeses made in
the village of Pont-l'Evêque were sent
all over France and were popular.

Soft pâte;
uncooked
unpressed

Washed, moist
or dry rind

It takes three litres of milk
to make one Pont-l'Evêque of
350–400 g. After washing, the rind
is moist and ochre in colour. The
pâte is creamy yellow, fine-textured,
and smooth. It sinks under finger
pressure but has no elasticity. As the
cheese ripens, the rind grows sticky
and reddens, and small holes spread
through the pâte. Further ripening
will result in a pâte that glistens with
fat when cut. There are lingering
traces of sweetness in the taste.
Cheeses that are washed and turned
during their affinage are strong, but
this mature flavour is not present
in younger cheeses.

Production of Pont-l'Evêque
may be *fermier, artisanal, coopérative,*
or *industriel.* However, only about
2% are *fermier* cheeses. Affinage
takes place within the specified
areas at least two weeks from the
date of production, although six
weeks is more usual. During
affinage, the cheeses are washed,
brushed, and turned.

◈	10.5–11 cm square, 3 cm high
⚖	350–400 g
❧	140 g min. per cheese
🗋	45%, 63 g min. per cheese
✓	All year
⚖	Raw or pasteurized
♀	Condrieu
Ⅱ	Cider

BASSE-
NORMANDIE
Calvados,
Manche, Orne;
HAUTE-
NORMANDIE
Eure, Seine-
Maritime; PAYS-
DE-LA-LOIRE
Mayenne

AOC Regulations: Pont-L'Evêque

1 The curd must be divided, kneaded, and drained.
2 Three different sizes are produced:
Petit-Pont-l'Evêque (small size): 8.5–9.5 cm square,
85 g minimum dry matter per cheese.
Demi-Pont-l'Evêque (half-size): 10.5–11.5 cm x 5.2–5.7 cm,
70 g minimum dry matter per cheese.
Grand-Pont-l'Evêque (large size):19–21 cm square,
650–850 g minimum dry matter per cheese.

AOC GRANTED 1976

PORT-SALUT

This cheese is a very popular *industriel* version of Port-du-Salut (*below*). The rind is slightly moist and uniformly coloured, with regular traces of the cloth used in production. It has a very faint smell. The pâte has little acidity and a slight aftertaste; it is elastic under finger pressure and sticks to the knife when cut. Affinage takes one month.

⊖	20 cm diameter, 4 cm high
⚖	1.3–1.5 kg
⟶	50%
✓	All year
⟲	Pasteurized
⟟	Chinon, Bourgueil

PAYS DE LA LOIRE
Mayenne

Washed, rubbed, and waxed rind, artificially coloured with beta carotene

Semi-hard pâte; uncooked, pressed

PORT-DU-SALUT / ENTRAMMES

This cheese was first made in an abbey in Entrammes in 1830. In 1959, rights were granted for an *industriel* version known as Port-Salut (*above*). The original method of production is still followed in abbeys and monasteries across France, but Port-du-Salut is rare. Affinage takes at least one month.

⊖	10 cm diameter, 4 cm high
⚖	300 g
⟶	40–42%
✓	All year
⟲	Pasteurized
⟟	Chinon, Bourgueil

PAYS DE LA LOIRE
Mayenne

Washed, waxed, and rubbed rind

Uncooked, pressed, semi-hard pâte

PITHIVIERS AU FOIN / BONDAROY AU FOIN

This *artisanal* cheese is produced in Bondaroy, near Pithiviers. Farmers used to make it in summer, when milk was plentiful, and store it in hay. Today it is available year round. The rind is white, with a slight smell of mould. Affinage takes three weeks.

⊖	10–12 cm diam., 2.5 cm high
⚖	300 g
⟶	45%
✓	All year
⟲	Pasteurized
⟟	Chinon, Bourgueil

CENTRE
Loiret

Soft pâte; uncooked, unpressed

Rind of white mould sprinkled with hay

FRENCH CHEESES
R

RACLETTE

This *artisanal* or *industriel* Savoie cheese, also called Fromage à Raclette, may be either round or square. The name derives from *racler*, meaning to scrape traditionally the cheese is heated on a spit so that it melts and can be scraped off with a knife. It is often eaten with pickles and potatoes boiled in their skins. The pâte is slightly hard, with a light smell of mould when warm, and a full, milky flavour. It has an affinage of at least eight weeks.

White to light yellow pâte, with small holes; supple and firm; uncooked, pressed

Thin, golden-yellow to light brown natural rind with uncoated sides

⊖	28–36 cm diameter, 5.5–7.5 cm high
◇	28–36 cm square, 5.5–7.5 cm high
⚖	4.5–7 kg (both formats)
⁂	53 g min. per 100 g cheese
⬭	45% min., 23.85 g min. per 100 g cheese
✓	All year
⟳	Raw or pasteurized
⚑	Vin de Savoie, Hautes Côte de Beaune

THROUGHOUT FRANCE

◀ **The large quantities of milk produced by these sheep in Les Landes are used to produce Roquefort**

The mountain villages of Savoie have a long tradition of making cheeses such as Reblochon

REBLOCHON DE SAVOIE / REBLOCHON (AOC)

Freshness, youth, and tenderness are the most noticeable features of this mountain cheese from Savoie. The name derives from the verb *reblocher*, which means "to pinch a cow's udder again". This is because Reblochon is made with the thicker, richer milk from the second milking of Abondance, Montbéliard, and Tarine cows.

Reblochon is a well-proportioned cheese with a thin, orange-yellow to pink, tight, velvety rind. Its fresh, clear aroma comes from the mould, and it has a moist, smooth and supple, fatty pâte. The flavour opens in the mouth, leaving a delicately nutty aftertaste.

Production may be *fermier* (sometimes in a *chalet*), *coopérative* (*fruitière*), or *industriel*, with an affinage of at least two (usually three to four) weeks from the date of production. The temperature of the cellar must be kept below 16°C. A regular and a small version (Petit Reblochon) are produced.

Reblochon bought in Thonon-les-Bains

Yellow to orange, washed rind with natural white mould

Smooth, soft, ivory pâte; uncooked, slightly pressed

Reblochon bought in Paris

⊖	9–14 cm diameter, 3–3.5 cm high
⚖	240–550 g
⁂	45 g min. per 100 g cheese
▯	45% min; 20.25 g min. per 100 g cheese
✓	From summer (*fermier* and *chalet*-made cheeses)
⬩	Raw, whole
❢	Vin de Savoie, Pommard

AOC Regulations: Reblochon

1 The milk must be brought to the place of production as quickly as possible after each milking.

2 Renneting must be done within 24 hours of the last milking.

3 *Fermier* cheeses must bear a green *casein* label.

AOC GRANTED 1976

RHÔNE-ALPES
Savoie, Haute-Savoie

Rigotte

Cheeses like *rigotte* were probably produced in Roman times. The name is a local word for cheese in the regions of Isère, Rhône, and the Loire. It might derive from the French *recuit* or Italian *ricotta*, which both mean recooked. Despite the name, however, *rigotte* does not involve recooking the milky whey (see *fromage de lactosérum* on *p. 181*). *Rigotte* used to have a low fat content, but now is usually between 40 and 45%. Made mostly in factories or *artisanal* dairies and almost always of cow's milk, *rigotte* is normally allowed a week to drain before it goes on sale. *Rigottes* are usually eaten while firm to the touch but soft inside and slightly sharp in flavour.

RIGOTTE D'ECHALAS

This is an *artisanal* cheese from Echalas in the Lyonnais province. It is best eaten with toast. The rind on the cheese shown has just formed. The fat content is almost 50%, which accounts for its smoothness. Affinage takes at least two weeks.

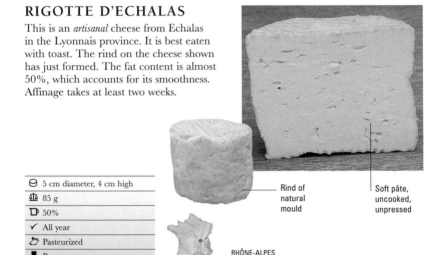

⊖	5 cm diameter, 4 cm high
⚖	85 g
🗗	50%
✓	All year
⊘	Pasteurized
🍷	Bourgogne

Rind of
natural
mould

Soft pâte,
uncooked,
unpressed

RHÔNE-ALPES
Rhône

RIGOTTE DE SAINTE-COLOMBE

This *artisanal* cheese from Saint-Genix-sur-Guiers in Savoie should be eaten young. The rind on the cheese shown has not yet finished developing. The pâte is yellow, rich, fine-textured, and smooth, with a slightly sour flavour. Affinage takes at least 15 days.

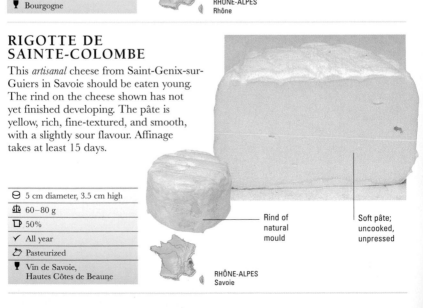

⊖	5 cm diameter, 3.5 cm high
⚖	60–80 g
🗗	50%
✓	All year
⊘	Pasteurized
🍷	Vin de Savoie, Hautes Côtes de Beaune

Rind of
natural
mould

Soft pâte;
uncooked,
unpressed

RHÔNE-ALPES
Savoie

RIGOTTE DE CONDRIEU

This is a *fermier* cheese from the Lyonnais province. Most *rigottes* are made with cow's milk, but this is a pure goat's-milk cheese and therefore quite rare. The pâte is fine-textured and robust, with a delicate aroma of honey and acacia. Affinage takes up to three weeks, although the cheese can be eaten fresh.

Rind of
natural mould

Soft pâte;
uncooked,
unpressed

**Fresh white
cheese**

⊖	4 cm diameter, 1.5–3 cm high
⚖	30 g
🡇	45%
✓	Spring to autumn
🐇	Raw, whole
♀	Condrieu

RHÔNE-ALPES
Rhône

RIGOTTE DES ALPES

This *industriel* cheese from the Dauphiné has a slightly sour but pleasant taste. When soaked in white wine for several days, it gains a new flavour. It must be eaten with wine, and perhaps sprinkled with fresh ground pepper. Affinage takes at least ten days.

⊖	4 cm diameter, 3.5 cm high
⚖	50 g
🡇	45%
✓	All year
🐄	Pasteurized
♀	Crépy, Seyssel

RHÔNE-ALPES
Isère, Rhône

Uncooked, unpressed, soft pâte,
with almost no rind; reddish-yellow
exterior, coloured with annatto

ROQUEFORT (AOC)

A cheese like Roquefort is said to date back to the time of Pliny in ancient Rome and is mentioned in his book of AD 79. In 1411, Charles VI granted the people of Roquefort the monopoly of ripening the cheese in their caves as they had done for hundreds of years. In 1925, they obtained an AOC, the first in France. Very soon, though, there were imitations.

Legal Protection

In 1961, the Tribunal de Grande Instance at Millau decreed that although the cheeses could be made in many regions of southern France (see map below), they could only be classed as true Roqueforts if they were ripened in the natural caves of Mont Combalou in the commune of Roquefort-sur-Soulzon. This eliminated imitation, and the modern monopoly was established.

Appearance and Flavour

With Stilton and Gorgonzola, Roquefort is one of the three greatest blue cheeses in the world. It has a clean, forceful flavour with strong salt, very different from the sweetness of milk. The pâte is damp and crumbly and should be cut with a pre-warmed knife. The cheese melts in the mouth, leaving an amazing flavour of mould and salt. When mature, it is exceedingly strong. Roquefort goes well with pasta or salad. It is rich and spicy and is best eaten at the end of a dinner, for example after venison, accompanied by a bottle of Sauternes. A young Roquefort might be accompanied by Muscat de Rivesaltes, served with raisin bread. Match a ripe, grey-blue-veined Roquefort with Banyuls, a naturally sweet wine from Roussillon.

Moist, soft, ivory and blue pâte crumbles under finger pressure; uncooked, unpressed

Varied Appearance
These three Roquefort cheeses illustrate the variations in colour and texture among different producers.

⊖	19–20 cm diameter, 8.5–10.5 cm high
⚖	2.5–2.9 kg
⁂	56 g min. per 100 g cheese
▯	52% min., 29.12 g min. per 100 g cheese
✓	All year
⌔	Raw, whole
♈	Sauternes, Banyuls (VDN)

AQUITAINE, MIDI-PYRÉNÉES, LANGUEDOC-ROUSSILON, PROVENCE-ALPES-CÔTE-D'AZUR, CORSE

Production and Affinage

Today, some 3.3 million cheeses per year are cured at Roquefort-sur-Soulzon. After Comté (*p. 112*), Roquefort is France's second most popular cheese. Around 60% of them are made by one company, the Société des Caves et des Producteurs Réunis. Roquefort is an *artisanal* or *industriel* cheese – there is no *fermier* version. All the cheeses carrying the name of Roquefort have been ripened for at least three months in natural caves as defined by the AOC. The usual affinage is four months, but may be extended by up to nine months. In a young cheese, the mould is pale and green; it becomes bluer and then grey as it ripens, while small, blue-grey holes begin to form. If the cheese is left for a long time, the mould becomes dominant.

Cheese produced by the Société des Caves et des Producteurs Réunis

Affinage of ten days

Affinage of one month

AOC Regulations: Roquefort

1 The milk may not be delivered by the producers fewer than 20 days after lambing.
2 The renneting must take place within 48 hours at the latest after the last milking.
3 The cultures of *Penicillium roqueforti* used to produce the cheese must be prepared in France, from traditional sources in the micro-climate of the natural caves in the specified area of the commune.
4 Dry salt must be used for salting.
5 The producers must keep a register available to the agents of control in which the quantities of milk delivered by the producers as well as the weight and number of cheeses made are entered every day.
6 The whole process of conditioning and packing Roquefort cheeses from the moment they enter the caves until they are sold must take place exclusively in the commune of Roquefort. The refrigeration rooms used for storage before the cheeses are sold must also be situated in the commune of Roquefort.

FULL AOC GRANTED 1979,
following the original law of 1925

Affinage of three months

Affinage of six months

The Home of Roquefort

The birthplace of Roquefort lies on a chalky mountain, called the Combalou or Cambalou. It has a flattish top, with slightly elevated sides, and resembles a saddle. The village of Roquefort hangs on a cliff to the north. Some two-thirds of the village are built into its side. The mountain's partial collapse was caused by water erosion in prehistoric times. This geological accident occurred three times; the third opened a series of caves in the debris. Vertical faults and fissures in these caves provide natural ventilation and are known as *fleurines*. These chimneys or wind holes may be up to 100 m high and connect the caves to the outside world. They serve as an immense storage area that maintains a constant temperature of 9°C and humidity of 95%.

Temperature and Ventilation

In winter, when the outside temperature is low, warm air from the caves is expelled

The Caves of Roquefort
This underground labyrinth of tunnels has changed little since the 17th century, and extends over a depth of 11 levels. Electricity was installed about 100 years ago. The insides of the caves are dark and cold. Except in the main alley, the rock along the walls is damp, if not wet. There is a constant through-draught of moist air.

through the *fleurines*. The more cheeses being ripened, the higher the temperature in the caves. In summer, the temperature outside is higher than within. Hot air is cooled at the northern surface of the cliff and falls to the muddy scree, where it is humidified and drawn into the caves.
In this way, the *fleurines* provide a highly sophisticated system of ventilation. The mould self-seeds naturally thanks to

Shaded, north face of mountain

Fleurines

Muddy scree humidifies the air

Layers of mud

Cross-section of the Combalou Mountain
Worn down by water erosion many thousands of years ago, the Combalou Mountain contains many faults and fissures, known as *fleurines* (see below). Layers of mud beneath the *fleurines* keep the humidity level at 95%.

Humid air enters the *fleurines*

◀ North wind

The cellars of Roquefort are built into different levels of the caves

Cheeses ripen in the naturally ventilated caves

Cross-section of Fleurines
The *fleurines* are similar to chimneys, providing a sophisticated ventilation system through the tunnels. The spores of *Penicillium roqueforti* are carried in the draught and permeate the caves. These naturally occurring conditions are unique in the world.

minuscule cheese particles on the cave walls. These serve as a culture pool for *Penicillium roqueforti* and yeasts. When wind blows through the *fleurines,* the air becomes laden with spores. (From *Rocailleux Royaume de Roquefort,* 1985.)

Penicillium Roqueforti

The blue mould that is found only in the caves of Roquefort is called *Penicillium roqueforti*. It lives in the soil and ferments the cheeses. Bread is used to extract it from its environment. Round rye and wheat loaves are specially baked and left where the air-flow is strong. After six to eight weeks, they are covered with mould, inside and out. The crust is discarded, the crumb dried. Any bad mould is discarded.

Eight days later, the white cheeses are taken to the caves, where they are pierced with needles. Carbon dioxide caused by fermentation in the pâte escapes, and spore-laden air is introduced. The mould multiplies until it spreads more or less evenly through-

The main cellar

Sheep eating while being milked by a milking machine

out. Four weeks after its arrival in the cave, the cheese is wrapped in tinfoil in order to eliminate contact with the air and prevent any bad mould from developing. It is thus ripened in an artificial environment that encourages the development of the desired mould.

The Ewes of Roquefort

In July 1925 a law was passed that decreed that Roquefort must be made from ewe's milk only. Before then, small proportions of cow or goat's milk were allowed. It takes four-and-a-half litres of milk to make one kilogramme of Roquefort. The ewes are Lacaune, Manechs, Basco-Béarnaise, and one Corsican breed. A good ewe produces some 200 litres of milk over six or seven months, equivalent to 45 kg of Roquefort.

With the increased demand for Roquefort that occurred at the beginning of the 20th century, the milk-producing regions acceptable under the law were then extended to the Pyrénées and Corsica.

In 1930, producers of ewe's milk united with the makers of Roquefort to register the Label de la Brebis Rouge. This meant that minimum standards regarding such things as the fodder and quality of milk were laid down. The first milking machine appeared in 1932, and the maximum number of ewes milked by hand rose from 20 to 40 per day per farmer. Today, technology has made it possible for 300 ewes to be milked by just one person in a single hour. The quality of hygienic conditions have also been improved, with the milk now being transferred into vats automatically.

FRENCH CHEESES
S

SAINT-MARCELLIN

This small cheese from the Dauphiné region is mild, acidic, and salty. As it matures from a fresh to a dry, ripe cheese the flavours develop. Saint-Marcellin is often made with cow's milk, but originally it was a goat's-milk cheese. Production may be *fermier*, *artisanal*, or *industriel*, with an affinage of two to six weeks.

Young Saint-Marcellin

Fresh Saint-Marcellin

Rind of natural mould

Soft pâte; uncooked, unpressed

Well-ripened Saint-Marcellin

Ripe cheese with a fine flavour

⊖	7 cm diameter, 2–2.5 cm high
⚖	80 g min.
⁂	50 g min. per 100 g cheese
⛛	40% min., 20 g min. per 100 g cheese
✓	All year
🖪	Raw or pasteurized
🖉	Raw or pasteurized
♉	Côtes de Ventoux, Gigondas, Châteauneuf-du-Pape

RHÔNE-ALPES
Drôme, Isère

◀ **The picturesque Alpine mountain town of Cordon**

Dry cheese, with a robust, ripe flavour

Ripe Saint-Marcellin

Raffia band for carrying more than one cheese at a time

Golden-orange rind of natural mould

Fine, pure-white pâte

Goat's-milk Saint-Marcellin

LE PITCHOU

This is an *artisanal* speciality made by marinating Saint-Marcellin cheeses in grapeseed oil with ample amounts of *herbes de Provence*. The cheese has a strong, salty flavour with some sourness. It is particularly good eaten with bread.

Le Pitchou

🥛 Sold in a pot	
🧀 50%	
✓ All year	
🧀 Pasteurized	
🍷 Côtes du Rhône	

RHÔNE-ALPES
Isère

SAINT-NECTAIRE (AOC)

Like Cantal (*p. 94*) and Salers (*p. 96*), this cheese, which is typical of the Auvergne, was brought to the table of Louis XIV by the Maréchal de Sennecterre. It has a greyish-purple rind, with dots and stains of white, yellow, and red moulds. The pâte is supple with a silky texture, heavy on the tongue, and resistant to the bite. It melts in the mouth to reveal a slight acidity. It also tastes of well-marinated salt, walnut, copper, and spices.

The soil, wild grass, and rich raw milk produced by Salers cows all contribute to this complex taste. Saint-Nectaire made with pasteurized milk does not have the same interesting combination of flavours. This cheese must be fully ripe before eating. Affinage takes from five to eight weeks. If it is any shorter than that, the smell and the taste do not develop sufficiently.

One of the characteristics of Saint-Nectaire is its distinctive smell, which could be described as old, the smell of a dark and humid cellar, of rye straw, on which it ripened, and of mould.

Rind of white, yellow, or red, natural moulds, according to level of ripening

Semi-hard pâte; uncooked, pressed

Affinage of just over six weeks

⊖ / ⚖	21 cm diameter, 5 cm high Approx. 1.7 kg
⊖ / ⚖	Petit Saint-Nectaire: 13 cm diameter, 3.5 cm high 600 g
⁂	52 g min. for 100 g of ripened cheese; 48 g min for 100 g of *fromage blanc*
ⅅ	45% min., 23.4 g min. per 100 g
✓	Best in summer (*fermier*); all year (*industriel*)
⟳	Raw or pasteurized
❢	St. Estèphe

AUVERGNE Cantal, Puy-de-Dôme

Mark of Quality
Casein label of Saint-Nectaire Fermier, indicating number of the department (63), and the codes of the maker (RG) and commune (Y).

AOC Regulations: Saint-Nectaire

1 The *fromages blancs* may be frozen before they enter the cave d'affinage. They must be thawed at below 12°C.
2 The rind may be coloured using E153, E160, E172, or E180.

3 The green elliptic *casein* label must indicate Saint-Nectaire Fermier and the registration number of the place of production for *fermier* cheeses. The label for *industriel* cheese is square.

4 All *affineurs* of Saint-Nectaire must be declared to the controlling commission.

AOC GRANTED 1979

HOW SAINT-NECTAIRE IS MADE

Saint-Nectaire is a *coopérative*, *fermier*, or *industriel* cheese from Auvergne and is cured and ripened within specified areas (departments of Cantal and Puy-de-Dôme) at a temperature of 6–12°C and almost 100% humidity. Production on the farms of Saint-Nectaire starts immediately after the morning and evening milkings. Around 15 litres of milk are needed for one cheese.

Affinage of one week

Coagulation

The milk is heated to 31–33°C. After renneting, it is left to rest for about one hour. The temperature and resting period depend on the weather and the amount of milk used. The curd is milled to the size of wheat grains. The whey is discarded. Finally, the curd is gathered into a big mass, called the *tomme*.

Moulding and Pressing

The *tomme* is cut into small cubes of about 2 cm that are pressed into the mould by hand. Four to six moulds are stacked, then pressed. The whey is discarded. The cheeses are taken out of the moulds and the *casein* labels are applied. Next, the cheeses are salted, returned to the moulds, and pressed for 12 hours, and then turned and pressed again for another 12 hours. The cheeses are taken out of their moulds and transferred to the drying room, at 9–12°C, for two to three days.

Affinage of just under a month

Affinage

The cheeses go into the *cave d'affinage* – at 9–11°C and 90–95% humidity – and are placed on rye straw. Ater two to three days they are washed in brine. Eight days later, they are washed for the second time. After one to two weeks of ripening, they are taken to the *affineur*. Only 5% of Saint-Nectaire are ripened at the farm. Affinage takes a minimum of three to eight weeks, until the cheese is covered in a red or yellow mould.

Affinage of ten weeks on straw

White, yellow, and, red mould

SAINT-PAULIN

This is one of many cheeses modelled on Port-du-Salut (*p. 209*). Once made exclusively in monasteries, a large and a small version are now produced by private companies, both *artisanal* and *industriel*, in Bretagne and Maine. Saint-Paulin was the first cheese to be made with pasteurized milk, around 1930. Production of the raw-milk version, shown here, did not begin until 1990. The rind is thin and moist, the pâte tender with a sweet and discreetly salty taste. Affinage takes two to three weeks.

Semi-hard pâte; uncooked, pressed

Washed, rubbed, and waxed rind

⊖	20 cm diameter, 4–6 cm high; 8–13 cm diameter, 3–4.5 cm high, (small)
⚖	1.8–2 kg; 500 g–1.5 kg (small)
♣	44 g min. per 100 g cheese
⎄	40% min., 17.6 g min. per 100 g cheese
✓	All year
⟲	Raw or pasteurized
⚱	Bordeaux *jeune fruité*

THROUGHOUT FRANCE

Monasteries such as Entrammes are closely associated with cheeses such as Port-du-Salut and Saint-Paulin

LE SAINT-WINOC

The name of this *fermier* cheese derives from the Abbey of Saint-Winoc in the extreme north of France, where it used to be made. Today, Mme Degraeve is probably the only person to continue its production there. Its beer-washed rind is slightly moist, and the pâte sinks under finger pressure, but springs back gently. The cheese shown here is extremely young. With further ripening, the taste and smell will become pungent, a characteristic of beer-washed-rind cheeses. Affinage takes at least three weeks.

Slightly elastic, semi-hard pâte; uncooked, pressed

⊖ 9–11 cm diameter, 4 cm high
⚖ 300–350 g
⌷ Not defined
✓ All year; best in spring to autumn
⌔ Raw, skimmed
⫙ Local beer
♀ Crémant d'Alsace

Washed, rubbed, waxed, pale orange rind

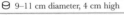

NORD-PAS-DE-CALAIS
Nord

SOUMAINTRAIN

This *fermier*, *artisanal*, or *industriel* cheese from Bourgogne has a light, creamy pâte and is generally eaten young. The method of affinage that is used for similar to Epoisses (*p. 166*) and Langres (*p. 186*) and usually takes six to eight weeks, during which time the cheese is washed in brine.

Matured for 7 to 8 weeks

Moist, orange, washed rind

Soft pâte; uncooked, unpressed

⊖ 10–13 cm diameter, 3–4 cm high
⚖ 350 g; 550 g for fresh cheese
⌷ 45%
✓ Spring to autumn
⌔ Raw or pasteurized
⌷ *Marc* de Bourgogne

BOURGOGNE
Côte d'Or, Yonne

FRENCH CHEESES

T

TAMIÉ

The Abbey of Tamié was founded in 1131 in the Bauges area of Savoie. It is an old monastery where cheese is still made by Trappist monks. Tamié is wrapped in blue paper, which is decorated with the white cross of Malta. It is a mild cheese from the same family as Reblochon (*p. 213*). Production is solely *artisanal*, with an affinage of at least one month, during which time the cheeses are washed in brine twice a week.

Semi-hard pâte; uncooked, pressed

Moist, pink, washed, rubbed, and waxed rind

⊖	18–20 cm diameter, 4–5 cm high
⚖	1.3 kg; 500 g
🍶	50%
✓	All year
🐄	Raw, whole
🍷	Roussette de Savoie

RHÔNE-ALPES
Savoie

TOMMES OR TOMES

Small cheeses made on small farms are generally called *tommes* or *tomes,* the spelling varying between the two forms. The names probably derive from Greek *tomos* and Latin *tomus,* meaning a slice or piece. These cheeses, which may be found in all regions of France, require little milk and do not keep for long but are easy to sell. *Tommes* may be made from cow, goat, or ewe's milk, or a mixture of milks. They are usually small to medium in size, and rounded in shape. The pâte may be unheated and pressed and therefore elastic; or soft and fresh as in Aligot (*p. 100*). The best-known *tomme* is probably Tomme de Savoie, made from cow's milk. There are goat's *tommes* in Savoie as well as in the Pyrénées. The following pages give details of the great variety of *tommes* to be found in France.

Tomme de Savoie

◀ A mouthwatering array of *tommes* and other cheeses on sale at a Provence market

Tomme de Savoie

Tomme de Savoie is a generic term, often coupled with a village name. It is said there are nearly as many *tommes* in Savoie as there are mountains and valleys. Their hard, grey rinds have patches of yellow or red mould. The sticky pâte has a smell of cellar and a softer taste than might be expected. The mountain *tommes* are pressed to eliminate as much water as possible, so that they keep for longer. This also makes the pâte firm, hard, and elastic, with small holes. Production may be *fermier, artisanal, coopérative, or industriel*, and affinage takes at least four weeks.

TOMME DE SAVOIE

The cheeses shown here are contrasting examples of Tomme de Savoie. The Vieille Tomme has been given a very long affinage. The rind and pâte are riddled with holes, and the cheese has partially disintegrated.

Most Tommes de Savoie are low in fat (20–40%), although whole-milk *tommes* are not uncommon today. Traditionally, if there is not enough milk to make a large cheese such as Beaufort (*p. 48*), it is instead separated, with the cream used to make butter and the remaining skimmed milk used to make *tomme*. Tomme de Savoie *maigre* is a very low-fat version – two examples are shown here.

Some versions of Tomme de Savoie, such as Tomme de Lullin (*p. 236*) are produced according to regulations that are as strict as those of the AOC. They may have a regional quality guarantee, indicated by a label showing four red hearts.

Vieille Tomme

Semi-hard pâte; uncooked, pressed

Tomme de Savoie with 30% fat content

Rind of dry, hard, grey natural mould with patches of red and yellow

⊖	18–30 cm diameter, 5–8 cm high
⚖	1.5–3 kg
🔀	40% min.
✓	All year (pasteurized); end of spring (raw milk); summer to winter (*chalet*)
�	Raw or pasteurized
♥	Vin de Savoie, Hautes Côtes de Beaune

RHÔNE-ALPES
Savoie,
Haute-Savoie

Tomme de Savoie *maigre* with 5% fat content

TOMME DE SAVOIE AU CUMIN

This cheese has a slightly viscous pâte containing seeds of cumin, which grows wild in the Savoie region. The cloth in which it is wrapped during pressing marks the rind. The cheese shown here has been ripened to perfection. Production of the cheese may be *fermier* or *artisanal*, with an affinage of three to four months.

Semi-hard pâte; uncooked, pressed

Rind of natural mould

⊖	17–19 cm diameter, 5–6 cm high
⚖	1.5 kg
▽	30–40%
✓	All year, depending on affinage
⟁	Raw or pasteurized
♀	Condrieu

RHÔNE-ALPES
Haute-Savoie

TOME ALPAGE DE LA VANOISE

The naturally red, mimosa-yellow, and violet-grey mould of this cheese is reminiscent of a meadow full of wild flowers. The variety of colours in the rind is said to be due to the high level of carotene in the milk produced by cows grazing on alpine meadows in the mountains of the Vanoise. This is a mild, full-flavoured *fermier* cheese made in summer in a *chalet*. Affinage takes two to three months.

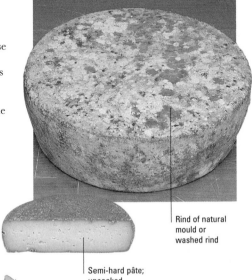

Rind of natural mould or washed rind

Semi-hard pâte; uncooked, pressed

⊖	17–18 cm diameter, 5–6 cm high
⚖	2 kg
▽	45%
✓	End of summer to winter
⟁	Raw, whole
♀	Crozes Hermitage

RHÔNE-ALPES
Savoie

TOME DES BAUGES
(AOC)

This is a *fermier* cheese from the Bauges mountains in the French Alps. The cheese shown has been made from whole milk and ripened for three months. It has a thick crust and a strong pâte. Affinage takes 40 days to three months. The AOC was granted in 2002.

Semi-hard pâte; uncooked, pressed

Rind forms naturally

⊖	17 cm diameter, 5 cm high
⚖	1–1.2 kg
🧈	45%
✓	Best from summer to winter
🐄	Raw, whole
🍷	Hermitage

RHÔNE-ALPES
Savoie

TOMME DU FAUCIGNY

The Faucigny region, where this *artisanal* cheese is made, lies on the edge of the Alps near the Swiss border. The Tomme du Faucigny has a reddish-brown rind covered with natural grey and white mould. The pâte, which is yellow when ripe, is full of small holes and sinks under finger pressure. It has a salty flavour. Affinage takes four to five months.

Pâte is semi-hard; uncooked, pressed

Rind of natural mould

⊖	18–20 cm diameter, 5–6 cm high
⚖	1.5 kg
🧈	40%
✓	All year
🐄	Raw
🍷	Côtes du Jura

RHÔNE-ALPES
Haute-Savoie

TOMME DE LA FRASSE FERMIÈRE

This *fermier* cheese originates in the town of Cluses in the Faucigny region on the edge of the Alps. It has a solid crust covered with patches of natural red and white moulds. The pâte is firm with holes throughout, yet the texture is supple in the mouth. The flavour is distinctly acidic. Since the milk used in production varies in richness, the fat content is not defined. Affinage takes four to six months.

Semi-hard pâte; uncooked, unpressed

Natural rind

⊖	18–20 cm diameter, 7 cm high
⚖	2 kg
⅊	Not defined
✓	All year, especially summer to winter
⟆	Raw
⚲	Crépy

RHÔNE-ALPES
Haute-Savoie

TOMME GRISE DE SEYSSEL

This *artisanal* cheese is produced in the town of Seyssel on the River Rhône. The cheese shown weighs 1.6 kg and is rather large for a Tomme. It is still young but already has a strong smell. The grey mould on the rind is called *poils de chat*, meaning cat's fur. During the affinage of two to six months, the cheese is rubbed by hand until the "fur" shortens to form the crust, which then hardens and thickens.

Semi-hard pâte; uncooked, pressed

Rind forms naturally during affinage

⊖	20 cm diameter, 6–7 cm high
⚖	1.6 kg
⅊	40%
✓	All year
⟆	Raw
⚲	St. Péray

RHÔNE-ALPES
Haute-Savoie

TOMME FERMIÈRE DES LINDARETS

The village of Lindarets, where this *fermier* cheese is made, lies close to the Swiss border at an altitude of 1,500 m. The dry, brown, burnt-looking crust is broken by patches of white mould and has a rough, uneven surface due to a long affinage of six to eight months. The pâte, which is suffused with holes, is neither too dry nor too salty. The flavour opens as the cheese is chewed.

Semi-hard pâte; uncooked, pressed

Rind of natural mould

⊖	17–19 cm diameter, 6 cm high
⚖	1.5 kg
🗋	Not defined
✓	Spring to autumn
🝆	Raw
🍷	Châteauneuf-du-Pape

RHÔNE-ALPES
Haute-Savoie

TOMME AU MARC DE RAISIN

This *fermier* cheese is made by soaking a ripened *tomme* in *marc* for a month in an air-tight container. The heat caused by the fermentation heats the inside of the container, making the pâte tighten and become viscous. The taste of the *marc* permeates through to the heart of the cheese.

Semi-hard pâte; uncooked, pressed

Rind appears naturally, covered with *marc de raisins*

⊖	19–21 cm diameter, 5–6 cm high
⚖	1.7 kg
🗋	40%
✓	End of autumn to winter
🝆	Raw
🗋	*Marc* de Savoie

RHÔNE-ALPES
Savoie

TOMME DE LULLIN

The village of Lullin, where this *coopérative* cheese is made, lies in the Alps at an altitude of 860 m. Tomme de Lullin is a Tomme Label Savoie, which is a regional guarantee of quality granted by the Association Marque Collective Savoie. Strict guidelines control the place of production of the milk, as well as the quality of the rennet, the animal fodder, the size and weight of the cheese, and the period of affinage. This label, which is specific to the Savoie region, may be applied to hams, sausages, and fruit.

Tomme de Lullin has a soft, mild-flavoured pâte with small holes throughout. It feels thick on the tongue and melts in the mouth.

Semi-hard pâte; uncooked, pressed

HOW TOMME DE LULLIN IS MADE

Some 15 farms share the same place of production and hire a *fromager* to produce both Abondance (*p. 40*) and Tomme from the milk of 200 cows. A Tomme of 1.5 kg needs 15 kg cow's milk, while the much larger Abondance of 9.5 kg requires 103 kg of milk.

Coagulation
The morning milk is heated to 33°C and coagulated with rennet. The curd is cut, then mixed while being heated to 37°C. After 30 minutes, it changes into rubbery grains.

Moulding
The curd is put into cloth-lined moulds. Once the whey has drained off, the "cheeses" are taken out of the moulds and turned. The cloths are removed and replaced by plastic net and red *casein* labels bearing the fat content, department number, and place of production. The cheeses are returned to the moulds.

Pressing and Salting
The moulds are stacked to create gentle pressure on the cheeses and enable drainage to continue. About ten hours after coagulation, they are taken out of their moulds and soaked in brine for 24 hours.

Affinage
Total affinage takes at least one-and-a-half months. Once salted, the cheeses are transferred to a cellar at 90–95% humidity and 10–12°C. Seven or eight days later, a mould resembling cat's fur forms on the cheeses. The mould is brushed. Its texture is like fine powder and its spores fill the air. This grey mould, also called *tomme grise*, is characteristic of the *tommes* of Savoie. It tastes of the soil and is the reason why the regions of production and location of the ripening cellars are specifically defined. Cheeses from other areas are brought to Savoie for this greying process. After four weeks, the cheese is given to an *affineur* or a *fromager,* who ripens it in a cellar.

1 Moulding
Cloth-lined moulds are filled with curds.

2 Turning
The cheese is turned quickly by hand.

⊖	18 cm diameter, 5–8 cm high
⚖	1.2–2 kg
⭗	40% min.; 20 g per 100 g cheese
✓	All year
⭗	Raw
♀	Côtes du Rhône

Rind of
natural mould

RHÔNE-ALPES
Haute-Savoie

3 After 48 hours
The cheese is still fresh and shows no signs of mould.

4 Seven or eight days later
The characteristic "cat's fur" mould appears.
This is brushed.

5 After a further 20 days
The hairs of the "fur" are soft and beginning
to shorten and turn grey.

6 Affinage of four weeks
After an affinage of four weeks, the grey rind
is starting to form.

TOME DE MÉNAGE / BOUDANE

De ménage means "household", which is an exact description of this homemade *fermier* cheese. The cheese's local name, *boudane*, is simply the dialect word for *tome*. The cheese shown has had an affinage of four months and is very mature, with a smell of the cellar. Its pâte has a good, strong, fatty, consistency and is the colour of egg yolk. Affinage usually takes two to three months.

Semi-hard pâte; uncooked, pressed

Affinage of four months

Rind of natural mould

⊖	30 cm diameter, 7–9 cm high
⚖	About 6.2 kg
🗖	45%
✓	Best from autumn onwards
🖰	Raw
♀	St. Joseph

RHÔNE-ALPES
Savoie

TOMME DU MONT-CENIS

This *fermier* cheese is produced in an area around Mont Cenis in the Alps, close to the Italian border. The pâte has small holes spread all over, and is moist, soft, and pleasantly sticky in the mouth. The taste of sweetness may be due to the alpine flowers on which the cows graze. The cheese shown has the appearance of a typical alpine *tome*, with shades of grey, brown, red, and white mould. It was made in September, just before the cows came down from the mountains at the end of the summer, making it one of the last *alpage* cheeses of the season. Affinage takes at least three months.

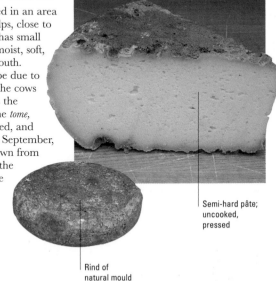

Semi-hard pâte; uncooked, pressed

Rind of natural mould

⊖	30 cm diameter, 5–6 cm high
⚖	3.5–4 kg
🗖	45%
✓	Best from autumn onwards
🖰	Raw
♀	Vinsobres

RHÔNE-ALPES
Savoie

TOMME DE THÔNES

This *fermier* cheese comes from the village of Thônes in the Aravis chain of mountains in the Alps. It has a hard, grey-brown crust covered with a white mould. The pâte is soft and yellow. Affinage takes at least six weeks.

Affinage of 12 weeks

Semi-hard pâte; uncooked, pressed

Rind of natural mould

⊖	10–12 cm diameter, 8–9 cm high
⚖	900 g–1 kg
🯄	40%
✓	Summer to autumn
⚗	Raw
♀	Vin de pays de l'Ardéche

RHÔNE-ALPES
Haute-Savoie

Tomme de Chèvre de Savoie

TOME DE CHÈVRE, BELLEVILLE

This mountain goat's-milk cheese is produced in the Vallée de Belleville in the Tarentaise region of Savoie. It is a pressed *fermier* cheese, with a thick, rubbery pâte riddled with holes. The cheese shown was made in September and kept in the cellar for 14 weeks, which is the usual period of affinage. It is at its best when bought and eaten from autumn onwards.

Rind of natural mould

Semi-hard pâte; uncooked, pressed

⊖	17 cm diameter, 7 cm high
⚖	1.6–1.8 kg
🯄	45%
✓	All year; best from autumn
⚗	Raw
♀	Condrieu, Château Grillet

RHÔNE-ALPES
Savoie

TOMME DE CHÈVRE D'ALPAGE, MORZINE

Morzine, where this *fermier* cheese is made, is a well-known ski resort in northern Savoie, some 10 km from the Swiss border. In summer, the region becomes a good grazing ground of alpine pastures and is well known for its cow's- and goat's-milk *tommes*.

The cheese shown is a *tomme d'alpage* made in an alpine chalet. It has a dry rind, covered with a grey to pale blue mould with red dots. When the cheese is young, the pâte has a light, flowery smell that becomes stronger as it matures. Affinage takes from two to 12 months.

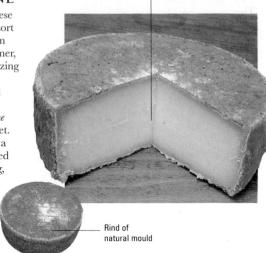

Semi-hard pâte; uncooked, pressed

Rind of natural mould

⊖	19 cm diameter, 6–7 cm high
⚖	1.8–2 kg
🏷	45%
✓	Best from autumn onwards
🥛	Raw
🍷	Vin de Savoie, Bourgogne Aligoté

RHÔNE-ALPES
Haute-Savoie

TOMME DE CHÈVRE, VALLÉE DE MORZINE

This is another *fermier* cheese produced from the milk of goats grazing in the alpine pastures of the Vallée de Morzine in northern Savoie. It has a moist and supple, reddish-brown rind and a heavy, cream-coloured pâte that sticks to the knife. The pâte melts in the mouth and has a surprisingly full after-taste. Affinage takes between one and two months, during which time the cheese is washed.

Semi-hard pâte; uncooked, pressed

Washed, rubbed, and waxed rind

⊖	18–20 cm diameter, 4 cm high
⚖	1–1.3 kg
🏷	Variable
✓	Spring to autumn
🥛	Raw
🍷	Graves *sec*

RHÔNE-ALPES
Haute-Savoie

TOMME DE CHÈVRE, VALLÉE DE NOVEL

This *fermier* cheese comes from the area around Novel, a small village beside Lake Geneva, near the Swiss border. It is an attractive, moist cheese with a firm, mimosa-yellow pâte that slightly resists cutting. This cheese smells of the cellar and is very different from the goat's-milk cheeses of the Loire (*p. 104*). Affinage takes from four to five months.

Soft pâte; uncooked, unpressed

Rind of natural mould

⊝	20 cm diameter, 5 cm high
⚖	1.7–2 kg
🗋	40%
✓	Autumn to winter
🗲	Raw
🍷	Vin de Savoie

RHÔNE-ALPES
Haute-Savoie

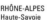

TOMME DE COURCHEVEL

This *fermier* goat's-milk cheese is produced in mountain chalets in the area around the town of Courchevel in the Alps. In the winter, the area is a famous Olympic sports centre, but during the summer, the alpine slopes provide excellent grazing for herds of goats. The cheese shown has a hard crust and a soft pâte, with a rich flavour. Affinage usually takes around two months.

Semi-hard pâte; uncooked, pressed

Rind of natural mould

⊝	20–25 cm diameter, 5–7 cm high
⚖	1.5–2 kg
🗋	45%
✓	Summer to winter
🗲	Raw
🍷	Condrieu

LANGUEDOC-ROUSSILLON
Lozère

TOME MI-CHÈVRE DU LÈCHERON

This *fermier* cheese, which is named after the Lècheron mountain, was made in a chalet in the Massif de la Vanoise. A decree of 1988 defines *mi-chèvre*, meaning half-goat, as a cheese containing 50% goat's milk. The other half, made up of cow's milk, softens the flavour. The cheese shown was washed with brine at the beginning of its affinage, but after four or five months the crust was quite dry.

Semi-hard, grey-yellow pâte; uncooked, pressed

Affinage of four or five months

Washed, dry, white, brown, and orange waxed rind

⊖	20–24 cm diameter, 4–5 cm high
⚖	2 kg
🗗	45%
✓	Summer to autumn
🥛	Raw (50%)
🐄	Raw (50%)
♀	Crépy

RHÔNE-ALPES
Savoie

TOMMETTE MI-CHÈVRE DES BAUGES

Tommette is a diminutive term, meaning a small *tomme*. The crust of this *fermier* cheese from the Massif des Bauges in Savoie is hard and dry, while the pâte is slightly moist, soft, and sticky. Affinage takes two to three months.

Rind of natural grey-brown mould

Semi-hard pâte; uncooked, pressed

⊖	10–11 cm diameter, 5 cm high
⚖	400 g
🗗	45%
✓	Best from autumn onwards
🥛	Raw
🐄	Raw
♀	Crépy

RHÔNE-ALPES
Savoie

Tommes from other Regions

TOMME D'ARLES

This *fermier* cheese was originally produced in the village of Montlaux in the Alpes de Haute Provence, but it disappeared some time ago. Production was resumed in 1988 by two women who began to make it with the milk from their small herd of 60 ewes. Their cheese has a soft, white pâte, which is barely ripened and has a distinct flavour. Affinage is short, lasting only about ten days.

Rind of natural mould

Soft pâte; uncooked, unpressed

⊖	8–9 cm diameter, 1.5 cm high
⚖	90–110 g
☊	50%
✓	End of winter to summer
⌣	Raw
♀	Cassis, Palette

PROVENCE-ALPES-CÔTE D'AZUR
Alpes-de-Haute-Provence

TOMME DE L'AVEYRON (PETITE)

This dry *fermier* cheese comes from the high plateaux of the Causse du Larzac in the department of Aveyron, from which it takes its name. The pâte is ivory-coloured, moist, and filled with small holes. It has a very slight acidity and a fairly strong flavour considering its low fat content of only 20%. It is an ideal choice for people who love cheese but who have to count calories. Affinage takes from one to three-and-a-half months.

Rind of natural mould

Soft pâte; uncooked, unpressed

⊖	12 cm diameter, 3 cm high
⚖	310–350 g
☊	20% or 40%
✓	Spring to autumn
⌣	Raw
♀	Cahors

MIDI-PYRÉNÉES
Aveyron

TOME DE BANON

This *artisanal* cheese takes its name from the town of Banon in Provence. A blue and white, natural mould has just appeared on the golden rind of the cheese shown here. The sprig of savory on top is not merely decorative, but adds the scent of Provence. The pâte of the cheese is fine in texture, with a light smell of goat's milk and savory. Affinage lasts from five days to three weeks.

Soft pâte; uncooked, unpressed

Rind of blue and white, natural mould

⊖	6 cm diameter, 2 cm high
⚖	60–75g
🝙	45%
✓	All year
🥄	Raw
♀	Cassis

PROVENCE-ALPES-CÔTE D'AZUR
Alpes-de-Haute-Provence

TOMME DU BOUGNAT

A *bougnat* is a native of Auvergne. If you ask the cheesemaker where his cheese comes from, all he will say is, "From the mountains of Auvergne". The maker's name and location are commercial secrets.

The pale yellow pâte of this cheese tastes cool on the tongue, and has a concentrated flavour. Production is *artisanal*, with an affinage of two months.

Semi-hard pâte; uncooked, slightly pressed

Natural rind

⊖	30 cm diameter, 5 cm high
⚖	4 kg
🝙	45%
✓	All year
🥄	Raw
♀	St. Pourçain

AUVERGNE

TOMME CAPRA

This simple goat's cheese comes from the village of St. Bardou in the Drôme region. Its name comes from the Italian word *capra*, which means goat. The rind is thin and the pâte is firm, even when fresh, with a light flavour of goat's milk. This *fermier* cheese is produced by F. Pozin and has an affinage of at least 12 days.

Soft pâte; uncooked, unpressed

Rind of natural mould

Θ	6 cm diameter, 1.5–2 cm high
⚖	50–60 g
🗋	45%
✓	All year, best in spring
🥛	Raw
🍷	St. Joseph

RHÔNE-ALPES
Drôme

TOMME DE CHÈVRE, PAYS NANTAIS

The Pays Nantais, from which this medium-sized *artisanal* cheese takes its name, lies at the mouth of the River Loire, a region famous for its white wine. The cheese shown has a moist, orange rind. The pâte is the colour of cream, with a fine texture, and is firm with no elasticity. The flavour is an unusual combination of goat and wine. Affinage takes three to six weeks, during which the cheese is rubbed with Muscadet wine.

Semi-hard pâte; uncooked, pressed

Washed, rubbed, and waxed, humid rind

Θ	20 cm diameter, 3–4 cm high
⚖	1.5 kg
🗋	45%
✓	All year
🥛	Raw
🍷	Muscadet sur Lie

PAYS DE LA LOIRE
Loire-Atlantique

TOME DE CHÈVRE DU TARN / LOU PENNOL

This *fermier* cheese is produced by the GAEC du Pic Agriculteurs in the department of Tarn, from which it takes its name. It has a dry rind covered in small bumps. The pâte is very white and fine-textured and has no elasticity. It has a sour taste, and melts in the mouth. At the beginning of its affinage, which lasts around three months, the cheese shown weighed 2 kg; two months later, it weighed 1.5 kg.

Semi-hard pâte; uncooked, pressed

Rind of natural mould

⊖	16–17 cm diameter, 7 cm high
⚖	1.5 g
🗋	45%
✓	All year
🖱	Raw
♀	Gaillac

MIDI-PYRÉNÉES
Tarn

TOMME LE GASCON

This *artisanal* cheese comes from the Lomagne region of Gascogne, which is well known for its *pâté de foie gras*. It has a dry rind that bounces under finger pressure. The pâte is yellow and supple, with a lot of holes and a rich, milky flavour. Affinage lasts four to five weeks.

Semi-hard pâte; uncooked, pressed

Natural rind

⊖	20 cm diameter, 9–10 cm high
⚖	3–3.5 kg
🗋	45–50%
✓	All year
🖱	Raw
♀	Tursan

MIDI-PYRÉNÉES
Gers

TOMME DE HUIT LITRES

A couple, originally from Paris, makes this *fermier* cheese in the village of Puimichel in Provence. They raise 45 goats in the Alps of Provence and make several kinds of goat's cheese that are distinctive by their methods of production, flavour, and aroma, but alike in the superior quality of their milk. The Tomme de Huit Litres, which is made following an ancient method, has almost no smell and a light flavour of rich goat's milk. Affinage takes from two weeks to six months.

Semi-hard pâte;
uncooked,
pressed

Rind of
natural mould

⊖	18 cm diameter, 3.5 cm high
⚖	1–1.2 kg
🗓	Not defined
✓	Spring to autumn
🥛	Raw
🍷	Cassis

PROVENCE-ALPES-
CÔTE D'AZUR
Alpes-de-Haute-Provence

TOMME DE MONTAGNE

The *fermier* cheese shown was made by couple of farmers who also make a fine Munster (*p. 192*) in the Vosges Mountains of eastern France. The rind is golden with red and white stains. The pâte is the colour of butter and firm, with a subtle flavour. Affinage takes two months, during which time the cheese is washed and brushed.

Semi-hard pâte;
uncooked,
pressed

Moist,
natural rind

⊖	19–20 cm diameter, 7–8 cm high
⚖	2.5 kg. – size and weight vary according to the quantity of milk produced each day
🗓	Not defined
✓	All year; best in autumn and winter
🥛	Raw
🍷	Sylvaner (good vintage)

ALSACE
Haut-Rhin

TOMME DE ROMANS / ROMANS

Some cheeses have continued to be produced in their region of origin, and are still known by their old names, while the milk used to produce them has changed with time. Romans is one such cheese. It used to be a *fermier* goat's-milk cheese, but now it is almost exclusively *industriel* or *artisanal*, made from pasteurized cow's milk. It smells slightly of the cellar in which it is matured. Affinage lasts for at least ten days.

Soft pâte; uncooked, unpressed

Rind of natural mould

⊖	8–9 cm diameter, 3.5 cm high
⚖	200–300 g
🗋	45–50%
✓	All year
⌔	Pasteurized
❢	Crozes Hermitage, Cornas

RHÔNE-ALPES
Drôme, Isère

TOMME DE SÉRANON

The town of Séranon lies at an altitude of 1,000 m just north of Grasse. The sea breezes blow in to the area and spread the scent of flowers. Even the cheeses produced here have a delicious, lingering aroma of flowers. Summer is the best season for Tomme de Séranon. The rind is thin and almost pink and the pâte is very supple and fragile. This is a *fermier* cheese with a short affinage of about two weeks.

Soft pâte; uncooked, unpressed

Rind of natural mould

⊖	9 cm diameter, 4 cm high
⚖	250–300 g
🗋	45%
✓	All year, best spring to summer
⌔	Raw
❢	*Rosé* de Provence

PROVENCE-ALPES-CÔTE D'AZUR
Alpes-Maritimes

TOMME DE VENDÉE

The pâte and rind of this large
artisanal cheese from France's
Atlantic Coast indicate that the
methods of production are
different from those of the
AOC goat's-milk cheeses of
the Loire Valley. The taste
of salt is quite strong, and
the flavour is partly due
to the careful affinage of
one-and-a-half months.

Semi-hard pâte;
uncooked,
pressed

⊖	20–22 cm diameter, 4 cm high
⚖	1.7 kg
⅌	45%
✓	Spring to autumn
⌣	Raw
♀	Fiefs Vendéens *rosé*

Rind of
natural mould

PAYS DE LA LOIRE
Vendée

TOMMETTE DE L'AVEYRON

This *fermier* cheese comes from the
Causse du Larzac, which is the home
of the famous Roquefort (*p. 216*).
It is named after Aveyron, the
department in which it is produced.
This cheese is made with rich milk
and has a dry rind and a white, grey,
and reddish-brown mould. The pâte
is firm and elastic under finger
pressure. The cheese melts in the
mouth and has a strong, salty taste.
Affinage takes two to six weeks.

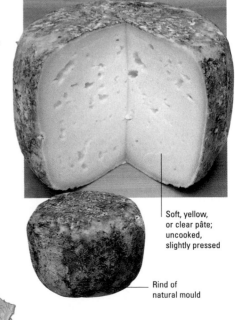

Soft, yellow,
or clear pâte;
uncooked,
slightly pressed

⊖	8 cm diameter 6 cm high
⚖	300 g
⅌	Not defined
✓	Made from December to 15 August
⌣	Raw
♀	Gaillac, Cahors

Rind of
natural mould

MIDI-PYRÉNÉES
Aveyron

TOMME DE CHÈVRE

This *fermier* goat's-milk cheese is made in the Provençal village of Puimichel by the producer of Tomme de Huit Litres (*p. 247*). It has a mild but complex flavour. Affinage lasts three weeks, during which time the cheese is washed in brine twice a week.

Washed, humid, red rind

Soft pâte; uncooked, slightly pressed

⊖	10 cm diameter, 2.5 cm high
⚖	220–250 g
🗔	Not defined
✓	Spring to autumn
🐐	Raw
🍷	Cassis

PROVENCE-ALPES-CÔTE D'AZUR
Alpes-de-Haute-Provence

Tomme de Chèvre, les Pyrénées

FROMAGE DE CHÈVRE FERMIER

Sheep's-milk cheeses have been produced in the Pyrénées for centuries, but goat's-milk cheeses like this one are rare. The curd is wrapped in a cloth, drained, and lightly pressed to discard the whey. This ensures that the cheese will keep for longer. The ripened cheese is solid, with a dry pâte that occasionally splits. The flavour is rich. The maker's mark – a heart – is embossed on the rind. Affinage of this *fermier* cheese takes one-and-a-half months.

Semi-hard pâte; uncooked, pressed

Natural rind, marked by the cloth; stamped with a heart

⊖	15–18.5 cm diameter, 8 cm high
⚖	2.3 kg
🗔	45%
✓	Summer to winter
🐐	Raw
🍷	Jurançon

MIDI-PYRÉNÉES
Hautes-Pyrénées

TOMME DE CHÈVRE LOUBIÈRES / CABRIOULET

This *fermier* goat's-milk cheese is produced at the Col del Fach farm in Loubières, near the town of Foix in southern France. The cheese shown has had an affinage of five months and the surface seems as hard as stone. The pâte is yellow-grey, with holes, and has little elasticity. This is a strong cheese with a smell of mould and the cellar. It is salty but well balanced, with rich flavours. During the affinage of at least two months, the cheese is washed in brine.

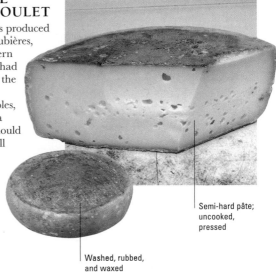

Semi-hard pâte; uncooked, pressed

Washed, rubbed, and waxed moist rind

⊖	20–21 cm diameter, 5–6 cm high
⚖	2–2.5 kg
⬠	Not defined
✓	All year except December and January
⟡	Raw
♀	Limoux

MIDI-PYRÉNÉES
Ariège

TOME PAYS BASQUE

This *fermier* cheese is produced by the Basque shepherd who makes Ardi-Gasna (*p. 67*) near the town of St.-Jean-Pied-de-Port, close to the Spanish border in southwest France. It is also ripened by the same *fromager*. The rind of the cheese shown here is dry and shows traces of the cloth used during pressing. The pâte is firm, with no elasticity, and breaks easily. Although it is dry, it contains a good balance of salt and fat and melts in the mouth to a sticky consistency. Affinage lasts for two months.

Semi-hard pâte; uncooked, pressed

Natural rind

⊖	12–13 cm diameter, 6–7 cm high
⚖	1–1.2 kg
⬠	45%
✓	Summer, autumn, and winter
⟡	Raw
♀	Irouléguy, Muscadet sur Lie

AQUITAINE
Pyrénées-Atlantiques

TOMME DE CHÈVRE DE PAYS

This *fermier* cheese is produced in Les Barronies in the region of Gascogne. It has a dry rind with a light brown and red mould showing traces of the cloth used in the production. After an affinage of three months, the taste is well developed with a balanced sweetness and no acidity.

Semi-hard pâte; uncooked, pressed

Rind of natural mould

⊖	19 cm diameter, 7–8 cm high
⚖	2–2.2 kg
🗘	45%
✓	All year; best in autumn and winter
🗇	Raw
♀	Tursan

MIDI-PYRÉNÉES
Hautes-Pyrénées

TRAPPE (VÉRITABLE)

The name of this *artisanal* cheese means "real Trappist" – it is made in the Trappist Abbaye de la Coudre close to the town of Laval in the province of Maine. It is a mild cheese with a slight smell of mould. Affinage lasts at least three weeks, during which time the cheese is washed in brine.

Semi-hard, elastic pâte; uncooked, pressed

Washed, rubbed, and waxed rind

⊖	20 cm diameter, 4–5 cm high
⚖	300 g, 400 g
🗘	40%
✓	All year
🗇	Pasteurized
♀	Chinon

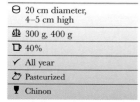

PAYS DE LA LOIRE
Mayenne

TRAPPE DE BELVAL

This *artisanal* cheese is produced in a convent called the Abbaye de Belval, in the province of Artois. The nuns originally came from Laval and started to make the cheese in 1892. Every year, the nuns make around 40 tonnes. The wrapper of the cheese is tangerine-coloured, with six blue crosses and a picture of the abbey in dark blue. The cheese has a soft, pink rind the colour of coral. Its pâte is ivory, with a cool, elastic texture and a slight scent. Affinage takes a minimum of six weeks.

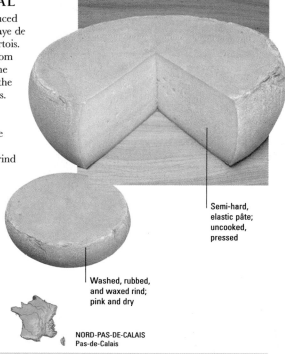

Semi-hard, elastic pâte; uncooked, pressed

Washed, rubbed, and waxed rind; pink and dry

⊖	20 cm diameter, 4–5 cm high
⚖	2 kg; 400 g
🗋	40–45%
✓	All year
🗋	Raw
🍷	Bordeaux, Médoc

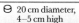

NORD-PAS-DE-CALAIS
Pas-de-Calais

FROMAGE D'HESDIN

This *artisanal* cheese is named after the town of Hesdin, which lies just 20 km from the village where Trappe de Belval is made. The cheese was probably modelled on a similar monastery cheese. Production of Fromage d'Hesdin began around 1960. The smell is soft and light and the aftertaste is slightly sweet. Affinage takes two months, during which time the cheese is washed occasionally in white wine.

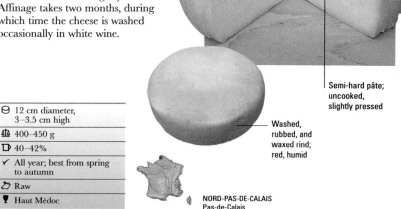

Semi-hard pâte; uncooked, slightly pressed

Washed, rubbed, and waxed rind; red, humid

⊖	12 cm diameter, 3–3.5 cm high
⚖	400–450 g
🗋	40–42%
✓	All year; best from spring to autumn
🗋	Raw
🍷	Haut Médoc

NORD-PAS-DE-CALAIS
Pas-de-Calais

TRAPPE D'ECHOURGNAC

Since 1868, Trappist nuns have been collecting milk from neighbouring farms to make and ripen this *artisanal* cheese in l'Abbaye d'Echourgnac, in Périgord. They use The same methods of production are used as for Port-du-Salut (*p. 209*) and succeed in producing 52 tonnes each year.

The rind of the cheese is very slightly moist and bounces under finger pressure. The flavour is balanced and simple. Affinage takes two weeks in the abbey cellars, plus a further month at the cheese shop.

Washed, rubbed, and waxed rind; slightly moist

Semi-hard, elastic pâte; uncooked, slightly pressed

⊖	9–10 cm diameter, 3–4 cm high
⚖	270–300 g; 2 kg
▯	45%
✓	All year
⟁	Pasteurized
🍷	Cahors

AQUITAINE
Dordogne

TRAPPISTE DE CHAMBARAN

This *artisanal* cheese made by monks comes from the town of Roybon on the Plateau de Chambaran, in the province of the Dauphiné. It has a moist, pale pink rind and a mild flavour. Production, which is modelled on that of Reblochon (*p. 213*) and Port-du-Salut (*p. 209*), began in 1932. The milk is bought from neighbouring farms and then pasteurized. During affinage, the cheeses are washed in brine over two weeks in the cellars of the abbey. Large cheeses need at least four weeks.

Washed, rubbed, and waxed rind; pink and moist

Semi-hard pâte; uncooked, slightly pressed

⊖	8–9 cm diameter, 2–2.5 cm high
⚖	160 g; 300 g; 1.5 kg
▯	45%
✓	All year
⟁	Pasteurized
🍷	Côtes Rotie

RHÔNE-ALPES
Isère

The milk of Blonde d'Aquitaine cows is ▶
used in many cheeses around the world

Triple-Crème and Double-Crème

Triple-crème and double-crème cheeses are popular because of their subtle, creamy flavour and they are often included on cheese platters. They are made by adding cream to the milk during production. *Triple-crème* has a minimum fat content of 75%, whereas *double-crème* contains between 60 and 75% fat. These cheeses generally have no rind at all, or a soft rind of mould. The pâte is soft, sweet, and tastes pleasant; there may also be a slight sourness. The smell is faint. Since these cheeses do not have strong flavours, they are often used in the production of other cheeses (*p. 261*). The length of affinage is usually short. The cheeses may be eaten fresh and go particularly well with a red wine such as Moulis, which is also known as Moulis-en-Médoc, a small vineyard in the Haut-Médoc.

LA BOUILLE

This rare *artisanal* cheese was first produced in Normandie at the end of the 19th century by the same man who made "Monsieur Fromage" (*p. 259*). Despite its high fat content, this *double-crème* cheese is ripened for two months.

Rind of white mould

Soft pâte; uncooked, unpressed

⊖ 8 cm diameter, 5–5.5 cm high	HAUTE-NORMANDIE Seine-Maritime
⚖ 220 g	
▯ 60%	
✓ Summer to winter	
⟳ Enriched with cream	
❢ Médoc	

BOURSAULT

This *industriel* cheese has a mild flavour, reminiscent of Brie (*p. 80*), and a slight acidity. It was first made after World War II and was named after its creator and maker. It is a soft, creamy cheese with a slight smell of mould. Affinage lasts two months.

Soft pâte; uncooked, unpressed

Rind of very light, white mould

⊖ 8 cm diameter, 4 cm high	ILE-DE-FRANCE Seine-et-Marne
⚖ 200 g	
▯ 70%	
✓ All year	
⟳ Enriched with cream	
❢ Bordeaux	

BOURSIN

The cheese on the right is a Boursin made with garlic and herbs; the one on the left is made with black pepper. Boursin is a soft, creamy, *industriel* cheeses from Normandie with no affinage. It goes particularly well with fresh bread and dry white wine.

⊖	8 cm diameter, 4 cm high
⚖	150 g
🡒	70%
✓	All year
⟳	Enriched with cream
♀	Graves

HAUTE-NORMANDIE
Eure

Fresh pâte shaped and kneaded; uncooked, unpressed

No rind

BRILLAT-SAVARIN

This cheese was created in the 1930s by Henri Androuët, who was the father of the French cheese expert Pierre Androuët. It was named after the renowned 18th-century food writer Brillat-Savarin. This is an *industriel* cheese with an affinage of one to two weeks.

⊖	12–13 cm diameter, 3.5–4 cm high
⚖	450–500 g
🡒	75%
✓	All year
⟳	Enriched with cream
♟	St. Emilion, Fronsac

MAINLY
NORMANDIE

Rind of white mould

Soft pâte; uncooked, unpressed

CAPRICE DES DIEUX

This *industriel* cheese from the Bassigny region of Haute-Marne was first produced commercially in 1956. There are three versions varying between 150 g and 310 g in weight. Affinage takes two weeks.

⊖	14 cm long, 6 cm wide, 3.5 cm high (medium)
⚖	210 g (medium)
🡒	60%
✓	All year
⟳	Enriched with cream
♟	Coteaux Champenois

CHAMPAGNE-ARDENNE
Haute-Marne

Soft pâte; uncooked, unpressed

Rind of white mould

CROUPET

The name of this cheese derives from a village in the Brie region of the Ile-de-France. It is produced in a small *industriel* dairy. Affinage takes one to two weeks.

Rind of white mould

Soft, creamy pâte; uncooked, unpressed

⊖ 11 cm diameter, 5 cm high	
⚖ 450 g	ILE-DE-FRANCE
🌡 75%	Seine-et-Marne
✓ All year	
⚗ Enriched with cream	
🍷 Bourgogne	

DÉLICE DE SAINT-CYR

This cheese from Saint-Cyr-sur-Morin in the region of Brie is similar to Boursault (*p. 256*). It is produced in a small *industriel* dairy. Affinage takes four to five weeks.

Soft pâte; uncooked, unpressed

Rind of white mould

⊖ 8–9 cm diameter, 4–6 cm high	
⚖ 300 g	ILE-DE-FRANCE
🌡 75%	Seine-et-Marne
✓ All year	
⚗ Enriched with cream	
🍷 Bordeaux	

EXPLORATEUR

This *industriel* cheese has a slight smell of mould and a creamy texture and taste. Affinage takes two to three weeks. As well as the cheese shown here, there are also larger versions weighing 450 g and 1.6 kg that are usually sold pre-cut.

Rind of white mould

Soft pâte; uncooked, unpressed

⊖ 8 cm diameter, 6 cm high	
⚖ 250 g	ILE-DE-FRANCE
🌡 75%	Seine-et-Marne
✓ All year	
⚗ Enriched with cream	
🍷 Bordeaux	

FIN-DE-SIÈCLE

This *artisanal* cheese from the Pays de
Bray in Normandie was given its name
by cheesemaker Henri Androuët.
It is a soft, creamy cheese with a slight
smell of mould. Affinage lasts two weeks.

⊖ 8 cm diameter, 5 cm high	HAUTE-NORMANDIE
⚖ 270 g	Eure
🗋 72%	
✓ All year	
🝖 Enriched with cream	
🍷 Bordeaux	

Soft pâte;
uncooked,
unpressed

Rind of
white mould

FROMAGE DE MONSIEUR / MONSIEUR FROMAGE

This *industriel* cheese was created by
Monsieur Fromage, as was Bouille
(*p. 256*). Affinage takes three weeks.

⊖ 7 cm diameter, 5 cm high	MAINLY NORMANDIE
⚖ 250 g	
🗋 60%	
✓ All year	
🝖 Enriched with cream	
🍷 Bordeaux	

Soft pâte;
uncooked,
unpressed

Rind of
white mould

GRAND VATEL

This is an *artisanal* cheese from
Bourgogne, with an affinage of six
weeks. It is a solid cheese with a buttery
taste. There is also a Petit Vatel, with
an affinage of only four weeks.

⊖ 13 cm diameter, 3–4 cm high	BOURGOGNE
⚖ 500 g	Côte d'Or
🗋 75%	
✓ All year	
🝖 Enriched with cream	
🍷 Côtes de Beaune	

Soft pâte;
uncooked, unpressed

Rind of
white mould

GRATTE-PAILLE

This is an *artisanal* cheese from the department of Seine-et-Marne, with an affinage of three weeks. It has an oily texture and a rich, creamy taste.

Soft pâte; | uncooked, unpressed

Rind of | white mould

◈ 8–10 cm long, 6–7 cm wide, 6 cm high	
⚖ 300–350 g	ILE-DE-FRANCE Seine-et-Marne
🜊 70%	
✓ All year	
⌔ Enriched with cream	
❢ Bordeaux	

LUCULLUS

This soft, creamy *industriel* cheese is named after Lucullus, the Roman general and gourmet. Affinage takes three to four weeks.

Soft pâte; | uncooked, unpressed

Rind of | white mould

⊖ 8 cm diameter, 4–5 cm high	
⚖ 250–300 g	ILE-DE-FRANCE Seine-et-Marne
🜊 75%	
✓ All year	
⌔ Enriched with cream	
❢ Bordeaux	

PIERRE-ROBERT

This artisanal cheese from Seine-et-Marne was conceived by cheesemaker Robert Rouzaire, who named it after himself and his friend Pierre. His son continues to make it today. It is a mild cheese that is popular with children. Affinage takes three weeks.

Soft pâte; | uncooked, unpressed

Rind of | white mould

⊖ 13 cm diam., 4.5–5 cm high	
⚖ 500 g	ILE-DE-FRANCE Seine-et-Marne
🜊 75%	
✓ All year	
⌔ Enriched with cream	
❢ Bordeaux	

IMAGINATIVE CREATIONS

The cheeses shown on this page are all *double-crème* and *triple-crème* cheeses that have been decorated by the *fromager* with a variety of herbs and spices.

Cannelle, covered with cinnamon

Gargantua à la feuille de sauge, decorated with sage leaves

Paprika, covered with paprika

Poivre, covered with coarsely ground black pepper

Trois-Epis, covered with cumin seeds

Soleil, covered with raisins and sultanas

Dried grapes marinated in rum cover the cheese entirely

FRENCH CHEESES

V

Vache des Pyrénées

The Pyrénées are some 250 miles long and extend over five French departments and 11 provinces. At the center of this area, in the departments of Ariège and Haute-Garonne, the cheeses that used to be made from sheep's milk are today being made with cow's milk. These cheeses are solid and quite large, with tough rinds that protect firm, fat, and fruity pâtes. They bear the names of their villages, although the local people simply call them *fromage de montagne*, meaning "mountain cheese." They are nearly all *fermier* cheeses made from raw milk, and have small eyes, or holes, in the pâte. Affinage develops the full character of a mountain cheese. The cheese becomes meaty and retains none of the softness, mildness, and sweetness of milk. It should be matched with a fruity red wine.

BAROUSSE

This cheese is named after the Vallée de Barousse de l'Ourse in the Pyrénées. Both Barousse and Esbareich (*below*) are produced by similar methods. The taste varies according to whether they are made with the milk of cows fed on spring and summer grass, or from cows fed dry fodder in their sheds in winter. The cheese shown was made by the Sost family from the village of the same name. It is a strong-smelling *fermier* cheese, with an affinage of at least one-and-a half months.

Washed, natural, pink-brown rind

Semihard, elastic pâte, with many small holes; uncooked, pressed

⊖	7½ in. diameter, 2¾ in. high
⚖	4½ lb.
🗋	Not defined
✓	All year
⚗	Raw
❢	Madiran, Côtes du Frontonnais

MIDI-PYRÉNÉES
Hautes-Pyrénèes

ESBAREICH

This cheese is the twin of Barousse. It is a *fermier* cheese from Esbareich, about a mile from Sost, with an affinage of two-and-a half months.

⊖	7½ in. diameter, 3 in. high
⚖	5½ lb.
🗋	Not defined
✓	All year
⚗	Raw
❢	Madiran, Côtes du Frontonnais

Uncooked, pressed, semihard cheese with a natural mold

MIDI-PYRÉNÉES
Hautes-Pyrénèes

◀ **Cows grazing in a mountainside meadow in the Pyrénées**

BETHMALE

This is the best-known of the traditional cow's-milk cheeses from the Pyrénées. It is named after the village where it is made, in the Couscrans region of the Comté de Foix. Legend has it that it was favoured by King Louis VI, who passed through the area in the 12th century.

Bethmale is probably the mildest of all the cow's-milk cheeses of the Pyrénées. The cheese shown here has a semi-hard, uncooked, pressed pâte and smells of the cellar. Affinage takes two to three months, during which time the cheese is brushed and turned.

Natural rind

⊖	25-40 cm diameter, 8-10 cm high
⚖	3.5-6kg
⟁	45–50%
✓	All year
⟁	Raw or pasteurized
❢	Collioure

MIDI-PYRÉNÉES
Ariège

E BAMALOU

This *artisanal* cheese is made in two sizes, large and small, in the town of Castillon-en-Couserans in Comté de Foix. It is probably the strongest of all the cow's-milk cheeses of the Pyrénées. The pâte is supple, greasy, and well wrapped in its solid rind, which is brownish with red spots. The taste and smell of this cheese blend well with a red wine with good tannin. Affinage takes about six weeks.

Semi-hard pâte; uncooked, pressed

Natural reddish-brown rind

⊖	24-29 cm diameter, 10 cm high (large); 11-13 cm, 7 cm high (small)
⚖	6 kg (large); 700-800 kg (small)
⟁	50%
✓	All year
⟁	Raw, whole
❢	Châteauneuf-du-Pape, Cahors

MIDI-PYRÉNÉES
Ariège

FROMAGE DE MONTAGNE

The tiny house of the two cheesemakers who produce this *fermier* cheese lies at an altitude of 1,300 m in the Pyrénées in Poubeau, close to the town of Luchon. The crust of the cheese is less strong-smelling than the pâte, and is orange and pinkish-white in colour, and soft and moist. The pâte is egg-yolk yellow and suffused with holes. It smells strong. The cheese shown here looks young, but it is already four months old, about the right age for eating. Affinage takes at least three months, during which time the cheese is washed and turned regularly.

Elastic, semi-hard pâte; uncooked, slightly pressed

Supple, natural rind

⊖	20–22 cm diam., 8–9 cm high
⚖	2.7 kg
🗋	Not defined
✓	All year
⟳	Raw
❦	Bergerac, Bordeaux, Fitou

MIDI-PYRÉNÉES
Haute-Garonne

FROMAGE DE MONTAGNE DE LÈGE

This *fermier* cheese is produced by the Camille Cazaux farm in the village of Lège. It has a reddish-brown, sticky, and slightly moist rind, and a dense, yellow pâte, which is full of holes. This cheese may be eaten after an affinage of just three months, but connoisseurs prefer to wait six months until it is completely mature.

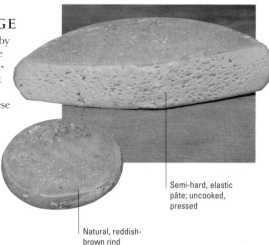

Semi-hard, elastic pâte; uncooked, pressed

Natural, reddish-brown rind

⊖	34–37 cm diameter, 7–8 cm high
⚖	6.5 kg
🗋	45%
✓	Summer to winter
⟳	Raw
❦	Madiran, Cahors, Fitou

MIDI-PYRÉNÉES
Haute-Garonne

FROMAGE DE MONTAGNE, LE PIC DE LA CALABASSE

This *artisanal* cheese is made in the village of Saint-Lary at the foot of the 2,210-m Pic de la Calabasse mountain. Besides the large cheese shown here, there is also a smaller version. The cheese shown is ripe and has hints of white, grey, pink, and brown on the rind, which is marked by the cloth. The pâte is yellow and brown, and full of holes; it is firm but melts in the mouth. The smell of this sticky cheese is strong and fruity, with a trace of flowers. Affinage takes three months.

Natural rind, marked by cloth

Semi-hard, elastic pâte; uncooked, pressed

⊖	28–37 cm diam., 7–8 cm high
⚖	6 kg
ⅅ	45%
✓	Best in spring
♻	Raw
🍷	Corbières, Minervois, Fitou

MIDI-PYRÉNÉES
Ariège

FROMAGE DE MONTAGNE/ LE ROGALLAIS

This *artisanal* cheese is made by the Fromagerie Coumes in Seix, in the Couserans region of Comté de Foix. It has a well-ripened, brown, or pinkish-brown rind, and a yellow to light brown pâte with "eyes" or holes in it. The pâte is thick and greasy and smells of the cellar and mould. The cheesemaker explains: "The eyes form during the affinage of one-and-a-half months and air the pâte.

Their quality depends on how the whey is drained. The cellar is at 14°C with a humidity of 95%. This humidity and the board of oak on which the cheese matures cause the mould to form and the pâte to ferment to create the eyes."

Slightly elastic, semi-hard pâte; uncooked, pressed

Natural rind

⊖	33 cm diameter, 5 cm high
⚖	4.5 kg; 2.5 kg
ⅅ	50%
✓	All year, especially spring to autumn
♻	Raw
🍷	Graves, Medoc

MIDI-PYRÉNÉES
Ariège

LE MOULIS

This is an *artisanal* cheese made by a long-established family business in Moulis in the province of Comté de Foix. Sixty tonnes are made each year, which amounts to some 17,000 cheeses.

Both young and mature Moulis have strong tastes. At first the pâte is straw-coloured, then it turns brown. Despite its many holes, it is moist, fatty, and melts softly in the mouth. The distinct taste of fermentation and decay stings the tongue. The cheese smells strong and is piquant when old. During affinage, it is washed in brine once every two days for the first two weeks, then brushed and turned for one to two months.

Semi-hard, elastic pâte; uncooked, slightly pressed

Young Moulis

Natural, dry, white, brown, and black mould marked by cloth

Pâte darkens and becomes harder with age

Moulis after an affinage of six months

Washed, rubbed, and waxed rind

⊖	22–24 cm diameter, 7 cm high
⚖	3.5 kg
🗗	48%
✓	All year
⟳	Raw
♀	Vin du Jura *sec*

MIDI-PYRÉNÉES
Ariège

VACHERIN D'ABONDANCE FERMIER

This *fermier* cheese is made in Abondance in Savoie. The unusual feature of this cheese is the strip of spruce bark in which it is wrapped. The bark protects the exterior and its scent permeates the cheese. The pâte is fine-textured, with a mild, creamy, slightly salty flavour. Affinage lasts three weeks.

Locally, Vacherin d'Abondance *fermier* is eaten with *patates au barbot*, which are potatoes boiled with their skins in salt water. On *p. 270–271* is an explanation of how this *fermier* cheese is made according to traditional methods.

Affinage of 24 hours

Affinage of 12 days

⊖	13 cm diameter, 3 cm high
⚖	400–500 g
🧀	Not defined (including wood covering)
✓	Winter and spring
🥛	Raw
🍷	Vin de Savoie, Marin

RHÔNE-ALPES
Haute-Savoie

Thin, washed rind with natural white mould

Soft, cream-like pâte that smells of spruce wood; uncooked, unpressed

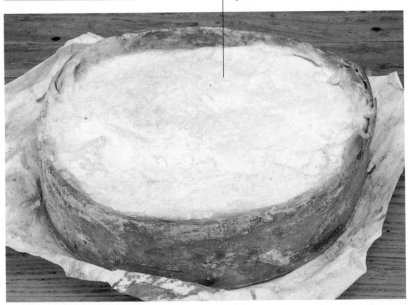

HOW VACHERIN D'ABONDANCE IS MADE

Cheesemaker Célina Gagneux produces this cheese following traditional methods. The only person who produces this cheese in Abondance, Célina learnt her technique from her mother-in-law.

Cheesemaking begins in December and goes on for 210 days of the year until July. With nine cows, which give 60 litres of milk every morning, she makes 15 cheeses. The evening milking is less productive and results in another 12 or 13 cheeses. Each cheese requires four litres of milk.

In July, the cows go up to the alpine pastures, where they join others in a herd of about 50. The summer milk is used to make the big Abondance cheeses (*p. 40*) in *chalets* in the mountains. The herdspeople and the

The peaceful town of Abondance

cows return in early October and the cows calve. The female calves are kept and reared for three years before they themselves start to produce milk. Each cow can continue to produce milk for around ten years.

1 At 6.30 a.m. the cows are milked and the milk is poured into a large copper bowl.

2 The rennet is mixed in with a ladle and coagulation begins. The mixture is left to rest for an hour at 12°C.

3 At 8 a.m. the curd is poured into 15 bowls lined with gauze.

4 The gauze is knotted around the curd to drain off the whey.

5 The whey is discarded and kept to extract the cream.

6 The balls of curd in cloth are bound with bands of spruce bark left to rest for about three hours, then transferred to the draining board. At 3 p.m. drainage continues.

Creamy Pâte
The soft, cream-like pâte of
Vacherin d'Abondance smells
of spruce wood. The cheese is
uncooked and unpressed.

Abondance cows

7 Once drainage is complete, the
cloth is removed.

8 The cheeses are laid on the
draining board until the next
morning. The whey continues to
drain off while the cheeses remain
sweet, light, and soft.

9 At 8 a.m. the following morning, the cheeses are moved to a cellar
at a temperature of 12°C, and salted on one side only. After 48 hours,
they are taken out of their bands, turned, and salted on the other side.
The bands are put back and tightened as the cheeses ripen.
    The cheeses are turned every morning for 15 to 20 days and the
cloth covering the board is changed, leaving marks on the surfaces of
the cheeses. About 15 to 20 days later, white mould appears on the
surfaces. The rind is not yet formed, but a thin, creamy-white skin has
appeared. The cheeses are ready for sale.

VACHERIN DES BAUGES

Two people make this *fermier* cheese in the Massif des Bauges in Savoie. According to a local cheesemaker, although it is best to allow the cheese to ripen fully, it can be eaten two weeks after the start of affinage, as long as it is wiped once every two days with water in which cream has been diluted. This is also done during the full affinage, which should ideally last a month. The cheese shown has been ripened for two weeks and includes patches of a bad grey mould that will impair the flavour.

Soft, white pâte with a smell of spruce resin; uncooked, unpressed

Bad grey mould

Spruce band

Washed rind

⊖	21 cm diameter, 4–4.5 cm high
⚖	1.4 kg in a band of spruce bark
▽	Not defined
✓	Winter
🜛	Raw
❢	Vin de Savoie, Arbois

RHÔNE-ALPES
Savoie

VACHERIN DU HAUT-DOUBS / MONT D'OR (AOC)

The Massif du Mont d'Or, which rises to a height of 1,463 m, lies near the French border with Switzerland. Although this winter cheese has been made on the French side for two centuries, for many years there was disagreement over the origins of this cheese, with both the French and the Swiss maintaining that they were the first to make it. The controversy ended when the Swiss conceded to the French.

Mont d'Or is simply called Vacherin in the shops. It is presented in a wooden box in which it continues to ripen. The cheese is bound by a band of spruce, the pleasant scent of which permeates the cheese. The spruce band also helps the cheese to keep its shape and should not be removed. The surface of the cheese is moist and the rind golden and slightly reddish, with imprints of the cloth. The pale yellow pâte is creamy. It can be spread on bread or boiled potatoes. The AOC permits both *artisanal* and *coopérative* production. Affinage must take place within specified areas over three weeks at a maximum temperature of 15°C. After three weeks of ripening, the aroma of spruce is distinct. The cheese is cured on a board of spruce wood and turned and rubbed with a cloth soaked in brine.

Band of spruce wood keeps cheese in shape and should not be removed, even when serving

Vacherin du Haut-Doubs in a wooden box

In the cheese shop, a piece of marble is used to stop the cheese from running

Vacherin du Haut-Doubs in a wooden box

⊖	12–30 cm diameter, 4–5 cm high
⚖	500 g–1 kg in a band of spruce bark
♣	45 g min. per 100 g cheese
☊	45% min., 20.25 g per 100 g cheese
✓	Best winter, autumn, and spring
⚘	Raw
▮	Beaujolais Nouveau, Côtes du Jura
♀	Champagne

Washed, wrinkled, yellow to light brown crust of natural mould

FRANCHE-COMTÉ
Doubs

Soft, runny, white to ivory pâte; uncooked, very slightly pressed

AOC Regulations: Vacherin du Haut-Doubs

1 The milk must be collected by or dispatched to the dairy every day.
2 The milk must be coagulated exclusively with rennet. It may be heated once to a maximum of 40°C, but only at the renneting stage.
3 Systems or machinery that would allow the rapid heating to above 40°C before renneting, may not be kept on the premises.
4 After being taken out of the mould, the curd must be bound in a strap of spruce wood and put inside a wooden box.

AOC GRANTED 1981

VIEUX-BOULOGNE

This is a new *pré-salé*, meaning pre-salted, cheese. It is made from the milk of cows raised by the sea near Boulogne. The rind, which is washed with beer, is moist and red. The cheese has a strong odour, although the smell of beer is quite faint. The pâte is elastic. Production is *artisanal*, with a long affinage of seven to nine weeks.

◈	11 cm square, 4 cm high
⚖	300–500 g
☊	45%
✓	All year
⚘	Raw
⚔	Local beer
♀	Champagne

NORD-PAS-DE-CALAIS
Pas-de-Calais

Semi-hard pâte; uncooked, pressed

Washed, orange-red, moist rind

Glossary

Affinage
The curing and maturing of cheeses, which can be anything from a few days to many months. (*See p. 17*)

Affineur
Specialist in the curing and maturing of cheeses.

Alpage
Movement of animals and herdspeople high into the mountains for summer grazing.

AOC
Appellation d'Origine Contrôlée – label applied to a range of cheeses that meet certain criteria. (*See p. 28*)

A Point
A cheese that is just at the right point of ripeness.

Artisanal
Used to describe a cheese that is made by hand rather than by machine.

Brebis
The French word for a ewe, or a ewe's-milk cheese.

Brine
Very salty water.

Brique
A rectangular, brick-shaped cheese.

Brousse
A cheese made from whey or skimmed milk.

Bûche
A log-shaped cheese.

Buron
A simple mountain dairy and cheese-store, with a sleeping space (Auvergne).

Cabane
Mountain chalet where cheese is made in summer (Pyrénées and Corsica).

Caillé
Curd.

Carré
Adjective used to describe a square cheese.

Casein
The main protein in milk, precipitated into curd by the use of rennet. It is used to make some edible cheese labels, which are embedded in the crust.

Causses
Limestone plateaux of the Massif Central.

Cave
Natural cave or cellar in which cheeses are ripened and stored until ready to eat.

Cendré
A cheese traditionally coated with ash from burned vine roots, but today usually covered with industrially powdered charcoal mixed with salt.

Cheese Iron
A small metal corer for removing a plug from the interior of a cheese to test aroma, flavour, and texture.

Chèvre
A nanny goat, or a goat's-milk cheese.

Coagulation
The clotting of milk, usually by rennet.

Commune
The smallest unit of French local government.

Curd
The coagulated fats and other solids produced from milk by natural ripening and renneting.

Department
(French *département*)
Modern administrative division of France, often disregarding old provincial boundaries.

Dry Matter
The remaining solids after all the water in a cheese has been eliminated.

Eau-de-vie
Spirit, usually made from wine-pressings e.g. *marc*.

Fat Content
Degree of fatness of cheese, expressed as a percentage of fat in total dry matter.

Fermier
Adjective used to describe a farm-made cheese.

Fourme
The old word for cheese derived from the form or mould in which it was made.

Frais, Fraîche
Fresh.

Fromage
Cheese.

Fromage Blanc
A fresh cheese that has been lightly drained.

Fromage Fort
Strong preparation usually made in a pot from cheese leftovers with alcohol and herbs added.

Fromage Frais
Cheese that has been salted, but sold unripened.

Fromager
1 Cheesemaker.
2 Wholesaler, or retailer of cheese.

Fromagerie
Cheese-dairy. Also used by some cheese shops.

GAEC
This stands for Groupement Agricole pour l'Exploitation en Commun, which is a kind of cooperative.

Halle
Covered market.

Industriel
Indicates a large-scale, factory-style creamery with mechanized cheesemaking.

◀ **Rows of Testa Mora and Brocciu maturing in the cellar of a cheese shop in Paris**

Lait
Milk.

Laurier
Bay leaf.

Maître Fromager
Master cheesemaker, or cheese expert. Fewer than 100 are listed by the Guilde des Fromagers.

Marc
Spirit made from distilled wine-pressings.

Moelleux
Soft and velvety.

Morge
Brine enriched with scrapings from old cheeses, used to rub the surfaces of some cheeses during affinage.

Mould
1 Wood, metal, or plastic container used in cheesemaking to shape the cheese.
2 Fungal species that form on the crust of cheeses or form veins within the pâte. Some moulds occur naturally, but many are artificially introduced.

Pâte
Everything that appears within the rind of a cheese.

Pavé
A thick, square cheese, shaped like a paving stone.

Pays
Village, district, or province.

Pelle
Round cutting-edged shovel used to handle curd (Brie).

Persillé
Blue cheese.

Petit Lait
Whey.

Rennet
The enzyme derived from the fourth stomach of a calf or goat, used in cheesemaking to break down the solids in milk into digestible form, helping coagulation. Some plants can have the same effect as rennet.

Tome, Tomme
1 Small, round goat's-milk cheeses.
2 Larger pressed cheese of all types of milk.

Transhumance
The movement of flocks or herds from winter pasture or stabling to high mountain pastures in summer.

Vache
A cow, or a cheese that has been made with cow's-milk.

Whey
Residue of milk after most of the fats and other solids have been coagulated into the curd.

VDN
Vin doux naturel – a naturally sparkling white wine.

A selection of *fermier* cheeses

Cheese Shops in France

SHOPS IN PARIS

Alain Dubois
80, rue de Tocquebille,
75017 Paris
*250 varieties including Époisses,
Comté, Camembert*

Alléosse
13, rue Poncelet, 75017 Paris
Over 200 varieties

Androuët
41, rue d'Amsterdam
19, rue Daguerre, 75014 Paris

Aux Bons Fromages
64, rue de la Pompe,
75015 Paris
*Speciality: Mont d'Or – 90% of
cheeses direct from producers*

Barthélémy
51, rue de Grenelle,
75007 Paris

Cantin
12, rue du Champ-de-Mars,
75007 Paris

Carmes
24, rue de Levis, 75017 Paris

La Cave aux Fromages
1, rue du Retrait, 75020 Paris

Cremerie Des Carmes
47 ter, boulevard Saint-
Germain, 75005 Paris

Cremerie Sainte-Hyacinthe
198, rue Saint-Jacques,
75005 Paris

Eric Lefebvre
229, rue de Charenton,
75012 Paris

La Ferme Saint-Aubin
76, rue Saint-Louis en l'Ile,
75004 Paris

La Ferme Saint-Hubert
21, rue Vignon, 75008 Paris

La Ferme des Arenes
60, rue Monge, 75005 Paris

Ferme de Passy
39, rue de l'Annonciation,
75016 Paris
*Specialities: Stilton with Port, Bleu
des Causses, Époisses*

Ferme Ste-Hyacinthe
198, rue Saint-Jacques,
75005 Paris

Ferme St-Hubert
21, rue Vignon, 75008 Paris

**Fil'O Fromage
(Cherif Boubrit)**
1, rue Poirier de Narçay,
75014 Paris

François Priet
214, rue des Pyrénées,
75020 Paris
*200 types, including Brie de Noix,
Brie aux Trois Bleux*

Fromagerie d'Auteuil
58, rue d'auteuil, 75016,
Paris
*Specialities: Époisses, Langres,
Camembert, Comté, Alpages
Beaufort, Saint-Nectaire, Chèvre*

La Fromagerarie Boursault
71, Avenue du General
Leclerc, 75014 Paris

Fromagerie Cler
31, rue Cler, 75007 Paris

Fromagers de France
39, rue de Bretagne,
75003 Paris

Fromagerie Lepic
20, rue Lepic, 75018 Paris
Specializing in farm cheeses, Comté

Fromagerie des Moines
47, rue des Moines,
75017 Paris
*Saint-Marcellin,
goat cheeses, Saint-
Nectaire*

Fromagerie de Montmartre
39, rue du Poteau,
75018 Paris
*300 types including Le Vigneron,
Roquefort Délice, Chevrot*

Fromagerie Mozart
48bis, avenue Mozart,
75016 Paris
Blue cheese specialist

Hamon Fromager
81, rue de Seine, 75005 Paris

Lasnier
51, rue de Tolbiac, 75013 Paris
*Specialities: Camembert au Calvados,
Tour Rilman*

Laurent Dubois
2, rue de Lourmel,
75015 Paris

Leverrier Marcel
25, rue Danielle Casanova,
75001 Paris

Lillo
35, rue des Belles Feuilles,
75016 Paris
*Mont d'Or, Chèvre, Cabron frais,
Tiramisu, Gâteau de Riz*

Lima
1, rue Marsoulan, 75012 Paris

Marie-Anne Cantin
12 rue du Champ-de-Mars,
75007 Paris
*Specialities: Saint-Marcellin,
Chèvre, Comté*

Au Palais du Fromage
129, avenue Victor-Hugo,
75016 Paris
*Vacherin, Brie de Meaux, Chèvre,
Old Gouda*

Quatrehomme
62, rue de Sevres,
75007 Paris

R 2 L
13, rue Rambuteau,
75004 Paris

Roger Alleosse
13 rue Poncelet

Serraz (Gerard Serraz)
110, rue Saint-Charles,
75015 Paris
*Farm cheeses, Saint-Nectaire,
Ossau-Iraty*

SHOPS OUTSIDE PARIS

Coopérative fermière Jeune Montagne
Laguiole, Aveyron
Tomme, Laguiole

La Maison du Fromage
84000 Avignon

Mille et un Fromages
8, Avenue Victor-Hugo,
64200 Biarritz

Roland Delannoy
88, rue Colonne,
Boulougne-sur-Mer

Philippe Olivier
43, rue Thiers,
62200 Boulogne-sur-Mer

La Maison Fromage et des Vins
1, rue André Gerschell, Calais

Nathalie Pinheiro
1, rue Montaigne, Calais

Domaine de Saint-Loup
14340 Saint-Loup de Fribois,
Calvados
Camembert

Fromagerie Thébault
La Houssaye,
14170 Boissey, Calvados
Pont l'Évêque specialist

Société Fromagerie Coopérative de l'Abbaye
01410 Chezery Forens
Bleu de Gex

Laiterie du Chalet
Route de Ricros
03410 Domérat

Laiterie Coopérative d'Etrez-Beauport, Etrez
Emmental

Fromagerie de Mondrepuis
02500 Hirson

Fromagerie Phillipe Olivier
3, rue du Curé St-Etienne, Lille

Fromagerie Renée Richard
Les Halles de Lyon, 102 Cours
Lafayette, 69003 Lyon

Fromagerie du Château
09200, Moulis

L'Edelweiss
55 rue de France, Nice

La Ferme Fromagere
7, rue Lepante, Nice

Ferme du Verger Pilote
59550 Maroilles

Fromageries George Grillot
29, rue Lattre de Tassigny,
25290, Ornans
Comté, Mont d'Or, Morbier

Earl Les Hirondelles
Le Bocage, 61470 Avernes
Saint-Gourgon, Orne
Livarot specialist

Chene Vert
B.P. 34, 24300 Saint
Front sur
Nizonne, Perigord
Goat's-milk cheeses

Volaillerie Saint-Antoine
7, rue Mirabeau, 66000,
Perpignan

André Fournier
63790 Chambon-sur-Lac,

Puy de Dôme
Saint-Nectaire specialist

Fromagerie Chabert
"Vallières"
74150 Rumilly

Crèmerie Clement
5 & 7, rue du Pre,
39200, Saint-Claude
*Bleu de Gex-Septmoncel, Mont d'Or,
Morbier, Canvillotte, Comté*

Fromagerie de Saligny
89100 Saligny

Stephane Brun
Le Chateau, 26400, Saou
Picodon

Fromagerie Bresse Bleu, B.P.
26, 01960 Servas

L'Ami du Chambertin
Le Palet de Bourgogne,
Soumaintrain
Époisses specialist

Fromages de la Costa Moliniere
Gerard et Line Cateau, 82110
Saverttre, Tarn et Garonne
Sheep's-milk cheeses

Compagnie Fromagère Edmond de Rotschild
Domaine des 30 Arpents,
77220, Tournan-en-Brie
Brie

Table et Terroir
Saint Germain, 47300
Villeneuve sur Lot

Fromagerie Cooperative Agricole de Villereversure-Cormorand
01250 Villereversure
Comté

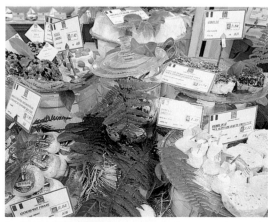

Fromagerie Phillipe Olivier

AOC Cheese Producers

THE INAO

The Institut National des Appellations d'Origine (INAO) oversees the AOC cheese producers and provides information about all AOC products. For more information about the AOC cheeses, *see p. 28.*

INAO
Champs Elysées, 138
75008 Paris
www.gouv.fr

AOC LABELS

This is a list of all the main collectives and *co-operatives* responsible for the AOC cheeses.

Abondance
Chambre d'Agriculture,
Chemin d'Hirmentaz, 16
74200 Thonon les Bains

Beaufort
15, rue A. Aubry
73270 Albertville

Bleu d'Auvergne
Rue du Lieutenant Basset, 20
15400 Riom Es Montagnes

Bleu des Causses
B.P. 9
12004 Rodez Cédex

Bleu du Haut-Jura, de Gex, de Septmoncel
Rout Félix Peclet, 146
39220 Les Rousses

Bleu du Vercors-Sassenage
Maison du Parc
38250 Lans en Vercors

Brie de Meaux
13, rue des Fossés
77000 Melun

Brie de Melun
13, rue des Fossés
77000 Melun

Brocciu Corse / Brocciu
Maison de l'Agriculture,
ave Noël Franchini,
20999 Ajaccio,
B.P. 104, 20250 Corte

Cantal
52, ave des Pupilles de la Nation, 15001 Aurillac Cédex

Camembert de Normandie
82, rue de Bernières
14000 Caen

Chabichou du Poitou
B.P. 191
86005 Poitiers Cédex

Chaource
Hôtel de Ville
10210 Chaource

Comté
Avenue de la Résistance
39800 Poligny

Crottin de Chavignol/ Chavignol
Route de Chavignol, 9
18300 Sancerre

Emmental de Savoie
1, rue du Château
73000 Chambery

Emmental
28, rue Proudhon
25000 Besançon

Epoisses de Bourgogne
Mairie d'Epoisses
21460 Epoisses

Fourme d'Ambert / Fourme de Montbrison
4, place de l'Hôtel de Ville
63600 Ambert

Laguiole
Syndicat de Défense et de Promotion du Fromage de Laguiole
12210 Laguiole

Langres
Maison de l'Agriculture,
avenue du 109e R.I, 26
52011 Chaumont Cédex

Livarot
82, rue de Bernières
14300 Caen

Maroilles / Marolles
U.R.I.A.N.E., B.P. 20,
148 avenue du
Général de Gaulle
02260 La Cappelle

**Mont d'or /
Vacherin du Haut-Doubs**
Rue Proudhon, 26
25006 Besançon

Morbier
Valparc Espace Valentin
F-25048 Besancon Cédex

Munster / Munster-Géromé
1, place de la Gare, B.P. 7
68001 Colmar Cédex

Neufchâtel
76270 Neufchâtel-en-Bray

Ossau-Iraty
Maison Bazatchartenea
64120 Ostabat

Pélardon
Domaine de Saporta
34970 Lattes

**Picodon de l'Ardèche /
Picodon de la Drôme**
Le Number One, Rue Frédéric
Chopin, 26000 Valence

Pont-l'Evêque
82, rue de Bernières
14300 Caen

Pouligny-Saint-Pierre
Rue Cabouin, 7
36300 Pouligny-Saint-Pierre

**Reblochon /
Reblochon de Savoie**
Rue Saint Blaise B-P 55
74230 Thones

Rocamadour
Maison de l'Agriculture du Lot
Avenue Jean-Jaurès, 430
48004 Cahors Cedex

Roquefort
B.P. 2, 12103 Millau Cédex

Saint-Nectaire
Route des Fraux, 2 -
B.P. 9
63610 Besse en Chandesse

Sainte-Maure de Touraine
Mairie de Sainte-Maure
de Touraine
37800 Sainte-Maure
de Touraine

Salers
52, avenue des Pupilles
de la Nation – Résidence
Auvergne - B.P. 124,
15001 Aurillac Cédex

Selles-sur-Cher
Route de Varennes, 15
36600 La Vernelle

Tomme de Savoie
Maison de l'Agriculture, 52,
avenue des Îles
74994 Annecy Cédex 9

Tomme des Pyrénées
183, Avenue des Etats-Unis
31016 Toulouse Cédex

Index

A

Abbaye de Bellocq 67
Abbaye de Cîteaux 8
Abbaye de la Coudre 38, 252
Abbaye de la Joie Notre Dame 38
Abbaye de la Pierre-qui-Vire 39
Abbaye du Mont des Cats 39
Abondance 40–41
affinage 17, 18
Aisy Cendré 42
Aligot 100
alpage 78
Ambert 112
Ami du Chambertin, L' 166
ancient Greeks 16–17
ancient Romans 16–17
Anneau du Vic-Bilh 112
AOC cheeses 29
AOC regulations 28–29
Apérobic 67, 112
Appellation d'Origine Contrôlée see AOC
Ardi-Gasna 68
Arômes au Gène de Marc 43
Arômes au Vin Blanc 43
artisanal 28
Aubisque Pyrénées 69
Autun 113

B

Baguette Laonnaise 189
Bamalou, E 265
Banon 46
Bargkass 47
Barousse 264
Bayard, Le Petit 57
Beaufort 48–50
Beaujolais Pur Chèvre (Petit) 113
Beaumont 47
Berger Plat 60
Bergues 169
Besace de Pur Chèvre 113
Bethmale 265
Bigoton 114
Bilou du Jura (Le Petit) 114
Bleu 51–57
Bleu d'Auvergne 51

Bleu de Costaros 52
Bleu de Gex, see Bleu du Haut-Jura
Bleu de Langeac 54
Bleu de Laqueuille 54
Bleu de Loudes 55
Bleu de Septmoncel, see Bleu du Haut-Jura
Bleu de Termignon 57
Bleu des Causses 52
Bleu du Haut-Jura 53
Bleu du Quercy 55
Bleu du Vercors Sassenage 56
Blue Fondu `la Poêle 53
blue cheeses 18
Bondard 197
Bondaroy au Foin 209
Bonde, see Bondard
Bonde de Gâtine 114
Bondon, see Bondard
Bonjura 23
Bouca, Le 113
Boudane, see Tome de Ménage
Bougon 115
Bouille, La 256
Boule de Lille 58
Boule des Moines 39
Boulette d'Avesnes 189
Boulette de Cambrai 189
Bourricot, Le 170
Boursault 256
Boursin 257
Bouton d'Oc 116
Bouton de Culotte 115
bread 22–23
Brebis 70
Brebis de Pays 60–65
Brebis de Pays de Grasse 60
Brebis des Pyrénées 66–79
Brebis de Bersend 61
Brebis du Lochois 61
Brebis Frais du Caussedou 181
Brebis (Pays Basque), Le Cayolar 69
Brebis Pyrénées 71
Bressan 116
Bresse Bleu 56
Breuil 181
Brie 80–85
Brie de Coulommiers 83

Brie de Meaux 80
Brie de Melun 82
Brie de Montereau 83
Brie de Nangis 85
Brie de Provins 85
Brie Fermier 81
Brie Noir 81
Brillat-Savarin 257
Brin d'Amour 149
Brique Ardéchoise 116
Brique du Forez 117
Briquette de Coubon 117
Broccio, see Brocciu
Brocciu 146–147
Brocciu poivré 147
Brousse du Rove 176
Bûchette d'Anjou 117
Bûchette de Banon 118
buying cheese 30

C

Cabécou 28
Cabécou de Gramat 88
Cabécou de Rocamadour 89
Cabrioulet, see Tomme de Chèvre Loubières
Cachaille 175
Cachat 174
Caesar 17
Caillé de Lait de Vache 68
Calenzana 148
Camembert 90–93
production techniques 90–91
Camembert Affiné au Cidre de la Maison 93
Camembert de Normandie 92
Cancoillotte 93
Cannelle 261
Cantal 94–95
production techniques 95
Capri Lezéen 118
Caprice des Dieux 257
Capricorne de Jarjat 118
Carré de l'Est 101
Cathelain, Le 119
cattle breeds
Abondance 40, 213
Aubrac 98, 99
Holstein 99
Montbéliard 40, 213

cattle breeds (cont.)
Normande 90
Pie-Rouge-de-l'Est 99
Salers 97
Tarine 40, 50, 213
Caussedou, Le 62
Cenberona, *see* Breuil
Cervelle de Canut 176
Chabichou 105
Chabichou du Poitou 105
Chabis 105
chalet 78
Chaource 102
Charolais 119
Charolles, *see* Charolais
Chaumes 102
Chavignol, *see* Crottin de
Chavignol
cheese
buying 30
cutting 31
nutritional values 25
origins 16–17
processed 23
storing 30
tasting 30
types 18–21
Chef-Boutonne 119
Chèvre a l'Huile d'Olive et
à la Sarriette 136
Chèvre de Coin 112–137
Chèvre de la Loire
104–111
Chèvre de Pays, *see*
Fromage au Lait de
Chèvre
Chèvre Fermier 120
Chèvre Fermier Alpilles 120
Chèvre Fermier du
Château-Vert 120
Chèvre Frais 177
Chévreton de Mâcon,
see Mâconnais
Chevrette des Bauges 138
Chevrotin d'Alpage, Vallée
de Morzine 139
Chevrotin de Macôt 140
Chevrotin de
Montvalezan 141
Chevrotin de Peisey-
Nancroix 141
Chevrotin des Aravis 139
Chevrotin du Mont Cenis
140
Civray 121
Clacbitou 121

Claqueret Lyonnais,
see Cervelle de Canut
Clochette 121
coagulation 21, 132, 194
Coeur d'Arras 190
Cocur d'Avesnes 190
Coeur du Berry 122
Coeur de Camembert au
Calvados 93
Comté 142–143
Confit d'Epoisses 174
coopérative 28
Cornilly, Le 122
Corse 144–161
Corsica *see* Corse
Couhé-Vérac 122
Coulommiers 84
cows, *see* cattle breeds
Crottin d'Ambert, *see*
Ambert
Crottin du Berry à l'Huile
d'Olive 136
Crottin de Chavignol 106
Crottin de Pays 123
Croupet 258
Curé Nantais, *see* Nantais
Curé, *see* Nantais
cutting cheese 31

D
Dauphin 190
Délice de Saint-Cyr 258
Double-Crème 256–261
Dreux à la Feuille 164

E
Emmental 164
Emmental Grand Cru 165
Entrammes,
see Port-du-Salut
Epoisses de Bourgogne 166
Esbareich 264
Explorateur 258

F
Faisselle de Chèvre 177
fermier 28
Feuille de Dreux, *see* Dreux
à la Feuille
Figue 123
Filetta, A (La Fougère)
150
Filetta, A (Pâte de Fromage)
156
Fin-de-Siècle 259
Fium'Orbo, Le 148

Fleur du Maquis 149
Fontainebleau 177
Fougerus, Le 84
Fourme d'Ambert 167
Fourme de Chèvre Ardèche
124
Fourme du Cantal, *see*
Cantal
Fourme de Montbrison, *see*
Fourme d'Ambert
fresh cheeses 18
Frinault 168
Fromage à Raclette, *see*
Raclette
Fromage Allégé 169–172
Fromage au Lait de Chèvre
127
Fromage au pur Lait de
Brebis 152
Fromage Blanc 178
Fromage Blanc
Fermier 178
Fromage Cendré 170
Fromage Corse 145; 153
Fromage Corse Niolo 153
Fromage d'Hesdin 253
Fromage d'Ossau,
Laruns 74
Fromage de Brebis (Corse)
150
Fromage de Brebis
(des Pyrénées) 71
Fromage de Brebis
(du Pays) 62
Fromage de Brebis et
Vache Fermier 72
Fromage de Brebis
Vallée d'Ossau 72
Fromage de Chèvre
Ariège 124
Fromage de Chèvre
de Coin 124
Fromage de Chèvre
Fermier 126, 250
Fromage de Chèvre
Larzac 126
Fromage de Lactosérum
181–182
Fromage de Lactosérum
(Corse) 146–147
Fromage de Lamastre
Rouge 132
Fromage de Monsieur 259
Fromage de Montagne 267
Fromage de Montagne
de Lège 266

Fromage de Montagne, Le
Pic de la Calabasse 267
Fromage de Montagne,
Le Rogallais 267
Fromage de Pays, Mixte 75
Fromage de Vache 74
Fromage de Vache Brûlé 68
Fromage du Jas 127
Fromage du Larzac 175
Fromage Fermier 127
Fromage Fermier au Lait
de Brebis 73
Fromage Fermier au Lait
de Vache 73
Fromage Fermier Brebis 151
Fromage Fermier de Chèvre
de la Tavagna 154
Fromage Fermier Pur
Brebis 63
Fromage Fort 173–175
Fromage Fort du
Lyonnais 173
Fromage Frais 176–180
Fromage Frais de Nîmes 178
Fromage au Pur Lait de
Brebis 152
Fromageé du Larzac 175
Fromageon Fermier au Lait
Cru de Brebis 63
fromager 17

G

Galet de Bigorre 128
Galet Solognot 128
Galette des Monts du
Lyonnais 129
Gaperon 183
Gardian 179
Gargantua à la Feuille de
Sauge 361
Gastanberra 179
goat farming 137
goat breeds 137
Alpine 137
Saanen 137
goat's-milk cheesemaking
137
Gournay Frais 179
Grand Colombier des
Aillons 128
Grand Vatel 259
Grataron d'Arèches 183
Gratte-Paille 260
Greuilh 182
Gris de Lille 191
Guerbigny 191

H

hard cheeses 20

I

industriel 28

L

labelling 41
Lacandou, Le 64
Laguiole 98–99
Langres 186
Laruns 76
Livarot 187
Loire 104
Lou Magré 171
Lou Pennol, *see* Tome de
Chèvre du Tarn
Lucullus 260

M

Mâconnais 129
Mamirolle 187
markets 27
Maroilles 188
Marolles, *see* Maroilles
Matocq 76; 77
Metton 93
Mignon (small version
of Maroilles)
milk 21
Mimolette Française,
see Boule de Lille
Mixte 70
Monsieur Fromage, *see*
Fromage de Monsieur
Mont d'Or du Lyonnais
129
Mont d'Or, *see* Vacherin
du Haut-Doubs
Morbier 194
Mothais à la Feuille
194
Mouflon, Le 155
Moularen 64
Moulis, Le 268
Munster 192
Munster au Cumin 192
Munster-Géromé, *see*
Munster
Murol 195
Murolait 195

N

Nantais 195
Neufchâtel 196–197
Niolo, Le 154

O

Olivet au Foin 200
Olivet Cendré 200
Ossau Fermier 77
Ossau–Iraty–Brebis

P

Pyrénées 66
Palouse des Aravis (Pur
Chèvre d'Alpage) 201
Paprika 261
Pâte de Fromage 156
Pâtefine Fort 175
Pavé Blésois 130
Pavé d'Auge 201
Pavé de la Ginestarié 131
Pavé de Roubaix 202
Pavé du Plessis, Le 202
Pavé, Le 130
Pélardon des Cévennes 203
Pélardon des Corbières 203
Pérail 65
Persillé 204
Persillé de la Haute-
Tarentaise 204
Persillé de la Tarentaise 204
Persillé de Tignes 205
Persillé du Semnoz 205
Petit Bayard, Le 57
Petit Pardou, Le 79
Petit Quercy 132
Petit-Suisse 180
Pèvre d'Aï, *see* Poivre d'Ane
Picadou 88
Picodon 206–207
Picodon à l'Huile
d'Olive 207
Picodon de Crest 207
Picodon de Dieulefit 207
Picodon de l'Ardèche 207
Picodon de la Drôme 207
Picodon du Dauphiné 207
Pierre-Robert 260
Pitchou, Le 223
Pithiviers au Foin 209
Poivre 261
Poivre d'Âne 46
Pont-l'Evêque 208
Port-Salut 209
Port-du-Salut 209
Pouligny-Saint-Pierre 107
Pourly 131
pressing 20, 41, 95, 237
processed cheese 23
Puant de Lille/Macéré, *see*
Gris de Lille

Q

Quatre-Vents 131
Quercy (Petit) 132

R

Rabelais 22
Raclette 212
Reblochon de Savoie 213
Reblochon, *see* Reblochon de Savoie
renneting 41, 95, 237
Rigotte 214–215
Rigotte d'Echalas 214
Rigotte de Condrieu 215
Rigotte de Sainte-Colombe 214
Rigotte des Alpes 215
rind 18–20
Rocamadour 88
Rogeret de Lamastre 132
Rollot 191
Romans, *see* Tomme de Romans
Roquefort 28, 216–219
Rustinu, U 161

S

Sainte-Maure de Touraine 108
Saint-Félicien de Lamastre 132
Saint-Marcellin 30, 222–223
Saint-Nectaire 224–225
Saint-Pancrace 133
Saint-Paulin 226
Saint-Rémy 101
Saint-Winoc, Le 227
Salers 96–97
salting 41, 95, 237
San Petrone 158
Santranges 133
Saulxurois, Le 101
scalding 41
seasonal cheeses 137
Séchon de Chèvre Drômois 133
Ségalou 180
Selles-sur-Cher 110
semi-hard cheeses 20
Sérac 182
sheep breeds Lacaune 60
soft cheeses 18
Soleil 261
Soumaintrain 227
Sourire Lozérien 171

Sumerians 16
storing cheese 30
supermarkets 26

T

Tamié 230
Tarentais 134
tasting cheese 30
Taupinière, La 134
tome 230
Tome Alpage de la Vanoise 232
Tome Chèvre 159
Tome de Banon 244
Tome de Chèvre 159
Tome de Chèvre, Belleville 239
Tome de Chèvre du Tarn 246
Tome de Ménage 238
Tome des Bauges 233
Tome Mi-Chèvre du Lècheron 242
Tome Pays Basque 251
tomme 230
Tomme 243–249
Tomme au Marc de Raisin 235
Tomme Capra 245
Tomme Corse 160
Tomme d'Arles 243
Tomme de Chèvre 250
Tomme de Chèvre d'Alpage, Morzine 240
Tomme de Chèvre de Pays 252
Tomme de Chèvre, Pays Nantais 245
Tomme de Chèvre, les Pyrénées 250–252
Tomme de Chèvre Loubières 251
Tomme de Chèvre, Savoie 239–242
Tomme de Chèvre, Vallée de Morzine 240
Tomme de Chèvre, Vallée de Novel 240
Tomme de Courchevel 241
Tomme de Huit Litres 27
Tomme de l'Aveyron (Petite) 243
Tomme de la Frasse Fermière 234
Tomme de Lomagne 172
Tomme de Lullin 236–237

Tomme de Montagne 247
Tomme de Romans 248
Tomme de Savoie 231–238
Tomme de Savoie 231
Tomme de Savoie au Cumin 232
Tomme de Savoie Maigre 231
Tomme de Séranon 248
Tomme de Thônes 239
Tomme de Vendée 249
Tomme du Bougnat 244
Tomme du Faucigny 233
Tomme du Mont Cenis 238
Tomme Fermière des Lindarets 235
Tomme Fraîche, *see* Aligot
Tomme Grise de Seyssel 234
Tomme le Gascon 246
Tommette de l'Aveyron 249
Tommette Mi-Chèvre des Bauges 242
Toucy 134
Tourmalet 78
transhumance 78
Trappe (Véritable) 252
Trappe de Belval 253
Trappe d'Echourgnac 254
Trappiste de Chambaran 254
Tricorne de Marans 65
Triple-Crème 256–261
Trois-Epis 261

U

unpressed cheeses 20

V

Vachard, Le 172
Vache des Pyrénées 264
Vache Frais 180
Vacherin d'Abondance Fermier 269–271
Vacherin des Bauges 272
Vacherin du Haut-Doubs 278–279
Valençay 111
Venaco, Le 161
Vendômois 136
Vieux Corse, Le 158
Vieux-Boulogne 280

W

whey 20
wine 22–24

BIBLIOGRAPHY

Androuët, Pierre, *Guide du Fromage,*
Stock, Paris, 1971 (in French). English
translation, Aidan Ellis, 1973; 2nd
edition, Aidan Ellis, 1977; revised 1983.

Androuët, Pierre, *Le Livre d'Or du
Fromage,* Atlas, Paris 1984

Androuët, Pierre, and Chabot, Yves,
Le Brie, Presses du Village, Etrepillat,
1985

Annuaire des Industries Laitières,
Comindus, Paris, 1991

Atlas Routier France, Michelin, London,
1989

Barthelemy, Roland, *Cheeses of the World,*
Hachette Illustrated, 2004

Bon, Colette, *Les Fromages,* Hachette,
Paris, 1979

Cart-Tanneur, Philippe, *Fromages et Vins
de France,* Trame Way, Paris, 1989

Charron, G. *Les Productions Laitières*

Chast, Michel, and Voy, Henry,
Le Livre de l'Amateur de Fromages,
Robert Laffont, Paris, 1984

Clozier, René, *Géographie de la France,*
Collection "Que sais-je?" Presses
Universitaires de France, Paris, 1970

Courtine, Robert J., *Grand Livre de la
France à Table,* Bordas, Paris, 1982

Courtine, Robert J., *Larousse des Fromages,*
Librairie Larousse, Paris, 1987

Downing Charpentier, Marolyn,
Les Fromages/French Cheese,
Brown Trout 2002

Eck, André, *Fromages,* Technique et
Documentation (Lavoisier), Paris, 1987

Evette, Jean-Luc, *La Fromagerie,* Presses
Universitaires de France, Paris, 1975

Foubert, Jean-Marie,
Guide de la Route du Fromage,
Charles Corlet, Condé-sur-Noireu, 1987

Girard, Sylvie, *Fromages,* Editions
Hermé, Paris, 1986

Handbook of Cheese, Hachette Illustrated,
English Translation Octopus, 2003

Le Jaouen, Jean-Claude,
La Fabrication du Fromage de Chèvre Fermier,
Itovic, Paris, 1982

Journal Officiel de la République Française

Le Liboux, Jean-Luc, *Nouveau Guide des
Fromages de France,* Ouest-France,
Rennes, 1984

Michelin Guide de Tourisme, Michelin, Paris

Michelson, Patricia, *The Cheese Room,*
Michael Joseph, 2001

**Montagne, Prosper, and Gottschalk,
Docteur,** *Larousse Gastronomique,* Librairie
Larousse, Paris, 1938

Petit Robert (I, II), Dictionnaires Le
Robert, Paris, 1989

Rance, Patrick, *The French Cheese Book,*
Macmillan, London, 1989

Ridgway, Judy,
*The Cheese Companion: The Connoisseur's
Guide,* Apple Press, 2002

Roc, Jean-Claude, *Le Buron de la Croix
Blanche,* Editions Watel, Brioude, 1989

Stobbs, William, *Guide to the Cheeses of
France,* Apple Press, London, 1984

Viard, Henry, *Fromages de France,*
Dargaud, Paris, 1980

CONTRIBUTORS

Kazuko Masui
The main author of this book lives in Paris and has written many books on food. Her vision for a comprehensive work on French cheeses goes back to 1980.

Tomoko Yamada
Co-author Tomoko Yamada has spent more than 25 years studying French cuisine in both France and Tokyo.

Yohei Maruyama
Photographer Yohei Maruyama has won numerous awards in his native Japan for his photography, including his two books *The Best of Sushi* and *The Taste of Paris*.

Joël Robuchon
The writer of the foreword has retired but is still considered to be one of the world's greatest chefs.

Randolph Hodgson
Consultant Randolph Hodgson is a founder of the British Specialist Cheesemakers' Association and owner of Neal's Yard Dairy in London.

Robert and Isabelle Vifian
Wine connoisseurs Robert and Isabelle run Tan Dinh restaurant in Paris. Also connoisseurs of cheese, their wine list ranks among the top five in France. Their suggested pairings of cheese and wine appear throughout this book.

PRODUCERS AND FROMAGERS

The publishers would like to thank the following producers and *fromagers*, who offered their invaluable knowledge and expertise to help with the creation of the first edition this book:

The nuns at Abbaye de la Joie Notre-Dame, Campénéac; Pierre Androuët; B. Antony, 17 rue de la Montagne, Vieux Ferrette; Roland Barthelemy, 51 rue de Grenelle, Paris; Batut, 22 rue Vieille-du-temple, Paris; J. Blanc, Crémerie des Halles, St-Jean-de-Luz; Daniel Boujon, 7 rue Saint-Sébastien, Thonon-les-Bains; Xavier Bourgon, 6 Place Victor-Hugo, Toulouse; Michel Bourgue, La Maison du Fromage, Les Halles Centrales, Avignon; R. Bousquet, Halles Centrales, Carcassonne; Le Cagibi, 17 allée d'Etigny, Luchon; Le Calendos, 11 rue Colbert, Tours; M. and Mme Cantin, 12 rue du Champ-de-Mars, Paris; Mme Cazaux, La Barthe-de-Neste; Gilbert Chemin, Crémerie du Couserans, 3 rue de la République, Saint-Girons; Edouard Ceneri, La Ferme Savoyarde, 22 rue Meynadier, Cannes; Brigitte Cordier and Françoise Fleutot, Montlaux; Jacques and Jacqueline Coulaud, 24 rue Grenouillit, Le Puy; M. and Mme Claude Dupin, 41 rue Gambetta, Saint-Jean-de-Luz; François Durand, La Heronnière, Camembert; Fromageries Bel, 4 rue d'Anjou, Paris; Henri Grillet, Crémerie du Gravier, Aurillac; M. and Mme Jacques Guerin, La Fromagerie, 18 rue Saint-Jean, Niort; Jean-Martin and Margot Kempf, 155 Ferme du Saesserlé, Breitenbach; Raymond Lecomte / Odette Jenny, 76 rue Saint-Louis-en-l'Ile, Paris; M. and Mme Jean-Pierre Le Lous, Marché des Grands-Hommes, Bordeaux; Michel Lepage, Conseils-Assistance-Fromagers, 3 Les Prés Claux, Oraison; Gérard Loup and family, Les Provins, Puimichel; M. and Mme Marius Manetti, Col de San-Bastiano, Calcatoggio; Marechal, Halle de Lyon, 102 Cours Lafayette, Lyon; Alain Martinet, 102 Cours Lafayette, Lyon; E. Millat, Halle Brauhauban, Tarbes; Jean-Pierre Moreau, Elevage Caprin de Bellevue, Pontlevoy; Philippe Olivier, 43-45 rue Thiers, Boulogne-sur-Mer; G. Paul, 9 rue des Marseillais, Aix-en-Provence; A. Penen and family, Préchacq-Navarrenx; Denis Provent, Laiterie des Halles, 2 Place de Genève, Chambéry; René and Renée Richard, Halle de Lyon, 102 Cours Lafayette, Lyon; Jacques Vernier, La Fromagerie Boursault, 71 avenue du Général Leclerc, Paris; Henry Voy, La Ferme Saint-Hubert, 21 rue Vignon, Paris

ACKNOWLEDGEMENTS

The publishers would also like to thank the following institutions:

Association Marque Collective Savoie; Association Nationale des Appellations d'Origine Laitières Françaises; Centre Interprofessionnel de Documentation et d'Information Laitières; Chambre d'Agriculture; Cheese & Wine Academy, Tokyo; Coopérative de Lullin; Coopérative A Pecurella; Crédit Agricole, Corsica; Institut National des Appellations d'Origine; Maison du Fromage, Valençay; Fermier S. A; Snow Brand Milk Products; La Société Fromagère de la Brie; Société des Caves et des Producteurs Réunis de Roquefort; Syndicat de Fromages d'Appellation d'Origine

The authors would like to thank the following individuals:

T. Basset, François Durand, Collette and Catherine Faller, A. Franceschi, Katsushi Kitamura, Katsunori Kobayashi, J.-E. La-Noir, Yohko Namioka, D. Pin, A. Vinciguerra

Special thanks to Kikuko Inoue, Takayoshi Nakasone, Kozue Tarumi, and Reiko Mori

Map illustrations: John Plumer
Illustrations on page 218: Claire Littlejohn
Picture research assistance: Celia Dearing

The publisher would like to thank the following for their kind permission to reproduce their photographs:
(Abbreviations key: t=top, b=bottom, r=right, l=left, c=centre)

1: Corbis/ © Owen Franken;
2-3: Corbis/ © John Heseltine;
4: Corbis/ © Adam Woolfitt;
5: Corbis/ © Owen Franken;
6-7: Alamy Images/ © Zyarescu;
14-15: Alamy Images/ © Robert Harding Picture Library Ltd (b);
14-15: Corbis/ Ludovic Maisant (t);
18: Corbis/ © Owen Franken;
20: Corbis/ © Franz-Merc Frei (b); © Owen Franken (t);
29: Corbis/ © Rob Howard;
32-33: Corbis/ © Ludovic Maisant;
36-37: Corbis/ © Ludovic Maisant;
37: Corbis/ © Owen Franken (t);
44-45: Alamy Images/ © Robert Harding Picture Library Ltd;
45: Corbis/ © Ludovic Maisant (t);
86-87: Corbis/© Adam Woolfitt;
87: Corbis/© Ludovic Maisant (t);
125: Corbis/ © Paul Almasy;
162-163: Corbis/ © Adam Woolfitt ;
163: Corbis/ © Ludovic Maisant (t);
168: Corbis/ © Paul Almasy (b);
184-185: Alamy Images/© Images-of-France (b);
184-185: Corbis/ © Ludovic Maisant (t);
198-199: Corbis/ © Sandro Vannini;
199: Corbis/ © Ludovic Maisant (t);
210-211: Corbis/ © Adam Woolfitt;
211: Corbis/© Ludovic Maisant (t);
220-221:Corbis/ © Adam Woolfitt;
221: Corbis/ © Ludovic Maisant (t);
226: Corbis/ © Yves Forestier/Sygma (b);
228-229: Alamy Images/ © Photolocate;
229: Corbis/ © Ludovic Maisant (t);
262-263: Corbis/ © O. Amamany & E.Vicens;
263: Corbis/ © Ludovic Maisant (t);
271: Corbis/ © Rougemont/Sygma (tr);
274-275: Corbis/© Owen Franken